RELIGIOUS LAW AND ETHICS

RELIGIOUS LAW AND ETHICS

Studies in Biblical and Rabbinical Theonomy

by

Ze'ev W. Falk

MESHARIM PUBLISHERS
JERUSALEM
1991

MESHARIM PUBLISHERS

10 Harav Berlin St., Jerusalem 92503, ISRAEL

Laser Typing and Printing by "SCORPIO"

P.O.B 2754 Jerusalem

ISBN 965-313-000-5

To the Daily *Minyan*
at Moreshet Israel Congregation, Jerusalem,
with its daily *Dvar Torah*
lefi hapshatot hamitchadshim bekhol yom
(R. Samuel ben Meir, Commentary, Gen. 37:1)

TABLE OF CONTENTS

B. POSTBIBLICAL ETHICS:

C. RABBINICAL ETHICS:

PREFACE

The writer on religious law and ethics should speak with the utmost humility vis-a-vis God, his teachers and all human beings[1] This, however, is not to say that he should always accept the teaching offered in the name of God, irrespective of his own moral reflection. Did not Moses claim that the divine statutes and judgements could be demonstrated to all nations as wise and righteous[2], and that the divine commandment was very near to every listener and should be close to his heart?[3]

In order to prove this claim right, one must have an ethical knowledge independently of the religious authority, even of God Himself, to be able to justify the message presented in His name. It would be a false humility, if one despised the additional sources of moral information: reason and conscience, which, like the Torah, are divine gifts.

"Surrendering our logic to the Almighty and embracing the logic of Sinai"[4], would render our moral faculties superfluous and constitute an act of ingratitude vis-a-vis their Creator. A meaningful evaluation of the Torah cannot be obtained only "from within" and cannot exclude rational, historical, psychological and utilitarian considerations.

In our time, the study of Torah must use the insights of contemporary thought, especially its sense of justice and its concept of human rights. True, opinions differ on many issues. However, just as nobody would renounce medical treatment because of the differences in medical opinion, we should not renounce the endeavour of ethics because of the differences among moral philosophies.

"The particular content of the voice of conscience is of course conditioned by all the relativities of history. Men may be mistaken in their interpretation of what life is essentially; and conscience may be, in its very content, a vehicle of sin. Yet even in its content the universalities of conscience are at least as significant as its varieties and relativities"[5].

Revealed rules must be brought into a synthesis with reason and moral feeling. Where the conflict cannot be solved by interpretation, use should be made of human legislation, epieikeia or exceptional rulings, to coordinate religious law with ethics. This is "the space which has been left to us for cultivation"[6], i.e. our chance for creative participation.

Instead of adopting a mathematical model of Jewish law[7], disregarding its vital and organic character, we should rather understand it as a constant challenge of human responsibility by the divine message. Sometimes, the challenge is to call for surrender to the Almighty, as in the offering of Isaac, but more often it is to make us an active and critical partner to the divine lawmaker.

Our interpretation of Jewish law is in the line of those Jewish philosophers, such as R. Sa'adyah Ga'on, Maimonides and Gersonides, who did not hesitate to use their own reason in the interpretation of revealed sources[8]. It follows the example of those rabbis engaged in the rational interpretation of the Torah[9], and of those prophets who called for disobedience to cultic rules, if they were not accompanied by moral behaviour[10].

Finally, it is in the line of the Torah itself, offering various reasons for its commandments, and thereby opening up to critical reflection by the audience. If "the divine judgments are true and altogether righteous"[11], this means that only what is true and righteous can be divine.

In Part A of this book, an attempt will be made to present biblical ethics, first in systematic chapters (1-7), and then in chapters arranged according to the sources (8-11). Postbiblical non-rabbinical sources are described in Part B (ch.12), while Part C (chs. 13-22) will examine Talmud and Midrash and Part D (chs. 23-25) the posttalmudic development.

Hopefully, the book has been written, and will be read, in the spirit of the advice: "Trust in God with all your heart, and do not rely on your own insight"[12] which does not mean we should quit reason, but that reason is a divine gift[13]. The author will be grateful to readers for any question or correction and will keep praying for further insight.

Jerusalem
On the Eve of New Year 5752   Z.W.F.

1.   M 'Avot 4:4, 10.

2.   Deut. 4:6-8.

3.   Deut. 30:11-14.

4.   From an address of Rabbi Dr. J.B. Soloveitchik to the Rabbinical Council of America Convention 5736 (published by Dr. Isaac Hersh, in **Light**, 17 Kislev 5736, pp. 11-18.

5.   Reinhold Niebuhr, **The Nature and Destiny of Man** (New York: Scribner, 1964) vol.1, p. 275.

6.   BT Chulin 7 a; cf. Rashi ad loc.

7.   Rabbi Soloveitchik, loc.cit. p. 18; and his **Halakhic Man**, passim.

8.   E.g. Sa'adyah's rationalization of laws of revelation (**Book of Doctrines and Beliefs 3:2**), Maimonides' stand on resurrection (**Mishneh Torah,** Teshuvah 8:2), mumbling over a wound (Avodat Kochavim 11:11); and **derekh 'erets** as a correction of law (Ishut 14:17), and Gersonides' methodological remarks on the interpretation of Torah (Levi ben Gerson, **Milchamot Ha-Schem; Die Kaempfe Gottes** (Leipzig 1866) Vorwort, p.7).

9.   E.g. R. Ishmael, pointing at the human character of language (A.J. Heschel, **Torah min Hashamyim be'aspaqlaryah shel hadorot,** Israel 1962).

10.   E.g. Hos. 1-3; Is. 1:10-17; Jer. 7: 21-23.

11.   Ps. 19:10.

12.   Prov. 3:5.

13.   Cf. Gersonides, **Commentary,** ad loc.: "He who relies on his own insight, is the one who thinks that he does not need for this purpose the help of God".

LAW, MORALS AND RELIGION

In discussing the three normative systems, or alternatively, the systems of behaviour control: law, morals and religion, we should begin with a short definition of each. All three systems are indicative of what ought to be, meaning that they are prescriptive, or justifying such prescriptions.

The **law** is usually understood to be the body of norms, structures and procedures which regulate the lives of individuals and groups within a given political society. These norms, structures and procedures are expressed in written or unwritten form, by way of legislation or judicial decisions. Obedience to the law is enforced by the judicial and executive organs of the state. In general, the law prescribes external behaviour rather than states of mind and intentions, and formulates rights and duties.

By the same token, **morals** control human behaviour, with a special emphasis on internal elements and intentions. Usually, morals call for a deeper commitment than law, their being based upon a person's soul and conscience, and not upon external legal sanction. Indeed, personal feelings of guilt, reproach and contempt often act as a more effective sanction than that of any organ of the state. The norms and principles of morals should be autonomous, i.e. based on the system itself and on reason, rather than on any external authority. Therefore, they should be presentable in philosophical discourse, and provable by rational argument. No moral norm should only apply to a single individual, rather morals should be general and even universal, i.e. applying to all human beings in the same situation.

Religion, while regulating human conduct, does so by giving meaning to our personal existence, and by providing us with a comprehensive world-view. Religion is generally based on theonomy, i.e. on the will of God, which does not necessarily exclude the function of human reason. Speaking about God, and human responsibility to God, religion provides a way for living within contradictions and overcoming crises. The various acts, omissions and teachings of religion provide the necessary enforcements, sanctions, and integration of its principles of faith.

The main problem with these three normative systems is their correlation and interdependence. Originally, they had all been part of one comprehensive body of rules, which later on became subject to greater differentiation[1].

While in the past the law had drawn upon the ideas of the latter two systems, contemporary legal positivism insists upon its autonomy. Moral and religious ideas still play an active role in the legal system through the legislator, who adopts and gives them legal standing. Even the judiciary occasionally draws upon moral principles, declaring them to be the "Law of Nature", in correcting an otherwise unsatisfactory situation.

Morals too, are said to depend upon religion and its beliefs. No alternative motivation has been found to make a person renounce his or her personal interests in favour of others. For instance, if we accept the utilitarian approach to build a system of ethics, we still lack an explanation as to why personal interests should not prevail in cases of conflict. Only the idea of God setting a personal example and commanding mankind to follow it, can prevail over human egoism.

Even a deontological system of ethics, like that of Kant, does not respond to the question 'why be moral?'[2]. Reason may lead us to the Categorical Imperative, but it does not demand that we look for any imperative, or other principle of action besides inclination and spontaneity.

Moreover, the ethical discourse by definition encourages argument and permits pluralism[3]. This must lead to a relativist attitude and bring about a loss of respect, not only towards any individual argument, but towards the entire endeavour of ethical discourse. In other words, the autonomy of morals spreads doubt concerning its authority, which in turn points in the direction of an extra-moral foundation, such as God and religion.

On the other hand, ethics does not permit the rationalist the adoption of a voluntarist belief, describing God as a despotic ruler. In order to understand the religious sources, he must engage in ethical discourse. Moral discourse is, therefore, not limited to philosophers, but is also the concern of believers, and provides a common language between religious and non-religious people.

Even within the study of holy texts, traditions and articles of faith, moral considerations belong to the rules of interpretation, e.g. the discourse on theodicy. The religious concepts of **imitatio dei** and **imago dei** refer the believer to ethics and to its autonomy. The question is raised, for example, as to whether God could command cruel behaviour or an injustice vis-a-vis another creature. In order to raise such a question, a fortiori to suggest an answer, an independent ethics is needed.

According to the opinion of some biblical scholars, law, morals and religion of the Hebrew Bible, especially in priestly scriptures, are removed from internal piety and conscience by an over-emphasis on legal aspects and casuistry. Only certain prophets, like Jeremiah, are said to have pointed out the decisive role of inwardness and subjective intention, rather than obedience to rules and objective conformism. As previously mentioned, such an opinion disregards the structure and function of all law as being distinct from morals and religion. Legal passages of the Bible should not be judged by criteria of morals or statements of internal piety, but by those of other legal texts.

The law and morality of the Hebrew Bible are, moreover, said to be preoccupied with the ideas of reward and punishment, the concept **of quid pro quo** and of the God of vengeance. Before expressing such criticism from the point of view of a comforting religion, the concept of justice should be examined. The Hebrew Bible and rabbinical tradition emphasize divine justice and human responsibility by the doctrine of reward and punishment. Reliance on the love of God and on divine grace have too often led to licentiousness and to the expectation of a cheap grace.

Moreover, if there could be an ethical system of ancient Israel and of Judaism at all, the argument of some critics goes, such a system must be seen as one based on eudaemonism, rather than on a deontology. Such an argument lacks, of course, appreciation of biblical this-worldliness and of the variety of motives for moral behaviour.

The following study is meant to rebut many of these criticisms. We will try to show that the rules of the Pentateuch, as well as the Prophets and the Psalms, are not satisfied with external behaviourism and legalism. If divine commandments do not cover the totality of good action, and if human beings have a responsibility beyond the letter of the law, the criticism that the biblical religion is removed from internal piety would be unjust.

The second characterisation of ancient Israel, that it had not yet perceived the concepts of love and grace, would likewise be refuted: we could trace a balance of strict law by the moral concept of relinquishing one's rights in favour of another person. Both God and human beings could indeed be shown to move on a double-drive path of loving-kindness along with strict justice. Provisions of law and the idea of **measure for measure**, if this is true, represent only part of the moral system and must be interpreted together with their corollary following from the love of God and of fellow human beings.

Finally, the discussion of deontological elements in the Hebrew Bible, as well as in rabbinical sources, is to put the eudaemonist elements in their proper place. Divine attributes and virtues, the concept of **imitatio dei** and of human ontology, and the idea of conscience present a more differentiated system of morality than that said to be sanctioned by reward and punishment.

The more we look for ethical arguments in Jewish legal and theological texts, the greater will be our understanding of the considerable variety of moral motives. The Hebrew Bible and its rabbinical interpretation go far beyond a single idea and concept, appealing thereby to a variety of listeners and readers, and speaking to the sophisticated audience as well as to the simple-minded.

1.   Cf. Reeder & Outka (eds.), **Religion and Morality**; Green, **Religion and Moral Reason**; Schwartz, **Analytische Ethik und christliche Theologie**; Burkhardt (ed.), **Begruendung ethischer Normen**. For further literature see bibliography.

2.   Frankena, **Ethics**, p. 114.

3.   Frankena, 109.

A. BIBLICAL ETHICS

1. BIBLICAL THEONOMY

(a) Heteronomy

The claim has often been made that the Torah, as well as other systems of theonomy, cannot be reconciled with ethics or moral philosophy. Torah derives what is good or evil from divine revelation and legislation, meaning that it is based on heteronomy, and that there is no room for human analysis or evaluation. Its norms are based on the listening and obedience to divine authority, on the uniqueness of the prophecy of Moses, and on the delegation of power to the Great Court, as constituted from time to time. The most striking example of this system is the divine commandment to Abraham to offer up his son, which was certainly in violation of his personal moral convictions[1]. Similarly, the rules of warfare, the harshness of punishment for certain sins and other portions of the Torah seem to subordinate individual moral feelings to the divine will.

Ethics, being based on human reason and the questioning of all assumptions, is therefore in conflict with this kind of authoritarian system. Indeed, ethics is part of human thought, it is **anthropocentric**, and according to Kant stands for human **autonomy**. Biblical thought, on the other hand, is **theocentric** and **theonomic**, so that a priori there can be no encounter between the two.

To take the concepts of the Platonic dialogue **Euthyphron**, we may say that the system of the Torah defines right and wrong as that which has been declared as such by God, while ethics would demand that God declared right and wrong as that which is so according to human reason[2].

This dichotomy seems to have deepened since the enlightenment. According to Kant's definition, autonomy is "the exit from the culpable dependence (selbstverschuldete Unmuendigkeit), i.e. from the incapacity to use one's reason without the guidance of others. Such an incapacity is culpable, if its cause is not lack of intellect but lack of will and courage... It is so convenient to be dependent. If I have a book which has reason for me, a keeper of my conscience, having a conscience for me, a physician determining a diet for me, etc., I do not have to take the trouble"[4].

Kant, therefore, rejected the ethical character of Jewish religion, and yet a whole generation of Jewish thinkers tried to establish the morality of Judaism vis-a-vis his ethics. They mainly pointed out expressions of moral freedom and autonomy in biblical and rabbinical sources, often disregarding other expressions of the opposite meaning, and sometimes even changing the meaning of the quotations.

Meanwhile, Kant's idea of autonomy has been developed by the **Existentialists** in their endorsement of human freedom. According to their view, rational determinism did not answer the questions of modern man: What is he to be? What is he to live for? What values shall he affirm? In the absence of an objective answer, the Existentialists maintained the right of every individual to formulate his own answer. Hence, freedom to select among the philosophies of life and freedom from determinism were seen as the logical conclusions of the human condition. Of course from the point of view of the Torah, this appears as a rebellion against divine law and authority.

The claim of freedom was also formulated by the psychoanalyst Erich Fromm in reply to totalitarian thought[4]. The studies of Jean Piaget[5] and Lawrence Kohlberg[6] have in turn traced the moral development of children from heteronomy to autonomy. Biblical morality could therefore be described as a perpetuation of Kohlberg's **intermediate** stage, that being the objectivation of rules instead of the total dependence on persons of authority. But it remains below the ideal attitude, viz. the assumption of full responsibility for one's decisions. The concept of **theonomy** seems to be a kind of **heteronomy** hampering the full moral development of the individual.

Beyond these psychological arguments, we should mention the claim of Samuel Hugo Bergman against the idea that there could be a biblical, Jewish, or indeed any particular kind of ethics. According to his teaching there is only one universal human ethics, while the so-called Jewish ethics reflects the tension in Judaism between universalism and particularism[7].

Leon Roth on the other hand, in a classical essay, denied the existence of an Ethics of Judaism, "a plain statement of the moral ideas of Judaism", and "the bringing of them together into one intelligible and coherent view"[8]. In his view, there was an urgent need to fill this lacuna, and he offered a few ideas in this direction.

Biblical reflection on the Torah seems to affirm the incompatibility of the latter with ethics. Jeremiah, for example, traces the source of moral rules in the **knowledge of God**: King Josiah had done justice and righteousness... judged the cause of the poor and needy, regarding which the prophet declares: "Is not this to know Me? says God"[9]. Justice is not realized for its own sake, but as the result of a close relationship with God. In other words, the only basis of justice is **theonomy**, not ethics or any other human-centered thought.

Even wisdom literature referred to the religious basis of morals: "Trust God with all your heart and do not rely on your own understanding... Do not be wise in your own eyes, fear God and shun evil"[10]. The wise of Israel were warned, lest they develop any anthropocentric system of correct behaviour. Instead, they should be satisfied with heteronomy.

Undoubtedly, moral concepts guide both legislators and judges in their formulation of the law[11], but they thereby cease to be part of ethical discourses. There must be a clear distinction between legislation, or adjudication, and ethics. While law may develop out of moral concepts, once a rule has crystallized in the form of law, it has ceased to be part of moral teaching. It has become a heteronomous command, and has lost the characteristics of ethical argument.

A similar distinction must be made between religious and moral norms. As formulated by Leibowitz, "ethics as an intrinsic value is indubitably an **atheistic** category"[12]. This means that a system of theonomy cannot permit any ethical discourse, because the latter confers authority on man. According to this concept, which is shared by Rabbi Soloveitchik, biblical and Jewish morals are theonomous, even heteronomous, and do not actually constitute a system of ethics[13]. Emphasis upon heteronomy is the constant theme in the writings of A. Lichtenstein[14], M. Fox[15], D. Bleich[16], A. Kirschenbaum[17] and I. England[18].

A synthesis between such an insistence on Jewish heteronomy and a concept of moral intuition was suggested by S. Spero[19], and W.S. Wurzburger[20]. Human conscience, according to this view, can supplement divine law, but never supersede it. On the other hand, a constant revision of Jewish law and tradition in light of ethics is demanded by the Conservative thinker Seymour Siegel[21], obviously on the grounds of human autonomy.

(b) Autonomy

Indeed, a system of ethics would be possible in biblical thought if we assumed that God did not act as an arbitrary despot but as an enlightened educator[22]. If we rejected ethical voluntarism and positivism in favour of reason, we could reconcile biblical theonomy with the moral aspiration of a humanity coming of age. God might have **limited** Himself, to use the metaphor of Lurianic mysticism[23], in order to lead human beings towards moral responsibility. In that case, the use of human reason and the application of human autonomy would be a realization of God's will, not a contradiction of theonomy[24].

In this context we would use the term **autonomy** in a particular way, which does not fit into the Kantian description of the concept. For an autonomy derived from theonomy will be limited to the area prescribed by the latter, whereas autonomy actually means human self-determination without limit. Nevertheless, we will use this term in the following work to describe human participation in moral responsibility, though not declaring man to be the **measure of all things.**

The most significant form of self-limitation on the part of God is the covenant relationship with Israel[25]. Instead of imposing His will by an outright command, the Almighty, by choosing the framework of the covenant, uses consensus and social contract as a basic norm of the Torah. God could have been satisfied with delivering His commandments, but He chose to enter into a **bilateral** agreement, and to assume certain duties. This choice recognized the personality of the other party in the way described Martin Buber as **I and Thou**[26], and gave the commandments an ethical character. In the final instance, the obligation of humanity to observe divine commandments is based on mankind's own commitment, and on the maxim of reason that **pacta servanda sunt.** This is a true idea of ethics, and of the moral capacity of human beings prior to revelation[27].

Indeed, various prophets[28] identified the Torah with the Covenant[29], and the narrative concerning the revelation at Mount Sinai, including the Ten Commandments, spoke of a Covenant[30]. The validity of the commandments is the result of the affirmation of the people[31], rather than of divine legislation, power or authority.

As a result of divine self-limitation, the rules of justice are binding on God as well as on mankind. If God made an oath or entered into a covenant, He was bound, according to biblical thought, to abide by His word. He could even be called to account by a human being, under human concepts of justice. This is the underlying idea of Abraham's argument in favour of the citizens of Sodom, and of Job's claim that he was treated unjustly.

The idea of self-limitation appears in the praise of the divine King for preferring right to might: "And the King's might is his love of right. You have established equity. You have applied judgment and equity in Jacob"[32].

If **theologically** God Himself was said to be submitting to human concepts of justice, the same could **politically** be expected of the king of Israel, and the latter could also be held responsible for the violation of justice. Although he had been granted extensive prerogatives[33], the king could be accused by the prophet for having taken the wife of a subject of his, or for having expropriated his land[34].

Just as God was described as compassionate and preferring grace to justice, the human ruler, and indeed everyone of Israel, was asked to practise lovingkindness towards his brethren, and not to insist on his rights. Hence, the legal system of Israel did not cover all facets of life, but rather referred everybody to his or her conscience.

(c) Ontology

Biblical thought does not derive all standards of behaviour from the divine will, but takes into consideration an ontological concept of morality[35]. The term ontological should describe the attempt to base moral norms not on positive legislation but on the very being of God, as well as on metaphysics and reason. It would represent the opposite of ethical voluntarism and of an overemphasis on revelation. The term ontology is preferable to the more common term of natural law, which does not include that which is beyond nature, such as divine and metaphysical concepts.

Both **yashar** ànd **mesharim** mean straightness, concretely spoken, and uprightness in the moral sense[36]. Similarly, the term **chanaf** means both crooked and morally perverse[37]. There is an assumption that moral behaviour is in line with nature, while immorality deviates from this standard[38].

There also seems to exist an ontological concept of goodness which corresponds with ethical discourse. The term **tov** describes the suitability of somebody or something for a certain goal, a quality, a characteristic of a person, a decision of the wise, and finally, a moral and a theological standard[39]. Again, such a variety of meanings points to the link between reason and experience on the one hand, and moral norms on the other.

The ontological, rather than positive character of morality, appears in the intercession of Moses in favour of the sinners: "And now I pray, let the power of God be great, as You have said that God is slow to anger and plentous in lovingkindness, forgiving iniquity and transgression..."[40]. The text here refers to the **self-presentation** of God at an earlier occasion[41], and describes Moses as quoting it against God Himself[42]. Once the readiness to forgive has been presented as a divine attribute, God was, so to speak, no longer free to act in violation of this attribute. It had thereby become part of the universalizing of ethics, existing beside the otherwise prevalent theonomy.

Furthermore, being created in the image of God, mankind is able to distinguish between good and evil[43], so that human behaviour follows nature[44]. To do good is actually a form of self-realization, perhaps the most basic one, according to the ontological approach. Even the rules of Torah, though revealed by God, can be described as "very near to you, in your mouth and in your heart, that you may do it"[45]. A parallelism between positive revelation, on the one hand, and human conscience on the other, is again due to the ontological approach allowing for ethics **within** theonomy.

Another element of biblical morality is **commutative justice** and its practical conclusion, namely the duty to show gratitude to God and to keep His covenant. If Israel ought to obey God, because otherwise their behaviour would not correspond to God's salvation[46], this follows from the nature of any relationship, from mutuality.

Similarly, the duty to keep the covenant "rests upon a presupposition that one ought to keep a promise... Thus, while the Torah contains a moral code revealed by God, it is urged upon Israel because of moral principles of gratitude and promise-keeping, with the implication that these are somehow binding prior to the Sinaitic covenant"[47].

(d) Human Evaluation

It may be said that the Torah emphasised the theonomic idea in the commandments and in the moral elements of the narratives. But even in the latter part, we find an ambivalence vis-a-vis the notion of human autonomy. The statement ascribed to the snake, that by defying the divine command mankind could become godlike, **knowing what is good or evil**[48], for instance, is a proclamation of human autonomy, but it comes from the mouth of the **seducer**[49].

Because of its theonomic attitude, the text perceives human autonomy as an act of **hybris**[50]. However, the text also saw the snake as God's creature and messenger[51], which means that God Himself had allowed mankind to achieve autonomy by way of sin[52]. Perhaps the rabbinical doctrine, that human beings are being guided in the direction of their own choice[53], could be used to explain the text. Originally, God had wanted to grant mankind autonomy in a legitimate way, but once humanity had chosen to disobey, it achieved the knowledge of good and evil through the path of sin. Hence knowledge is tied with suffering[54], whereas originally it should have been a source of enjoyment.

Autonomy is represented in Abraham's moral argument with God[55], the assumption being that man has the capacity to evaluate the acts of God. This could have been considered an even more extreme example of hybris, but on this occasion God is perceived as willing to submit to moral criticism. This obviously preceded the insight of the Book of Job, viz. that God's ways were beyond the perception of human beings.

Again, the reader may assume that God had purposely announced his intention to destroy the city, so as to challenge the moral sensitivity of Abraham. The patriarch was to become an active partner in the formulation of the moral system of his descendants, not just a passive recipient of divine decisions. Human autonomy was therefore no longer **hybris**, but a creative contribution to the moral growth of the world.

This is remarkable in light of the other story concerning Abraham, namely the offering of Isaac, where the patriarch was lauded for the total abdication of his own moral responsibility in order to submit to the will of God. When he himself was tested, he was no proper judge of divine acts. However, God's relations towards other beings could be analysed and evaluated by Abraham's sense of justice.

The problem is, obviously, why Isaac's life was not protected by Abraham's conscience. "Kant, to whom the imperatives of universal morality were absolute, condemned Abraham, and argued that the Patriarch should have doubted the authenticity of the call. The Danish theologian Soeren Kierkegaard saw in the Akedah evidence that faith could sometimes make demands that went beyond morality; he called this doctrine 'the teleological suspension of the ethical'"[56].

The story indeed conveys the idea that human autonomy has its limits, not only where a person pleads **in sua causa**, but also where his test is just that, whether he is ready to surrender everything he believes in as a sign of his fear of God. Although biblical faith referred at other occasions to human reason and responsibility, it ascribed enough freedom to God to use this most valuable moral concept as a test. It is the exception meant to prove the rule, viz. that moral autonomy is so important, that it should become the supreme sacrifice and act of obedience.

Thus, the description of Abraham's test is not intended to be a theological discourse or a statement of ethical voluntarism, but to set an example of faith in God. Socrates or Kant would have been closer to the principles of ethics, but further away from God. On the other hand, the same set of facts in another situation would have called for moral reasoning and for independence of judgment, even vis-a-vis God. Abraham's intercession on behalf of Sodom shows him, in fact, to be ethical as well as believing.

A moral argument with God appears, for instance, in Moses' prayer on behalf of the people[57]. God is said to have changed His mind in response to the human sense of justice. But we could also argue that from the beginning God wanted to let Moses have a share in the decision, and therefore challenged him by a seemingly unjust declaration of intention. The same can be said regarding another prayer[58], which too was the result of a divine challenge.

A direct impact of moral argument on legislation, said to be divine, can be found in the case of the inheritance of daughters[59], and in that of the second Passover celebration[60]. In both cases a complaint was raised against the law ascribed to God: that it discriminated against some people. Again, rather than assuming that a divine mistake had to be corrected through human criticism, we understand these passages as a warning to always use one's moral sense, even when it comes to the highest authority.

Moral judgment is appealed to as a supreme test of the Torah[61]. Thus, divine law can be evaluated by human conscience. Whenever a rule of the Torah would violate the principles of justice according to ordinary human standards, it would not be supported. A new interpretation, or an amendment, would then be necessary to allow the Torah to maintain the said claim of being altogether just.

The tradition of wisdom called for ethical insights to be gained through reason and observation. The Book of Proverbs presents its purpose: "that men may know wisdom and morals, understand words of insight, receive moral instruction of reason, equity, judgment and righteousness"[62]. The value of observation is contained in the passage on the field of the sluggard, teaching the observer: "A little sleep, a little slumber, a little folding of the hands to rest, and poverty will come upon you like a robber, and want like an armed man"[63].

By the same token, the Prophets appealed to reason and experience to establish their points. The devastation of other nations should have led Judah to learn their lesson, without having to be addressed by a similar fate[64]. Accordingly, the afflictions of Israel should be taken as a warning and moralizing speech to the neighbouring nations[65].

(e) Legal and Moral Norms

As already mentioned, the moral character of the Torah expresses itself in the concept of covenant. Although God could have created a unilateral relationship with Israel, He is described as relating to the people within a bilateral agreement. Thus, the Torah is not a set of commands, but a contract: it calls for the active participation of human beings in the relationship.

Israel, therefore, was said to have submitted to the commandments in order to give them effect[66]. Legitimacy and consent, rather than power and authority, are the moral bases of the Torah. A true servant of God must first realize his autonomy before submitting to the Kingdom. Surrendering to God is meaningful only if one appreciates the alternative[67].

Human beings are treated as responsible partners in a dialogue. They are to be convinced by the so-called motive-clauses of the commandments[68]. Take, for example, the remark explaining the moral duty towards the bondwoman[69]. A legislator or a judge would have no need for such an explanation, which is used in order to convince by moral argument. The inclusion of such a remark is a recognition of the moral personality of the listener. He is not addressed like a politically inferior, but like an equal, who may or may not obey the norm.

Likewise, the call for humane behavior towards poor debtors takes the form of an ethical argument, and not that of a command[70]. The stranger is to be treated in the same way as the listeners had hoped to be while being strangers in Egypt[71]. The argument is based on the principle of universalism or more particularly, on the **Golden Rule**.

The commandments of social solidarity, though based on divine will, do not usually provide the exact measures, but leave it to the conscience of the person concerned[72]. This means that such norms belong to moral rather than legal obligations, and could be the subject of ethical discourse.

The rules of behaviour in the Torah can be classified according to their sanction, i.e. according to the reward and punishment attached to their observance or violation. On the one hand, we have true legal provisions, where the community or the court are called upon to inflict punishment in case of transgression. On the other hand, we have strictly moral appeals directed towards conscience only, without any reference to reward and punishment. In between there are a number of commandments with divine reward or punishment attached.

An example of the true legal provisions is the rule regarding brawling men causing the spontaneous abortion of a pregnant woman[73]. The strictly moral category can be represented by the inhibition of coveting the wife or property of a neighbour[74]. Between these extremes we can analyse and categorize a great number of commandments according to their consequences.

Take for instance the rule of levirate. It relies on a social sanction which has been put into legal language[75]. The rule belongs to the larger framework of family-solidarity, which is called "redemption", whether of the blood[76], of a woman[77], of property[78], or of a debtor[79]. The duty of redemption is enforced by way of social sanction, through public praise or disapproval.

The same can be said about the rule of the seventh year. True, according to a rabbinical interpretation, this is a kind of "royal expropriation"[80], which means that by law the ownership lapses during the seventh year. Nevertheless, it was held that the spirit of the sages approved of the repayment of debts in the seventh year[81]. The creditor might even stretch out his hand to indicate his willingness to collect the debt, in spite of the rule of remission[82].

The rule of the seventh year is therefore not a legal one, but only an appeal to the conscience of the property-owner. This is the meaning of the Hebrew **shamat** and **natash**[83], describing the idea of letting something go out of one's control. The text does not speak of expropriation, but recommends that the owner should let go. It is as if the text says: in the seventh year do not insist on your right, but be generous.

Likewise, the rule demanding restoration of the pledge at dawn, if the debtor needs the pledge as night-clothing[84], is a moral appeal. According to the law, the creditor has the right of possession until payment, but he is called upon to perform an act of charity[85].

(f) Conclusion

Biblical theonomy appeals to human conscience and builds upon existing morality. It is a system of cooperation between two poles, the divine and the truly human. Biblical theonomy is therefore not a form of heteronomy, but a responsible autonomy. This is so as a result of divine will and self-limitation, allowing humankind to serve God by their own decision. We have found ontological criteria of human behaviour, such as divine attributes and human nature, so that there is room for ethical discourse beside theology.

There appear clear references to the possibility of human evaluation of the good and of divine acts, which is another proof for the existence of ethics in theonomy. Even the commandments themselves testify to the ethical approach of the Hebrew Bible, since they are addressed to reason and to the participation of the listeners, and often depend upon human conscience alone.

1.   Gen. 22; cf. Green, pp. 77-102.

2.   See Eichrodt, **Theologie**, p. 218 ff.; van Oyen, **Ethik;** Smend, **Ethik;** I. Englard, "The Interaction of Morality and Jewish Law", JLA 7 (1988) 114-124.

3.   I. Kant, Beantwortung der Frage Was ist Aufklaerung, **Gesammelte Werke**, 9, p. 53; see also Kant, **Grundlegung zur Metaphysik der Sitten**, (Stuttgart: Reclam, 1961); cf. E. Fackenheim, "The Revealed Morality of Judaism and Modern Thought: A Confrontation with Kant", in Kellner, **Ethics**, pp. 61-83.

4.   Erich Fromm, **Escape from Freedom,** (1941); **Man for Himself,** (1947); **You shall be as gods**, (1966).

5.   Jean Piaget, **Das Moralische Urteil beim Kinde**, 4th ed. (rpt. Frankfurt M., 1981).

6.   Lawrence Kohlberg, "Moral and Religious Education and the Public Schools", in T. Sizer (ed.), **Religion and Public Education**, (Boston, 1967); Kohlberg, **The Philosophy of Moral Development** (San Francisco, 1981).

7.   S.H. Bergman, **The Quality of Faith: Essays on Judaism and Morality**, trans. Y. Hanegbi, (Jerusalem, 1970), pp. 32-40; cf. Leibowitz, **Yahadut,** pp. 303-321; Steven S. Schwarzschild (and respondents) in **Shema**, 7, (1977).

8.   Leon Roth, "Moralization and Demoralization in Jewish Ethics", **Judaism**, 11, (1962), pp. 291-302.

9.   Jer. 22:15-6.

10.   Prov. 3:5-7.

11.   Cf. M. Greenberg, "Some Postulates of Biblical Criminal Law", in M. Haran (ed.), **Y. Kaufman Jubilee Volume**, (Jerusalem, 1960) pp. 5-28.

12.   Y. Leibowitz, "Commandments", in Cohen & Mendes Flohr, p. 71; see also Leibowitz, **Yahadut,** pp. 28, 72-82, 310-313, and 344-345.

13.   Cf. W.S. Wurzburger, "The Maimonidean Matrix of R. J.B. Soloveitchik's Two Tiered Ethics", in J.V. Plaut, **Through the Sound of Many Vocies**, (Toronto, 1982), pp. 172-183; L. Kaplan, "Rabbi Joseph Soloveitchik's Philosophy of Halakhah", JLA 7 (1988) 139-197.

14.   In "Does Jewish Tradition Recognize an Ethics independent of Halakhah?" in Fox, **Ethics**, 62-88. Cf. also D. Weiss Halivni, "Can a Religious Law be Immoral?" in A. Chiel (ed.), **Perspectives on Jews and Judaism**, Wolfe Kelman Vol., (New York, 1978) 165-170.

15. In "Law and Morality in the Thought of Maimonides", in N. Rakover (ed.), **Maimonides as Codifier**, (Jerusalem, 1987), pp. 105-120.

16. In **Proceedings of the 9th World Congress of Jewish Studies**, (Jerusalem, 1986), C, pp. 55-62; id. "Judaism and Natural Law", JLA 7 (1988) 5-42.

17. "Maimonides and Equity", in Rakover, op. cit. pp. 143-153.

18. "The Interaction of Morality and Jewish Law", in **JLA** 7 (1988), pp. 114-124.

19. Spero, **Morality**, pp. 64-91.

20. "Law as the Basis of a Moral Society", in **Tradition 19**, (1981), pp. 42-54.

21. "Ethics and the Halakhah", in his **Conservative Judaism and Jewish Law**, xxiii, (New York, 1977), pp. 124-132.

22. Cf. BT 'Avodah Zarah 3 ab, "God is not a tyrant issuing arbitrary rules"; and Fromm, **You shall be as gods**, 24 ff. In Christian thought the possiblity of human moral autonomy is implied in Paul's doctrine about the law being written on the heart of man (Romans 2:14-15) and Thomas Aquinas, **Summa Theologica** 2:1:93:2; 2:1:94:2,4 (cf. Reinhold Niebuhr, **The Nature and Destiny of Man**, (New York, 1941) I, p. 275)‒. The recognition of autonomy within the system of Christian theonomy has been developed by Paul Tillich in his article "Theonomie" in **RGG** 2nd ed. (1931), and recently by the Catholic theologian Alphons Auer, **Autonome Moral und christlicher Glaube**, (Duesseldorf, 1971), and his article published by the Catholic Academy Freiburg in **Die Autoritaet der Kirche in Fragen der Moral**, (Freiburg, 1984). On Judaism and ethics see L. Jacobs "The Relationship between Religion and Ethics in Jewish Thought", in Kellner, **Ethics**, pp. 41-57; D. Novak "Natural Law, Halakhah and the Covenant", JLA 7 (1988) 43-67.

23. Gershom Sholem, **Major Trends in Jewish Mysticism**, (New York, Schocken 1961), p. 260 ff.

24. See also P. Tillich, **Systematic Theology**, vol. 3, (Chicago, 1963), pp. 249-275; Schrey, **Einfuehrung**, p. 30 f.; K. Hilpert, "Autonomie", in Stoeckle (ed.), **Woerterbuch**, pp. 28-34; and Fromm, **You shall be as gods**.

25. Cf. E. Kutsch, in TRE, s.v. **Bund**; Eichrodt, **Theologie** 1, 8th ed. (1968), p. 9; and E. Dorff "The Covenant: The Transcendent Thrust in Jewish Law", **JLA** 7, (1988) pp. 68-96.

26. M. Buber, **Ich und Du**, (Leipzig, 1923); and Buber **Koenigtum Gottes**, (Heidelberg 1956).

27. Contra Kaiser, **Ethics**, p. 4.

28. Hos. 8:1; Is. 24:5.

29. Cf. Ps. 78:10.

30. Ex. 19:5; Deut. 4:13, 5:2.

31. Ex. 19:8, 24:7.

32. Ps. 99:4; cf. Midrash Psalms ad loc.

33. 1 Sam. 8: 11-17.

34.   2 Sam. 12; 1 Kings 21.

35.   Cf. Pieper, **Ethik,** p. 47; Schrey, **Einfuehrung,** pp. 34-45; and Green, **Religion,** pp. 77-102. For the Jewish attitude toward Natural Law cf. **JLA 6** (1987) and 7 (1988).

36.   G. Liedke, in **Theologisches Handwoerterbuch zum AT,** (hereafter ThHWB), 1, p. 790.

37.   R. Knierim, in **ThHWB,** 1, p. 597.

38.   On human nature cf. G. Carey, **I believe in Man,** (1977); and R.S. Anderson, **On being Human,** (1983).

39.   H.J. Stoebe, in **ThHWB,** 1, pp. 652-664.

40.   Num. 14:17-18.

41.   Ex. 34:6-7.

42.   BT Sanhedrin 111 b.

43.   Gen. 3:22.

44.   Spero, p. 75 ff.

45.   Deut. 30:14.

46.   Deut. 32: 6-18; and Spero, p. 81.

47.   Spero, p. 81.

48.   Gen. 3:5.

49.   See H.J. Stoeber, "Gut und Boese in der j-istischen Quelle des Pentateuchs", **ZAW** 65, (1953), pp. 188-204; and the various opinions in C. Westermann, **Genesis,** 2nd ed., (Neukirchen, 1976), vol. 1, pp. 330-333.

50.   Cf. the Greek myth of Prometheus.

51.   Gen. 3:1.

52.   Cf. Karl Barth, **Die kirchliche Dogmatik,** Zollikon-Zuerich ii, (1942) p. 573, that human attempts to engage in ethical questions and to be autonomous are sinful.

53.   BT Makkot 10 b.

54.   Cf. Eccl. 1:18.

55.   Gen. 18:25; cf. Westermann, pp. 344-357.

56.   Spero, **Morality,** p. 93. See also Samuel Hugo Bergman, **The Quality of Faith,** transl. Y. Hanegbi, (Jerusalem, 1970), pp. 24-31; Emil L. Fackenheim, **Encounters between Judaism and Modern Philosophy,** (New York, 1973), pp. 9-29; Ronald M. Green, "Abraham, Isaac and the Jewish Tradition", **Journal of Religious Ethics,** 10, (1982) pp. 1-21; Green, **Religion;** Reeder & Outka, **Religion;** Shalom Spiegel, **The Last Trial, On the Legends and Lore of the Command to Abraham to offer Isaac as a Sacrifice: The Akedah,** (New York: Schocken, 1969); criticism of Kierkegaard's presentation of the problem in J.H. Gumbiner, "Fear and Trembling", **Commentary,** 2, (1948), pp. 143-148; M. Fox, **Judaism,** 2, (1953), pp. 160-169; M. Steinberg, **Anatomy of Faith,** (New York: Harcourt, 1960), pp. 130-152; E.L. Fackenheim, **Quest for Past and Future,** (Indiana: U.P., 1968), pp. 52-65; J.L. Halevi, **Judaism,** 4, (1955), pp. 13-28, and 8, (1959), pp. 291-302.

57. Ex. 32:12-13; cf. J. Muilenburg, "The Intercession of the Covenant Mediator" in P.R. Ackroyd (ed.), **Words and Meanings... Esays to D.W. Thomas**, (Cambridge, 1968), p. 159 ff.

58. Num. 14: 13-18; cf. Jacob Milgrom, **Numbers**, (Philadelphia: JPS, 1990), pp. 392-396.

59. Num. 27:1-5.

60. Num. 9:7.

61. Deut. 4:8.

62. Prov. 1:2-3.

63. Prov. 24:30-32.

64. Zeph. 3:6-7.

65. Ez. 5:15.

66. Ex. 24:3.

67. This is like the unleavened bread which must consist of dough which could ferment: BT Pessachim 35 a.

68. B. Gemser, "The Importance of the Motive Clause in OT Law", VT, Suppl. 1, (1953), pp. 50-66; R. Sonsino, **Motive Clauses in Hebrew Law: Biblical Forms and NE Parallels**, (Chico, 1980); and Kaiser, **OT Ethics**, pp. 239-342.

69. Ex. 21:8.

70. Ex. 22:25; Deut. 24:6.

71. Ex. 23:9.

72. M Pe'ah 1:1.

73. Ex. 21:22-25.

74. Ex. 20:13.

75. Deut. 25:9-10.

76. Num. 35:19; Deut. 19:6; cf. E. Neufeld, "Ius redemptionis in Ancient Hebrew Law", **RIDA**, 3rd ser., 8, (1961), pp. 29-40.

77. Gen. 38; Deut. 25:5-10; Ruth.

78. Lev. 25:25-35; Ruth; cf. D.A. Legget, **The Levirate and go'el Institutions in the OT**, Diss. (Cherry Hill, NJ, 1974).

79. Lev. 25:47-55.

80. BT Bava Metsia 106 a; ET s.v. **'afqa'ta de malka.**

81. M Shevi'it 10:9.

82. JT Shevi'it 10:7, 39 d.

83. Ex. 23:11; Deut. 15:1.

84. Deut. 24:12-13.

85. Cf. BT Bava Metsia 82 a.

2. BIBLICAL VIRTUES

(a) Human Virtues

The anthropocentric aspect of biblical teaching appears in the existing balance between the system of duties and that of virtues[1]. Such a balance can be found not only in the description of human virtues, but also in the meaning of divine attributes and models. The discussion of the latter definitely belongs to ethical discourse, and does not follow from the divine **fiat**. Moreover, biblical appreciation of the body, of material values and of temperance, points to the room left for ethics beside theonomy.

While the system of commandments occupies the central place in the Torah, the alternative system of virtues can be found as well, especially in the narratives which describe the virtues or educational ideals of Israel. The listener to these narratives is called upon to imitate these virtues in order to lead a meaningful life.

We distinguish between virtues of direction, such as justice and lovingkindness, and those relating to attitudes, such as wisdom, courage, patience, prudence and diligence. Indeed, both categories are used by the authors of biblical narratives.

Thus, the ancestors of the people were described by reference to various virtues of direction, in a way which called for the imitation of those virtues. For instance Noach, Abraham and Jacob were shown to be perfect, integral and sincere[2], which means their total devotion to living a good life, and their being without inner conflict. All of these virtues make sense only within the context of human responsibility to God, and within the framework of His direction[3].

Abraham also represents the virtue of trust in God[4]; likewise, Moses is said to be the trustee in the house of God[5]. These virtues refer, therefore, to the relationship of the individual with God, but they equally play a role in the relations between humans. A trustworthy person is said to be able to keep secrets[6], and to be a faithful messenger vis-a-vis his principal[7]. Even the wounds inflicted by a friend are considered to be faithful[8], meaning that they must be for a good cause, and valuable acts of relationships.

The virtue of righteousness is mentioned as a general characterization of Noach as a person[9], but it is also ascribed to specific acts[10]. Corresponding to this is the virtue of straightforwardness of the heart[11], which is also understood as a parallel to true piety[12].

Virtues of attitudes are often linked with those of direction. Joseph, for example, is described as wise and insightful[13], aside from his being righteous before God. By keeping the commandments, the people of Israel are said to acquire these characteristics as well[14], besides their merit in the eyes of God. The same virtues are mentioned regarding the judges and leaders of the people[15], which obviously enable them to do their duty towards God as well as towards human beings.

While art is usually seen as an achievement of human cognitive faculties, the artistic perception is also described as a wisdom derived from the divine spirit[16]. Synonymous to this virtue is that of knowledge[17], which is again a relation with God. Joseph, Solomon and Daniel represent these virtues, all in connection with dreams and divine intuition.

The humility of Moses is another virtue of attitude to be aspired to in education and self-improvement[18]. Obviously, the biography of the greatest prophet is not only of historical interest, but represents a model of behavior which should be followed by the listener.

Every individual is called upon to relate to his fellow man as a brother, brotherly feelings and action being a central virtue. This idea is expressed in the negative in the stories of Cain and Abel, and that of Joseph and his brothers. In the positive, the idea is behind many rules of solidarity[19]. This concept is not an exclusive one, but extends even to the Edomites, a nation which had often been at war with Israel[20].

The virtue of joyfulness is part of the ethos of family life and of the religious cult[21], especially at the celebration of festivals[22]. According to the rabbinical definition, this refers to the **simchah shel mitswah** (joy of the commandment)[23], which is a form of internalization and participation.

Many commandments are understood to be the means of creating a habit and developing a virtue. The concept of holiness serves as the heading of a series of commandments[24]. Just as God is perceived as set apart from anything else, the people of Israel are destined to be set apart from secularity and materialism. By keeping the commandments they could become godlike, and transcend their natural weakness and limitation.

The virtues of awe and love of God give meaning to many practical rules of behaviour[25]. Instead of declaring each commandment in a deontological way, i.e. as a specific command of obedience, the commandments in general are seen as part of a program of self-improvement.

Moreover, by stressing the justice and wisdom of the Torah, the speaker puts the particular message addressed to the people of Israel into a general framework of virtues, common to all mankind.

Every discourse on specific virtues must be understood as a rejection of alternatives. While Plato considered prudence, temperance, courage and justice to be the cardinal virtues of man[26], Jeremiah had already rejected the values of prudence, courage and richness **per se**[27]. According to the ethics of the prophet, only the knowledge of God was a true virtue, and its consequence was **imitatio dei**, in particular the practice of mercy, justice and righteousness[28].

A woman's virtue, in turn, was defined vis-a-vis other potentialties: "Grace is deceitful and beauty is vain; a woman should be praised for fearing God"[29]. Again, ethics in the environment of Israel must have declared the former virtues to be significant for woman, and the author of the text wanted to reject the prevalent view.

In accordance with biblical views, a person excelling in these virtues was designated as **tov** (good), as young Saul for instance[30]. Moreover, courage was said to befit the pious rather than the ordinary man[31].

The prophets speaking of the end of days tend to ascribe the change to the prevalence of certain virtues. The future king is described as being in possession of the spirit of God[32], and the state of peace is explained as being a result of the knowledge of God[33]. Correspondingly, the promise that the teaching would be put within the people and written upon their hearts[34], is a reference to the importance of virtue in human behaviour.

The Bible also ascribes negative traits of character to the Patriarchs and to other personalities. Abraham, for instance, is shown as lying in order to protect his wife. Other vices are mentioned in the biblical narratives as well[35]. This is evidence of the realism in biblical teaching, which does not pretend that the Patriarchs were super-human and completely without fault. The listener and reader are invited to use his or her understanding in the evaluation of these narratives, and thereby continue the moral discourse offered by the text.

(b) Divine Attributes and Models

Some of the divine attributes described in the Torah are virtues themselves, and are meant to be used as models for the development of human character. Human beings should follow in the path of God[36], who is described as merciful, gracious, long suffering and abundant in goodness and truth[37]. This is a call for **imitatio dei**, i.e. for the adoption of these virtues of the divine model[38]. These divine characteristics are also called **God's Way**[39]. The whole idea of **imitatio dei** is based on a system of virtues, which should provide guidance for human behaviour. If God is described as compassionate or holy[40], this is to proclaim these virtues as supreme values in human life.

A person seeking a new way of life is called upon to take God as a model: "Good and straightforward is God, therefore he instructs sinners in the way. He guides the humble in justice and teaches the humble His way"[41]. By describing the character of God, the speaker has put his finger upon one of the central ideas of biblical ethics: the correlation between faith and behaviour[42].

The first application of the **imitatio dei** concept is the idea of the Sabbath, calling for a weekly rest, like that which God is said to have taken after creation. If man is called upon to keep the Sabbath, this means that he is able to overcome his drive for creativity and acquisition, and can devote time to spirituality. On the Sabbath man can be like God. Likewise, the commandment to be holy because God is holy[43], develops the concept of **imitatio dei**. God's love for the stranger, the orphan and the widow, is the paradigm for the same virtue on the part of the people of Israel[44].

The confluence of divine and human virtues appears in the concept of walking in God's ways, which is a corollary to the concept of being created in the image of God. Abraham was chosen "in order that he might command his children and his household after him to keep God's way, to do righteousness and justice"[45]. "This would indicate that these values are not merely the ways which God has commanded man to walk in, but that they are actually God's ways - i.e. the ways in which God Himself walks"[46]. The same meaning should probably be ascribed to the commandments employing the phrase "Go in the ways of God"[47], so that they called for using divine attributes as models of human behaviour.

The problem with biblical ethics lies in the various texts ascribing what we consider as being negative character traits, or vices, to God. Such statements should be seen as anthropomorphisms and anthropopathisms, which are used to impress the listener and reader. God is described as regretting and changing his earlier decision, because this is how a human being would have behaved in the situation[48]. The same applies to texts which reveal the hatred of God, His wrath, His taking revenge[49], or His use of falsehood and deception[50]. The vicarious suffering of descendants for the sins of their ascendants, in reference to God's measures of justice, was said to have been abrogated by the prophet Ezekiel[51].

The idea of **imitatio dei** is therefore selective, and not meant to relate to these negative characteristics, though the listener and reader obviously might sometimes be inclined to use them as models. This is indeed proof of the need for ethical criticism, lest the Bible itself, if read in a fundamentalistic way, set a negative example.

(c) Theodicy

Biblical thought had difficulty in vindicating God in the face of evil and suffering[52]. The question of why should the righteous be afflicted and prosperity be granted to the wicked, was raised time and again[53]. The philosopher would formulate this problem as how to harmonize the divine attributes of justice and benevolence with those of omniscience and omnipotence. Originally, these events were explained as the reward or punishment of the people concerned; Job's friends, for instance, served as spokesmen of this attitude.

At a very early stage, probably during the tribal age, the doctrine of punishment was extended to cover vicarious responsibility of ascendants and descendants, as well as of brothers, kinsmen and members of the covenant[54]. Perhaps the doctrine of the Suffering Servant[55] still belongs to this stage.

Another justification of unfair suffering is the doctrine of divine test, which could also serve as a catalyst for moral growth. Abraham's supreme test was the commandment that he should offer his son. Likewise, any suffering inflicted upon man by God could be a test of his faith[56]. The best example for this doctrine is Job, who through his suffering rises to the highest level of faith in God: "Though He dealt a death blow to me, yet will I trust in Him"[57].

A similar idea appears in the psalm of trust: "Nevertheless, I am continually with You; You hold my right hand. You will guide me with Your counsel, and afterwards receive me with glory. Whom do I have in heaven but You? And beside You I desire no one on earth. My flesh and my heart fail, but God is the rock of my heart and my portion for ever"[58].

(d) Temperance

Biblical thought perceives the unity of human beings, rather than the distinction between soul and body. The same can be said about the unity of all phenomena, which is stressed, rather than the distinction between spirit and matter[59]. The concept of **shalem** (wholeness), includes the integrity of the body as well as the peace of the soul, and the goal of biblical teaching is material **and** spiritual wellbeing of individuals and nations.

The various commandments are meant to sanctify the secular sphere, not to abolish it. Fast days, vows of abstinence and priestly restrictions are exceptional measures, rather than expressions of an ideal of asceticism. The aim of the service to God is a balanced life - of man together with woman, blessed by children and material goods, in a mood of joy and fulfillment. Hence the Aristotelian middle path had been anticipated in the teaching of Israel.

The tension existing in biblical thought between the observance of the golden mean and ascetic tendencies appears in the rule of the Nazirite[60]. On one hand, the vow and the observance of the rule are meant to raise him to holiness; on the other hand, he is in need of a sin offering at the end of the period, for having perhaps been extreme in his abstinence[61].

Similarly, the perception of Israel as a people, occupying a territory and being involved in matter as well as in spirit, is a sign of the virtue of temperance. The balance of power by king and prophet, or by priest and prophet, is another factor of moderation. Biblical religion in general, represents a golden mean between realism and piety, or between the concern with matter and spirit.

It may therefore be said, that biblical thought does not derive the norms of human behaviour from divine commandments alone, but also refers to a system of human self-realization and of human values. Though the ethics of virtues was not meant as an alternative to theonomy, it did serve towards its completion.

A person following in the footsteps of the Patriarchs or imitating the characters described in the narratives is not simply obedient to theonomy. He must evaluate traits of character, his own as well as those of the person described in the holy tradition. He must be selective and critical and cannot be satisfied with mere obedience to divine law. The message of the biblical sources, therefore, reaches us by two parallel media: by the arguments of virtue as well as by normative commandments. While the latter might perhaps be taken as an indication of heteronomy, the former is definitely an appeal to human hermeneutic autonomy.

1.   Cf. Frankena, **Ethics**, pp. 63-69; Hoeffe, **Lexikon,** pp. 257-259; and Erik Erikson, **Insight and Responsibility**, (London: Faber, 1964), ch. 4.

2.   Gen. 6:9; 17:1; 25:27.

3.   Cf. E. Wuerthwein & O. Merck, **Verantwortung,** (Stuttgart: Kohlhammer TB).

4.   Gen. 15:6.

5.   Num. 12:7.

6.   Prov. 11:13.

7.   Prov. 25:13.

8.   Prov. 27:6.

9.   Gen. 6:9.

10.   Gen. 15:6; Deut. 24:13; cf. Ps. 106:31.

11.   Deut. 9:5.

12.   Mic. 7:2.

13.   Gen. 41:33, 39.

14.   Deut. 4:7.

15.   Deut. 1:13, 15.

16.   Ex. 28:3; 31:6; 36:1-2.

17.   Ex. 31:3; 35:31: Num. 24:16.

18.   Num. 12:3.

19.   Lev. 19:17; 25:35-48; Num. 32:6; Deut. 15: 2-12; 17: 15,20; 18:15,18; 19:18-19; 20:8; 22:1-4; 23:20-21; 24:7, 14; 25:3.

20.   Deut. 23:8.

21.   Deut 24:5; 28:47.

22.   Lev. 23:40; Deut. 12:7,12.

23.   Cf. BT Berakhot 31 a.

24.   Lev. 19:1 ff.

25.   Ex. 20:6; Deut. 12:12; 19:9.

26.   Cf. Plato's dialogues: **Charmides, Laches,** and **Protagoras.**

27.   Jer. 9:22-23.

28.   Likewise, in biblical thought, intellect and love directed towards God, and hence towards fellow human beings, are of great importance. While biblical thought appreciates greatly the virtue of justice, there seems to be less of an emphasis on temperance. See however Eccl. 7:16-18.

29.   Prov. 31:30.

30.   1 Sam. 9:2; cf. 1 Kings 20:3.

31.   Ps. 112:2.

32.   Is. 11:2.

33.   Is. 11:9.

34.   Jer. 31:33.

35.   Kaiser, **OT Ethics**, pp. 270-283.

36.   Deut. 10:12; 11:22; 26:17.

37.   Ex. 34:6; Num. 14:18; Ps. 103:7.

38.   Cf. D.S. Shapiro, "The Doctrine of the Image of God and Imitatio Dei", in Kellner, **Ethics** pp. 127-151.

39.   Gen. 18:19; Deut. 11:22; 13:5; 28:9; and see Sifre Deut. 11:22; BT Sotah 14 a; Shapiro, "The Doctrine", p. 129; and Spero, **Morality**, p. 86.

40.   Ex. 34:6; Num. 14:18; Lev. 11:44; 19:2; 20:26; 21:8.

41.   Ps. 25:8-9.

42.   Cf. Kaiser, **Ethics**, pp. 29-30; and infra.

43.   Lev. 19:2; cf. Sifra Lev. 19:2; and Shapiro, "The Doctrine", p. 130.

44.   Deut. 10:18-9.

45.   Gen. 18:19; cf. Ex. 33:13; Ps. 103:9.

46.   Cf. Ps. 25:10; D.S. Shapiro, "The Doctrine", p. 129 f., p. 145, nn. 12-14; and Spero, **Morality**, p. 86.

47.   Deut. 11:22; 28:9.

48.   Cf. Midrash Tanchuma, **Wayishlach** 10; Shapiro, "The Doctrine", p. 131; and Kaiser, **Ethics**, pp. 249-251.

49.   Kaiser, pp. 251-261.

50.   Kaiser, pp. 256-258, 264-266.

51.   Ez. 18:4; BT Makkot 24 a.

52.   Cf. N. Pike, **God and Evil**, (Englewood Cliffs, 1964).

53.   Cf. Jer. 12: 1-3; Job21:7.

54.   Ex. 20:4; 32:10; 34:7; Num. 14:12,18; Deut. 5:8.

55.   Is. 52:13 - 53:12.

56.   Cf. Deut. 8:2.

57.   Job 13:15.

58.   Ps. 73: 23-26.

59.   Cf. my **Law and Religion**, pp. 97-103.

60.   Num. 6:1-21.

61.   Cf. BT Ta'anit 11 a; Nedarim 10 a.

3. BIBLICAL FAITH AND ETHICS

Ethical discourse must take into account the meaning of faith in God in addressing the personal and social aspects of human behaviour. Faith presents an answer to the question of meaning, which in turn is relevant to the personal and social life of every individual. An attempt must therefore be made to explain the moral attitude of biblical sources in correlation with the teachings of biblical faith. We will concentrate here on the image of God, human relations, and the religious concept of law.

(a) God

Biblical tradition derives many moral concepts from the belief in God. While under God's control, every human judge is called upon to administer justice in His name, God being the ultimate Judge of the whole world[1]. This means that both the rules of substantive law and of procedure are founded in divine authority. God is perceived as the author and center of the moral order, which is comprised of animate, inanimate, Israelite and non-Israelite, elements and concerns. This idea would be in accordance with religious positivism and ethical voluntarism.

However, various prophets took it for granted that the people would be obliged to obey God's will and commandments at least out of gratitude; ingratitude towards God being the basis for all sin[2]. Human beings were supposed to believe in the benefits of divine creation and to feel responsible for its preservation[3]. Therefore, expressions of ungratefulness are mentioned as primary causes of evil[4]. The religious duty is thereby based upon a moral principle.

On the other hand, the belief of **imago dei** is a religious source of various ethical concepts. The absolute value of human life, and the public responsibility for the suppression of killing, are derived from this doctrine[5]. The impression of God as the merciful father of all creatures, animals as well as man, leads to the ethical value of human compassion vis-a-vis all other beings[6].

Worshipping God means not only being sensitive to His will, but also to the needs of His creatures[7]. At the same time, the concept of God as the judge of individuals and nations imposes ethical responsibility for any human act or omission.

However, the concept of **imago dei** also allows for human argument with God[8]. If mankind has been created in the image of God, it has been elevated to the level of a **Thou**, according to the terminology of Buber, and therefore God Himself is responsible to man for His acts or omissions.

The belief in creation is the basis for human responsibility towards his brother, neighbour, property, and for the preservation of the earth. It is likewise the basis for Israel's title to the Holy Land, having been allotted to them by God. God is said to have brought Israel out of Egypt, and to have given them the land of the Canaanites[9]. The story of creation is the basis of the concept of human stewardship and of Israel's title to the Holy Land, both originating from divine dominion over the whole earth[10].

According to the same principle, however, the conquest of the land of Israel by the Babylonians is ascribed to divine disposition[11]. This is a good example of the universality of moral concepts, such as the legitimization of Israel, and of the ethical character of the statement.

Moreover, this universality includes even God Himself. He is considered as being bound by His decisions and by His sense of justice. The land could have been given to Israel only after the native population had forfeited their title through their wickedness[12]. Thus, the Creator of Heaven and Earth was considered to be under the rule of law and justice, which shows, again, the legitimacy of ethics in the biblical belief system. Divine acts of salvation are called **tsedakot**, meaning acts of justice[13], as if God was judged for his relationship with Israel. Divine revelation and legislation provide ethical challenges as well as ethical impulses. Any case of divine revelation sets an example of outreach and transcendence, to be applied in inter-human relations as well.

If God had transcended to speak to human beings and reveal His will, inter-human relations were no longer exclusively a concern of mankind. The human **I and Thou**, to use again the terminology of Buber, can no longer be seen in isolation without the prior **I and Thou** between God and man. Therefore, certain human rights cannot be renounced, but other human rights, such as the right of life of a murderer, may have to give way to the commandment of justice, according to the will of God.

The concept of God as effecting redemption of individuals, nations and mankind, corresponds with the ethics of family solidarity. God is perceived as caring for, and sympathizing with human beings, and this is to be taken as a model for mankind's duty to extend care and protection to their kin

and to others in need[14]. Hence, redemption is not only the basis of hope
and security, but even more so the basis for **imitatio dei**.

Biblical eschatology is an ethical programme, based on the belief in
God. From the House of the God of Israel justice would, finally, be
administered among the nations, and eternal peace would be the result[15].
Such a programme, combining social with personal morality, as well as
international with national order, is indeed unthinkable without faith.

(b) Human Relations

The belief that human beings were created **imago dei** became a basis for
the concepts of human dignity and of human rights. Both can be modelled
after the concept of God. Every human being represents God and enjoys
His protection. Therefore, human relations form the basis of a triangle, of
which the opposite angle points to God. Furthermore, every human being
has the potential to walk in the path of God and be godlike, and it is this
potential which embodies him or her with a special dignity. The Israelite
can become holy and godlike by living according to God's special
commandments[16], which means that he too, must be treated with the
respect and reverence accorded to the divine being.

Human relations should be based upon the divine commandment and
the divine example, especially the ideals of justice and love[17]. Moreover, it
is the vocation of human beings to serve God, and this vocation requires
their prior independence from other human beings[18].

The description of the first man, and the lists of genealogy at the
beginning of the Book of Genesis, stress the brotherhood of all mankind.
Their common descent from that first man, and the fact that all are united
in their being creatures of one God, are the basis of their mutual duty of
loyalty[19]. Their responsibility to God, and the common concerns in the
preservation of the earth, as well as the prevention of cruelty to animals,
should unite otherwise conflicting human beings. These responsibilities
should lead them to overcome animosity and hatred between themselves,
and thereby bring about peace[20].

The experience of national suffering should sensitize the people of Israel
to the feelings of strangers[21], which means that the belief in one's history is
an element of practical ethics. The concept of brotherhood was extended
even to the Edomites, a neighbouring nation often at war with Israel. The
duty of gratitude was even to be applied to the Egyptians, who long ago
had offered hospitality to the Hebrew tribes, though afterwards had enslaved
and persecuted them[22].

The communal service to God, and the idea of the covenant, provided a framework of unity and a common consciousness of biblical society. Both the individual and the people as a whole were responsible for their fellow human beings and for their society, and even for all of humanity[23].

(c) The Law

The laws delivered by God to Moses were not only seen as an example of theonomy, but also made an important contribution to ethical thought. Being part of the covenant between God and the people, the laws have an element of consent and equality, setting an example for human institutions. Many laws are accompanied by words of motivation and justification[24], which is the ethical approach to be applied in human relations as well.

The idea of equality before the law follows from the divine lawgiver, who relates equally to both natives and strangers[25]. Not only is human life of unlimited value, but compensation for personal injury should not be dependent upon the status of the plaintiff or defendant[26].

The law consists of cultic and ritual norms, as well as of legal and moral ones, and it realizes the ideas of love and of justice in relation to God and to fellow human beings. By observing the divine commandments, a man or woman gives expression to their love and awe of God[27], which means that the intention is the goal of the act.

The law gives every Jew the opportunity to experience the presence of God, and to feel the divine concern for his life. By studying and observing, he practises **devequt** (cleaving unto God)[28], an experience similar to the **unio mystica**.

Similarly, the love of one's fellow man is the purpose of the moral commandments[29], and of quite a number of rituals. The discipline practised through this system makes room for the other, and sensitizes those who observe the commandments to the needs of their fellow human beings.

A major ethical question pertaining to the law of the Torah, is how to understand its hatred towards other faiths and towards assimilation and secularization. Religion usually tends to sensitize the person to the concern of others, but in this case the commitment to God creates fanaticism and motivates the believer in a negative direction. Monotheistic faiths have, indeed, been accused by Eastern thinkers of fanaticism and imperialism, especially vis-a-vis adherents to other religions.

Various biblical laws against other cults, unauthorized prophecy and other acts of non-conformism, present great difficulties for pluralistic ethics and liberal humanism. Indeed, if the law was meant to serve the people, rather than to be an end unto itself, it should have reacted to pluralism in a creative manner, rather than suppress non-orthodox opinions.

Although freedom of religion and of religious non-conformism was unknown in biblical times, there existed certain tendencies towards a more comprehensive understanding of other cults by Israel. God was said to be worshipped from the East to the West[30], which meant that the other cults were also addressing the one and only God of the world, who is also the God of Israel[31].

Moreover, biblical faith is based on piety as well as on revelation. The former is a subjective, human-centered virtue, while the latter expresses the objective formulation of the divine will. The commandments of the Torah and the speeches of the prophets are of the latter category, the psalms and the books of wisdom reflect the former. Just as theonomy and ethics should complement each other, commandments of the Torah were meant to be applied, interpreted and, where need arises, to be amended by sensitive individuals.

Rules of intolerance vis-a-vis religious deviations, acts of discrimination against women and foreigners and other norms conflicting with ethics should probably be set aside by an inner voice of the pious. The Talmud knows of exceptional cases permitting transgressions of the law, in order to serve a higher purpose, e.g. the sanctification of the Divine Name[32]. Similar considerations may have played a role, whenever the moral conscience of the pious was confronted with such a moral dilemma.

1.   Deut. 1:17; Ps. 82:1.

2.   Am. 2:9-11; cf. Hos. 11:1 ff..; Is. 1:3; Mic. 6:3-5; Jer. 2:6-7.

3.   Cf. Deut. 20:19-20.

4.   Gen. 3:12; Num. 21:5. Cf. BT Avodah Zarah 5 ab.

5.   Gen. 9:6.

6.   Cf. Ex. 22:26.

7.   Deut. 16:11, 14.

8.   Gen. 18:25; Ex. 32:11-13.

9.   Lev. 25:38; Deut. 6:10 ff., 9:4 ff.

10.   Cf. Gen. Rabba 1:2.

11.   Jer. 27:5 ff.

12.   Gen. 15:16.

13.   Jud. 5:11.

14.   Cf. Ex. 3:7-9.
15.   Is. 2:1-4; Jer. 23:5-6.
16.   Lev. 19:1-2.
17.   Gen. 18:19; Deut. 11:22; Mic. 6:8.
18.   Lev. 25:42,55; BT Bava Metsia 10 a.
19.   Mal. 2:10.
20.   Ex. 23:4-5.
21.   Ex. 22:12; Lev. 19:33-34; Deut. 10:18-19; 15:15.
22.   Deut. 23:8.
23.   Gen. 12:3.
24.   Cf. Ex. 22:25-26; 23:8; Deut. 5-13-14; 24:6; 25:3.
25.   Ex. 12:49.
26.   Ex. 21:23-25: Lev. 24:19-22: Deut. 19:21.
27.   Deut. 6:5; 11:1,13,22; 19:9; 30:6,16,20.
28.   Ps. 119:33-35.
29.   Lev. 19:18,34.
30.   Ps. 113: 3; Mal. 1:11.
31.   Cf. my "From East to West", in J. Hick & Hasan Askari (eds.), **The Experience of Religious Diversity**, (Aldershot: Gower, 1985), pp. 25-33.
32.   Cf. ET s.v. **Chillul hashem.**

4. SOCIAL CONVENTION IN THE BIBLE

(a) Social Origin of Commandments

Ethics deals with inter-human relations and communications based, inter alia, upon the social role and expectations applying to the individual. Human behaviour is conditioned by social learning processes, which form the various concepts, values and norms that are used as guiding principles in situations of doubt. The greater mobility and dynamism in modern society leads on the one hand to a growing independence of the individual vis-a-vis his original environment, and on the other hand to a constantly growing dependence upon the social values of one's chosen group, party or other setting.

Hence, a discussion of biblical as well as of any other moral philosophy, must include an examination of the social factors which influence the behaviour of the individual. Within the framework of a theonomic ethics especially, based on the covenant concept, consideration must be given to a differentiation between personal and social elements of human responsibility towards God.

In a theonomic system, the will of God will usually be accepted as the direct source of law and morality. However, this does not exclude the possibility that the divine will is the indirect source of a rule. Take, for instance, certain rules of law and morality being constituted by tacit or explicit social agreement, and **a posteriori** sanctioned by God.

The same could be said if one derived law or morality from nature or reason. In general, this would mean that nature or reason were the direct sources, but we could also declare them to be indirect sources, viz. ascribe to them the function of giving sanction **a posteriori** to rules of social convention.

In all the latter cases we would call God, nature or reason, respectively, the indirect source, or the source of recognition. The following examples do indeed show that a social convention could transform into a theonomic rule of law.

We are first told of a custom of refraining from the consumption of the sciatic nerve, and this observance is later incorporated in the dietary commandments[1]. This means that divine recognition was given to the social convention, and thereby the rule turned into a commandment.

The division of spoil was likewise said to be based on a precedent laid down by King David, and on the ensuing custom of the people[2], but it is also mentioned as a theonomic rule[3]. Historically, therefore, social convention preceded theonomy and later merged into the latter.

We will now speak of the social origins of additional divine commandments, of changes in the social consciousness, and finally of social pluralism in the biblical ethos.

Although ethics exercises the reason and experience of individual thinkers, it cannot be developed in a vacuum. The test for the validity of moral norms is always whether they have social sanction[4]; what is right or wrong is then derived from the social group to which one belongs. This has been established by researchers in the fields of psychology and sociology.

According to Sigmund Freud, the first (proto)-moral authority of the individual is the instinct, which might be called **id**. In a second phase, the id is superseded by the **ego**, which in turn is instrumental in the development of the **super-ego**, constituting the internalized parental authority and the conscious, and often influencing the individual's **sub-conscious**. This third stage is reached by the individual through the development of a personality of his own, and through learning from his experiences. Only the latter is to be considered the true I[5].

The educational conclusions from this differentiation were demonstrated by Erik Erikson and Lawrence Kohlberg[6]. Every child learns right from birth to respond to the expectations of his environment, and to evaluate himself by the recognition granted him by this environment. In the course of moral development, independence from the environment becomes the basis of individual conscience.

A similar process is depicted by sociologists. F. Toennies described the well-known distinction between the total living **Gemeinschaft** (community), like the family, village or small town, and the artificial, purpose-oriented **Gesellschaft** (society), based on utility and economic function. The former is an organic entity having hierarchical values, traditions and a sense of solidarity. Its morals are unquestioned and binding on all the members. These group values remain in existence beside the emerging systems of religious, moral and legal institutions, and often leave their imprints upon the latter. Conventional concepts are mainly defined in the negative, for consensus can better be reached on what should be avoided, rather than on what should be done[7].

In the Torah such norms are designated as **acts which must not be done**[8], and occasionally take the form of a special term expressing public censure. Thus, the thing which "is not done" is also called **nevalah** (outrage)[9], **to'evah** (abhorrent thing)[10], **zimmah** (depravity)[11], as well as other synonyms[12]. All these examples of violent language date from a time when this was the only effective sanction. There would have been little need for such expressions if the law had already provided for capital punishment.

However, even after the law had prescribed the gravest sanction, and after these expressions had become redundant, they were still preserved. This was probably done to stress the fact that the legal rules had originated in public morality, and that they were still in need of this justification.

A case in point can be found in the rule of unshoeing the unwilling levir, which is part of the law of levirate[13]. There is no legal sanction to enforce the duty of maintaining the name of a deceased relative. Instead, the rule prescribes a ceremony intended to express the popular feeling at such a lack of solidarity. The institutional stage of the concept had not done away with its roots in social morality.

A positive structure of social convention is custom, as recognized and adopted by theonomy. Wisdom demanded that one "went in the way of good men and kept the paths of the righteous"[14], which meant submitting to the social convention of the elite. Hence, social convention in itself was not recognized. The wise refer only to the custom of a special group of elite, but subsequently this custom was used as a model for all to follow.

(b) Change of Social Consciousness

While the authority of social convention persists in the realm of religious and legal institutions, sometimes the latter has to purify and reform the former. Just as sensitive individuals stand in opposition to public opinion and follow the guidance of their own conscience, at times the Torah calls everyone to transcend the concepts of social convention. Take, for example, the attitude towards the stranger. The spontaneous feeling of xenophobia vis-a-vis the old Egyptian and Edomite enemies of Israel must be dissolved and overcome. The people should rather remember those factors which would allow them to develop an empathic relationship towards them[15].

The laws in the legal collections of the book of **Exodus** introduced quite a number of changes in public morality and opinion. The leniency in property offences, the humane attitude towards slaves, as well as the evaluation of human life and dignity were certainly beyond the prevalent social conventions of the people. They could only have been introduced by an exceptional law-giver or teacher, by reference to super-human authority and by a critical attitude towards contemporary social conventions.

The tales concerning the exemplary behaviour of the patriarchs were likewise offered in order to improve the public opinion and custom of their descendants. Their manner of dealing with members of other nations[16] was stressed in order to universalize moral norms, which public morality had developed only within the limits of its own **Gemeinschaft**[17].

(c) Varieties of Group Morals

Biblical tradition preserves various group morals, or sub-cultures, relating to civilization. The prophets proclaimed the value of the ancient life in the desert in contradistinction to the contemporary permissiveness of the cities[18]. We have here an example of the different moral standards to be found within the tradition of Israel.

Each of the various tribes of Israel probably preserved the moral standards of their respective ancestors, in addition to those adopted by the religious covenant of Israel. While some tended to cherish the separate existence and independence expressed in the maxims: "Everyman does what is right in his eyes"[19], and "Everyman to your tents, O Israel"[20], others aspired to unite the people under the rule of one king[21].

There were probably special reserve duties within the different tribal units. The marksmen of Benjamin must have practised to maintain their high standard[22], and the participation in such practice was part of their individual social convention. If trades and industries were passed down within families[23], this also must have been linked with particular norms of behaviour amounting to social convention. Likewise the priests in general, and the separate priestly families in particular, developed various norms of what we would today call professional ethics. They were supposed to behave in a way befitting the servants of God and to observe the rules in connection with their office.

The descendants of Jonadav ben Rekhav constituted a congregation for the maintenance of ancient simplicity. According to the will of their ancestor they refrained from the consumption of wine, from agriculture and from living in houses. The idea was to live in tents in the style of the nomads, and to do so while living beside, and in connection with, their rural and urban compatriots[24]. Their ethos could therefore be used as a model for the rest of the people[25].

This means that the one covenant between God and Israel was to be realized in a number of ways, in a more hierarchical as well as more liberal structure. The covenant was above and beyond the distinctions of social culture, and revealed itself in spite of the tension and dialogue between various human values.

Although the system of monotheism and theonomy could not easily be reconciled with the pluralism of social convention, the Bible made use of the latter. In this sense, social convention represents decentralization and liberalization, as well as recognition of the will of human society by divine law.

1.   Gen. 32:32; cf. BT Chullin 101 b; Maimonides ad M Chullin 7:6.

2.   1 Sam. 30:23-25.

3.   Num. 31:27.

4.   On social convention as a moral authority see Brandt, **Ethical Theory**, pp. 57-61; Schrey, **Einfuehrung**, pp. 119-131; and B.N. Kaye & G. J. Wenham (eds.), **Law, Morality and the Bible**, (Downers Grove, Il.:1978).

5.   S. Freud, **Das Ich und das Es**, (1923).

6.   E. Erikson, **Insight and Responsibility**, (London: Faber, 1964); **Identity, Youth and Crisis**, (New York: Norton, 1968); **Identity and Lifecycle**, (New York, 1959); and L. Kohlberg, **The Philosophy of Moral Development**, (San Francisco, 1981).

7.   F. Toennies, **Gemeinschaft und Gesellschaft**, 1887 (8th ed. Leipzig 1935).

8.   Gen. 20:9; 29:26.

9.   Gen. 34:7; cf. Deut. 22:21; Jos. 7:15; Jud. 19:23; 20:6,10; 2 Sam. 13:12; Jer. 29:23.

10.   Lev. 20:13; Deut. 17:4-5.

11.   Jud. 20:6; Lev. 18:17.

12.   Eichrodt, **Theologie**, ch. 22, p. 218 ff.

13.   Deut. 25:9-10.

14.   Prov. 2:20.

15.   Deut. 23:8-9.

16.   Gen. 20:4; 39:9.

17.   Eichrodt, **Theologie**, ch. 22, p. 222.

18.   Hos. 2:16-17; 12:10; Jer. 35:6-10.

19.   Jud. 17:6; 21:25.

20.   2 Chron. 10:16.

21.   Deut. 17:14 and the various royal psalms.

22.   Jud. 20:16; 1 Chr. 12:1-2.

23.   Cf. 1 Chron. 2:55; 'Avot deR. Nathan, A:35.

24.   Jer. 35:1-11.

25.   Jer. 35:12-19.

5. BIBLICAL TELEOLOGY AND DEONTOLOGY

(a) Reward and Punishment

Ethical systems are either finalist-teleological or conceptual-deontological. The former refers to the centrality of the end and effect of any moral choice, while the latter recognizes only the duty itself in the making of moral decisions. If a system of morality belongs in the first category, it could employ pleasure or inclination as a criterion for correct behaviour, but a system of the second category must reject such an approach[1].

The Bible seems to include ideas from both types of systems, i.e. it lends itself to conflicting interpretations and even tolerates conflicting attitudes concerning such a central point. In this chapter we will first examine those passages which seem to be in agreement with the teleological theory, and then speak of the deontological alternative.

The student of the Torah will generally be inclined to understand its provisions as a system of service to God[2], or as a way of demonstrating one's love as well as awe of God[3]. This type of motivation, based on the concepts of duty, could be classified within the deontological system, viz. by tracing their reason in relation to God or the authority of the divine will.

However, on other occasions we also find teleological elements in the Torah, i.e. purpose-oriented explanations of norms, such as reward for obedience and punishment for disobedience[4].

Indeed, the idea of a covenant between God and Israel implies that obedience to the commandments ensures divine reward, while the violation of God's will effects punishment. The well-being of the people in general, and of every individual in particular, depends upon their loyalty to God[5]. Hence, the sum-total of the commandments could be seen as an egoistical goal, namely happiness in this world, or as perhaps implied by the insights of Job and Ecclesiastes, happiness in a future life.

While the doctrine of reward and punishment could, therefore, be classified as a theory of ethical egoism[6], the concepts of national solidarity, as implied in the idea of covenant, represent a theory close to that of utilitarianism. Every individual is called upon to keep in mind the happiness of the whole of Israel, rather than his own. The biblical system of reward and punishment seems to be directed towards the greatest happiness for the greatest number, as formulated by Jeremy Bentham[7]. This is especially so if we understand the commandments as befitting a majority of the people, but also realize that they might sometimes conflict with the needs of an individual[8].

(b) Spiritual Perfection and Altruism

The **telos** of the commandments, however, may also be found in spiritual perfection, which is unlike the idea of pleasure or happiness. As a result of keeping their commitment of the covenant, the people would become **a special treasure** to God[9]. It is also said that by abiding by God's statutes and judgments, a person would **live**[10], the terminology here pertaining to quality of life, no less than to physical existence itself. The Torah itself is considered to constitute **life**, and only after having made this statement, the text goes on to promise longevity as well[11].

Such promises, while perhaps within the framework of teleology, are not necessarily in conflict with deontology. The duty remains the focus of the rule, but is extended to include spiritual perfection instead of mere obedience. The listener is not only rewarded by being granted life, but is actually asked to raise the quality of his life and to be a special treasure to God.

By the same token, a number of commandments given as reminders and pedagogical devices could be interpreted as the means towards an end[12]. But at the same time, the observance of these commandments results in the production of an effect, so that the **telos** is actually part of the **deontos**. The observance of the Sabbath, for example, is meant as a recognition of creation[13], which is obviously part of the duty towards God. It is, however, also a means of ensuring a weekly rest for the employees, servants and animals of the household[14], which is a duty towards others.

Commandments defining a person's relationship towards fellow human beings are all duties belonging in the teleological category. Thus, the commandment to fence the roof of one's house is to be justified, lest someone fall down[15], and the owner of land should leave part of his harvest behind, in order to support the poor[16].

The entire Torah, besides being a divine commandment to human beings and calling for obedience, is also intended to promote the holiness or saintliness of its observers[17]. This means that the commandments should not be seen as an end in and of themselves, but as a means to that end. The rules providing for the visits in the sanctuary and the consumption of tithes are designed to instill within us awe of God[18], likewise the king is asked to keep the Book of the Torah constantly with him, so that he will learn to be in awe of God and keep all the provisions of the Torah[19]. In all of these texts, the duty extends to the end, so that teleology is in harmony with deontology.

(c) Happiness

The end of all practical endeavour, according to Aristotle, is eudaimonia, which may be translated as happiness. It is "the highest good in the realm of action", and "the aim of all knowledge and will for a good"[20]. This does not necessarily mean hedone, the equivalent of pleasure, though very often, as for instance in Kant's writings, the two are used interchangeably.

On the other hand, according to Freud, "the plan of creation does not show an intention to make mankind happy"[21]. This is actually strange to attribute to Freud, who had established the **libido** as the main drive of human beings.

In fact, the biblical report of creation seems to view happiness in a positive light, declaring as it does, that creation is "very good"[22]. The narrative about Paradise being put at the disposal of the ancestors of mankind and being lost through their sin, is a mythical expression of the human quest for happiness[23]. Moreover, the promise of longevity as a reward for the observance of certain commandments reflects a positive evaluation of human life[24].

The appreciation of life and of the world is reflected in various commandments which are to be performed with joy[25]. In these cases the duty extends to the enjoyment, just as above we found the duty to extend to the **telos**. A person is asked not only to obey, but to internalize the divine will to the degree of enjoyment, if not actual pleasure. Instead of drawing pleasure from mundane or even sinful matters, he or she should connect it with the doing of duty[26].

Similarly, the deontological idea of the divine commandment does not necessarily contradict the **eudaemonism** implied in reward and punishment[27]. Man is called upon to enjoy life by doing his duty, and biblical teaching presents a method of how to combine obedience with happiness.

The real question, however, lies in the definition of happiness. Here again, biblical thought describes Paradise at the beginning and the state of bliss at the end of days, to indicate a combination of spiritual and material satisfaction.

There seem to exist alternative forms of happiness, as determined either by human or by divine choice. The very duplicity of motivation suggested in biblical sources, viz. reward and punishment on the one hand, and the spiritual ideas of love or awe of God on the other, indicate this insight. God, in His freedom, may determine the form of happiness for every individual, and to a certain extent every individual may determine the form of happiness aspired by him.

Hence, the humble and the poor are often mentioned in the sense of being righteous[28], and from the point of view of the speaker, their state is one of happiness. This is to say that happiness can also, or perhaps only, be attained through having a good conscience and through righteousness.

Likewise, wisdom has been understood as the highest good, even for people lacking other essential goods. Therefore, the servants of King Solomon could be declared to be happy by virtue of always being in the presence of a wise master[29]. The manifestation of wisdom is more valuable, in the eyes of the wise, than any material goods[30].

In this context, even pain, which is accepted as a way of correction, can be seen as compatible with happiness[31]. This is again a harmonization of the principle of **eudaimonism** with that of **deontology**.

(d) The Non-Finalist Good

The question must eventually be put as to whether Biblical thought includes a true deontological position, i.e. a general principle of good behaviour independent of any desirable end, or even of the will of God. In order to be able to speak of biblical ethics, we must indeed look for an idea which goes beyond all teleology and heteronomy.

While purpose-oriented arguments seem to be more prevalent than purely normative ones, we sometimes come across an assertion of the latter category. Take, for instance, the formulation of the prophet Micah: "He has shown you, O man, what is good; and what does God require of you, but to do justice and love kindness and walk humbly with your God"[32]. These three norms, though proclaimed in the name of God, are presented as good in and of themselves, and therefore satisfy the requirements of the deontological theory.

The **apodictic** formulation of the Decalogue, along with other apodictic laws of the Pentateuch, belong in this category as well. The prohibitions against killing, adultery, stealing, lying and coveting are meant to be categorical and independent of utilitarian or religious speculation.

The commandment of loving one's neighbour and the stranger, "for you yourselves were once strangers in Egypt"[33], is the most perfect example of this ethical category. Although included among the commandments headed by the call for holiness, that of love is not meant to promote any purpose other than that of the object of such love. This follows from its parallel, the commandment of loving God, which cannot be fulfilled with ulterior motives. By the same token, loving a human being means adopting the attitude of **I and Thou** as described by Buber, and does not allow for any further **telos**.

Hence, biblical pluralism regarding the teleological and the deontological attitude is another example of freedom accorded to everybody according to his or her needs. Again, the divine message reaches us by alternative media, to be chosen by us humans.

1.   On deontological and teleological thought in ethics see Brandt, **Ethical Theory**, pp. 353-356; Frankena, **Ethics**, pp. 12-33. On these attitudes and the Bible see L. Hodgson, "Ethics in the OT", **The Church Quarterly Review**, 134, (1942), pp. 153-169; E.H. Martens, "The Problem of OT Ethics", **Direction**, 6, (1977), pp. 25-26; B.C. Ollenburger, op.cit., pp. 35-37; and Kaiser, **OT Ethics**, p. 16 ff.

2.   Deut. 6:13; 10:20.

3.   Deut. 10:12; 11:22; 19:9; 30:16.

4.   E.g. Lev. 18:5; Deut. 11:13 ff., 26-28; 28:1-69. See Kaiser, **OT Ethics**, pp. 301-304.

5.   Cf. Spero, **Morality**, pp. 98-100.

6.   Cf. Brandt, **Ethical Theory**, p. 369 ff.; Frankena, **Ethics**, p. 15 ff.

7.   Cf. Raphael, **Moral Philosophy**, p. 38.

8.   See Maimonides, **Guide to the Perplexed**, 3:34; and my **Dat haNetsach**, pp. 22-24.

9.   Ex. 19:5.

10.   Lev. 18:5.

11.   Deut. 32:47; see Eichrodt, **Theologie**, ch. 22, p. 241 ff.

12.   Lev. 23:43; Num. 15:40.

13.   Ex. 20:7-10.

14.   Ex. 23:12; Deut. 5:11-14.

15.   Deut. 22:8.

16.   Lev. 19:10.

17.   Num. 15:40.

18.   Deut. 14:23.

19.   Deut. 17:19.

20.   Aristotle, **Nic. Ethics**, i. 2, 1059 a, pp. 14-18.

21.   Freud, "Das Unbehagen in der Kulter", in **Abriss der Psychoanalyse**, 105. This idea was first expressed by Kant who saw happiness in opposition to duty and refused to base

any ethical system on the notion of happiness, which he tended to identify with **hedonism.**

22.   Gen. 1:31.

23.   Gen. 2-3; cf. Ez. 28:11-19; 31:8-9, 16-18.

24.   Ex. 20:12; Deut. 11-21 etc.; cf. S. Greenberg, **A Jewish Philosophy and Pattern of Life,** (New York: JTS, 1981), p. 78.

25.   Lev. 23:40; Deut. 14:26; 24:5; 28:47.

26.   The rabbinical equivalent is **simchah shel mitswah** (joy of commandment). This is in line with Schiller's critique of Kant's rejection of the inclination: "Gern dien' ich den Freunden, doch tu ich es leider mit Neigung, und so wurmt es mich oft, dass ich nicht tugendhaft bin". Kant himself rejected inclination as a motive of moral action, but he called for the fulfilling of the duty with "froehlicher Gemuetsstimmung".

27.   In Christian thought the attempt was made by Augustine and Thomas Aquinas to harmonize eudaimonist and theonomic or deontological concepts.

28.   E.g. Ps. 34:19; 37:11; 147:6; Is. 11:4; 57:46; 66:2.

29.   1 Kings 10:8.

30.   Prov. 3:13-15.

31.   Ps. 94:12; Prov. 3:12 (to be understood within the context of the pursuit of wisdom, mentioned in v. 13); Job 5:17.

32.   Mic. 6:8.

33.   Lev. 19.:34.

6. BIBLICAL JUSTICE, GENERALITY AND UNIVERSALITY

(a) Concepts of Justice

Every ethical theory must address the concept of justice and its various manifestations[1]. Legal systems and states in general are evaluated by this concept, as are individuals in their relations with others. In this chapter we will therefore discuss the biblical concepts and forms of justice, and examine them vis-a-vis the ideas of **chosenness**, the attitude towards **other nations**, and in regard to the status of **women**.

The term **tsedek** (justice), and its synonyms, **tsedakah** (equity), **yosher** and **mesharim** (literally, straightness) and **'emeth** (truth), describe both institutions and individuals.

The law of Israel is said to be just and righteous[2]. Weights and measures should be just as well[3]. Jerusalem is to be the City of Justice[4], and God is often described as just and as a fountain of justice. Furthermore, the term is used to describe the virtues and actions of human beings in their dealings with others, and in their performing of judicial functions.

The common element of these institutional and personal characteristics of justice is the equal treatment of people and situations, and the avoidance of arbitrary and discriminatory decisions.

On many occasions this principle of justice demands that the same norm be used for the stranger as is used for the native[5]. The commandments of loving one's neighbour, and even the stranger, like oneself[6], are based on the concept of equality and justice. If the king was called upon to abide by the legal restrictions of his power and to always consult his copy of the law[7], this was to preclude his feeling himself to be above the law, and to prevent him from behaving in an arbitrary manner. Both precepts follow from the idea of justice. Obviously, the demand made of the judge to pursue justice[8], means that he should apply this value in forensic practice.

Justice is a relationship between people, i.e. a quality of social behaviour. An individual who acted justly would speak of his justice, which is testifying in his favour[9]. This concept already presumes that there may be justice in the arguments of both litigants. Correspondingly, a party admitting to the justice of his adversary would say that the other was closer to justice than himself[10]. The speaker here refers to the possibility of finding justice even in conflicting claims, though one claim may be more just than the other.

Often, the distinction is made between a judicial decision **per se** and a just decision. The king of Israel was expected not only to apply the law, but to act justly as well[11]. The same is demanded of all judges[12], and indeed of anyone[13]. Among the various attributes of God, two forms of justice, **tsedek** and **mesharim**, are mentioned in describing His adhering to the concept of justice in making judgments[14].

(b) Commutation, Retribution and Distribution

Biblical thought contains a strong element of **quid pro quo,** i.e. the need for adequate reward and compensation. The seller of any object should not wrong the purchaser by demanding an exaggerated price[15], and a tortfeasor should pay damages in the amount determined by a judge[16].

The concept of justice is also central in biblical theology, and is the basis of its teachings concerning divine reward and punishment[17]. God is described as maintaining the equilibrium of merit and reward, as well as of wrongdoing and punishment. This was thought to be necessary in preserving the moral perfection of the world.

To illustrate this point, the killing of the newborn sons of Israel by throwing them into the **Nile,** is offered as the reason behind the death of Pharaoh and his army in the sea[18]. Another case of retribution in kind is the story concerning Absalom's death through his beautiful hair, after he had used its beauty in his rebellion against his father[19].

The absolute freedom of God, however, permits Him to replace justice with divine grace[20]. Such an act of grace, pardon or amnesty is a form of gift, made by a ruler toward one of his subjects, to make up for the latter's shortcommings.   The principle of commutative justice was primarily applied in inter-human relations. If the owner of a goring ox had been negligent, he was obliged to amend the damage by the substitution of another animal; and if he himself had caused the loss, he had to make restitution in the same manner[21].

The same principle was used in cases of killing or the causing bodily harm, according to the maxim: a life for life, an eye for eye, etc..[22] However, in practice the principle was not realized as such, but was commuted by the payment of a ransom[23].

In any event, a person was not to take revenge on his kinsman, but to act graciously towards the wrongdoer[24]. This follows from the above-mentioned idea of divine pardon, which should be imitated by the pious. By renouncing one's right in favour of a needy person, one performs a meritorious act[25]. This is perhaps a higher form of maintaining the equilibrium, viz. by making up for the insufficiencies of others through one's own generosity.

Accordingly, the Kings of Israel in general had the reputation of being lenient in the treatment of their enemies, and King David in particular was shown to have granted pardon to an insurgent[26].

Another correction of harsh justice was the doctrine that one should do what was straight and good in the sight of God[27]. This formulation was flexible enough to infer responsibility upon the individual beyond the letter of the law.

The equilibrium in the relationship between God and Israel was called **tsedek** (justice), and the term is used to describe divine and human behaviour, and inter-human relationships in particular. This again reveals the universal and ethical character of biblical teaching[28].

Prophetic accusations concerning a lack of gratitude towards God on the part of the people, were based on the assumption of commutative justice. Take for instance the Song of Moses mentioning the good bestowed upon Israel by God, and the fact that no corresponding expression of thankfulness on the part of the people had taken place[29]. Samuel is said to have listed the divine **tsedakot,** meaning the acts in favour of God, in an imaginary law-suit with the people. This was done to emphasize the ingratitude of the people[30].

Biblical criminal law and theology are both based on the concept of retribution[31], particularly on the retributive theory of criminal justice. The omission or commission of any act prescribed or prohibited by the law, respectively, had to result in appropriate consequences which corresponded with the gravity of the offence.

(c) Equality

The principle of a basic human equality followed from the ideas of **imago dei** and of the creation of mankind[32]. Nevertheless, the centrality of family relations, the rejection of strange cults and cultures, as well as the perpetuation of slavery prevented the ultimate realization of this equality. **De facto,** strangers living in ancient Israel may have enjoyed a considerable number of human rights, but no moral or legal recognition of their basic equality, such as first established by the **Stoa,** can be found in the Bible.

However, the Torah does encompass a number of rules against the discrimination of strangers, orphans and widows, which go beyond a mere **de facto** recognition of equality[33].

By the same token, the principle of an eye for eye is actually based on the notion of equality of all human beings, irrespectively of their social status. Nevertheless, the literal implementation of this rule would actually violate the principle of equality, for the situation of the attacker is never identical with that of the victim. Therefore the very goal of equality could not be reached by the application of the **ius talionis**. Instead, the original method of compromise and payment prevailed. Only murder could never be compounded for payment, for every human life is invaluable and therefore equal to that of another[34].

According to biblical thought, the distribution of resources should be equalized by a series of social measures which operate in favour of the underprivileged[35]. Likewise, the concepts of equal taxation, and of equal protection under the law as well as in court, appear in a number of biblical commandments. While the protection of life, as already mentioned, follows the principle that all persons are equal, duties toward the poor follow the criterion of need. Divine reward and punishment and the human administration of justice follow the criterion of desert and merit.

For us however, the concept of equality also refers to equality of opportunity[36]. According to the systems of chosenness, such as that of the covenant and of divine legislation, the central institutions of kingship, priesthood, and the allegiance to the people of Israel were determined by birth rather than by merit. Since God is believed to act justly, even if His acts are sometimes beyond human comprehension, we would expect a basic equality of all Israelites, without regard to their respective status. We must therefore assume that the status by birth was justified by consideratioms of utility, division of labour, stability, desert of an ancestor, or by other purpose-oriented principles. Of those who had to put up with some minor status, it was probably believed that they received their compensation in some other way.

As to the basic equality of all mankind, established by virtue of their being created in the **image of God** and by being descendants of one single ancestor, there was obviously a need for a justification of the existing discrimination. Biblical tradition assumed that the greater part of mankind had lost equality of status through sin. In retrospect however, the question of how to justify the discrimination of the other nations from the point of view of divine economy and justice arises if there was never an equal chance for them to earn merit or to lose it.

The assumption was therefore made that other nations had, indeed, been given equal opportunities to adopt the faith of Israel and that they had refused to take advantage of them. The question must then be raised concerning which moment in world history this chance had been given, and for how long had the offer been open. If the opportunity given to other nations was unequal to that of Israel, our sense of justice would have difficulty accepting it.

Even if we assume that the people of Israel had demonstrated a greater ability to represent the divine concern and were therefore the proper candidates for chosenness, there still remains the doctrine of divine benevolence, calling for the consideration of the needs of the others. But again, inequality between Israel and the nations might have been functional only, and not have excluded the possibility of all to achieve an equal quality of life and the same standing before God. There may also be utilitarian considerations which justify a certain deviation from the principle of equal treatment, e.g.affirmative action, taken to promote greater equality in the long run.

(c) Generality and Universality

Aside from the problem of equality mentioned above, we also must contend with that of generality and universality, which are basic qualities of ethical systems[37]. Even if the special character of Israel justified a deviation from the realization of equality, the question still remains as to whether biblical thought is general and universal enough to qualify as an ethical religion. We previously mentioned the negative reply of Kant, which has been challenged by the Jewish philosophers Lazarus and Hermann Cohen.

The moral teaching of Israel is indeed based on the particular concepts of the covenant and chosenness, but with a universal justification: "You only have I known of all the families of the earth; therefore I will punish you for all your iniquities"[38]. This means that the particular status of the chosen people corresponds with their special responsibility, and that their rights are justified in general and universal terms.

In fact, chosenness was connected with service to the rest of the world. Israel was chosen to be a treasure to God, not as an end in itself, or as a form of **sacro egoismo**. They were to be a **realm of priests** and a **holy nation**[39]. The former clearly being meant as a vocation for the spiritual elevation of mankind. The whole land of Israel was a kind of sanctuary for the world, and the people of Israel were to serve God on behalf of all nations.

The idea of the holy nation was likewise to be understood as being related to the rest of the world, rather than describing withdrawal from it. Israel was called upon to become holy, so that the other nations would recognize the name of God, who called upon Israel, as their God and would hold it in awe[40].

Just as the choice of the Aaronites and of the Holy Place was a reaction to the people's apostacy[41], the choice of Israel was a reaction to the sins of humanity. Only Abraham is shown to recognize God, and among his descendants only Isaac and Jacob are said to have continued his tradition. The nations around Israel were described as unwilling to join the covenant[42], so that only the people of Israel remained as candidates for being chosen[43].

Moreover, the invitation to become a party to the covenant was said to still be open. This is indicated by the need to publish the Torah by an inscription in stone[44], and by the peace offer to be made preceeding any battle[45]. The Gibeonites' submission may be used as an illustration of this process[46].

The openness of the covenant for the accession of other nations is implied in the arrangement of the Book of Genesis, which describes the ancestors of Israel as a part, and as brothers, of the rest of mankind. Every human being, not only the Israelite, was created in the image of God and under His protection. The stories about creation, the first brothers, the flood and Sodom and Gemorah are addressed to all of humanity[47], and not only to one chosen people[48].

The **Adamite** or **Noachide** Commandments were addressed to all nations, which means that all were invited to join in the framework of Torah[49]. The sexual practices of Egypt and Canaan were censured, meaning that the rules of morality had been addressed to them as well as to Israel[50]. Likewise, the prohibition against killing was general and to be applied to all human beings[51].

Israelites were called upon to overcome their animosity towards some former enemy nations[52]. The same effort was to be made vis-a-vis the strangers in the midst of Israel[53]. The fact that human beings are all descendants of one ancestor and creatures of one God, as described at the beginning of the Torah, is a good basis for biblical humanism and universalism. Not only is the life of every person under the special protection of God[54], but his dignity and value are almost as great as that of God[55]. Just as God is good to all, and His mercy extends to everyone of His creatures[56], the concept of **imitatio dei** called for equal treatment of all mankind[57].

By reference to the experience of being strangers in Egypt, the Torah provided for an inclusive attitude towards all human beings[58]. Since every one had been a stranger, they were also entitled to the understanding and love of any other person. The property of the enemy, or of the person hating you, should be as much a concern to you as that of your brother[59]. Subsequently, wisdom provided a utilitarian motive for this altruistic rule[60].

The universality of Israel's moral system expressed itself in various laws, in addition to in the words of the prophets[61]. The benefit of the weekly rest for example, was granted to slaves as well as to free Israelites, and even to their animals. One law should be applied to everyone[62], and the prophets assumed that there existed a universal standard of rights. While in the rest of the world people would identify themselves by the allegiance to their god, and this god would relate to his people only, biblical monotheism universalized the validity of morality, and related it to all mankind. Amos criticized the behaviour of all the nations in his surrounding area[63], and declared that God related to all of mankind and not to Israel alone[64].

Another expression of the universality of these moral rules was the concept of divine attributes setting models for human behaviour. God is described as merciful and gracious, long-suffering and abundant in goodness and truth[65]. This means that these virtues were "prior to our knowledge of God not only in an epistemological sense but in an axiological sense as well... In a sense, God has no choice but to ordain moral rules. The moral God cannot command rules that are not moral... It is because of this logic that Abraham with complete confidence is able to confront God with the demand for justice."[66].

On the other hand, the Torah also includes extreme expressions of particularism and exclusivity. The war of extermination against the peoples of Canaan and Amalek was seen as a divine commandment, though biblical tradition showed that these norms were not followed to their full extent. Hatred and revenge were propagated by some prophets and psalmists, which obviously weakened the impact of the greater number of universalist and humanist texts.

A distinction must therefore be made between the humane conclusions drawn from monotheism and the morality of God on the one hand, and the conclusions drawn from the existential war situation of ancient Israel, on the other[67]. Likewise, the toleration of slavery by the Torah, and its legitimization by the story of Noach, reflected negative feelings harbored towards other nations[68].

Nevertheless, both the conquest of Canaan and slavery were justified by reference to universal principles. God is said to have delayed the realization of His promise to Abraham regarding Canaan because of the prior rights of the Canaanites: "Know well that your offspring shall be strangers in a land not theirs, and they shall be enslaved and oppressed four hundred years... And they shall return here in the fourth generation, for the iniquity of the Amorites will not be fulfilled until then"[69].

The same idea appears in the admonition: "It is not because of your virtues and your rectitude that you will be able to occupy their country, but because of the wickedness of those nations the Lord your God is dispossessing them before you, and in order to fulfill the oath that the Lord made to your fathers, Abraham, Isaac and Jacob"[70]. Again the rights of other nations are recognized in principle, but these rights are said to have lapsed due to the misbehaviour of the people concerned.

Even the narrative regarding the justification of slavery showed that capture, acquisition and descent were not sufficient justifications by themselves[71]. Without derogating from the achievements of international legislation against slavery, we should keep in mind the difference between the human-centered context, demanding equality, and the theocentric system of the Bible. If God is recognized as the ruler of everything, there is also room for the justification of slavery. After an initial state of equality of all human beings, God could have decided on the loss of liberty of some, certainly as a reaction to their sins.

Just as the Torah uses human language to express divine ideas, it also uses the world of ideas of a patriarchal society to express universal truths. It therefore still requires feminist analysis and critique in order to create a more general and universal interpretation[72]. The story concerning the daughters of Zelophehad, who brought about a correction of the law of inheritance[73], should be used as the model for this process, which is an ongoing responsibility of each generation, and the special challenge of ours.

In summation, we have found the realization of justice, and of generality and universality in many parts of biblical sources and institutions, though not in all. Faith in the unity of mankind, both as descendants of one ancestor and as creatures of one God, provide the foundation for the further development in the direction of the concept of human rights.

This further phase of Torah derives from its general spirit of justice and universality, but needs active collaboration on the part of sensitive human beings. The proclamation of equality and of human rights cannot be made from above but has to be worked out by men and women facing the existential need for it.

1. On the concepts of justice see J. Rawls, **A Theory of Justice,** (Oxford: UP, 1972); Ch. Perelman, **Justice et Raison,** (Bruxelles, 1963); Frankena, **Ethics,** pp. 48-52; Raphael, **Moral Philosophy,** pp. 67-80; Brandt, **Ethics,** pp. 407-432, 480-505; and my **Erkhey Mishpat,** p.91.

2. Deut. 4:8

3. Lev. 19:36

4. Is. 1:26

5. Ex 12:49

6. Lev. 19:18,34

7. Deut. 17:14-20

8. Deut. 16:20.

9. Gen. 30:33.

10. Gen. 38:26

11. 2 Sam. 8:15; 1 Kings 10:9.

12. Lev. 19:15; Deut. 33:21.

13. Ez. 18:5.

14. Ps 9:9; 98:9; 99:4.

15. Lev 25:14.

16. Ex. 21:22.

17. Deut. 7:9-10; 32: 35, 41; 1 Kings 8:32; Ps. 9:16; 59:13; 62:13; 141:10; Prov. 1:31; 11:6; 12:13; 29:6. Cf. M Sotah 1:7-9; Mekhilta ad Ex. 18:11.

18. Ex 1:16,22; 14:15 ff.

19. 2 Sam. 14:25; 18:9.

20. Ex 34:6ff.; Lev. 23:28; Num. 14:19f.: Deut. 21:8.

21. Ex 21:36; Lev. 24:21.

22. Ex. 21:23-25; Lev. 24:18-20; Deut. 19:21.

23. Ex. 21:30; Num. 35:31-32.

24. Lev. 19:18.

25. Deut 24:13.

26. 1 Kings 20:31; 2 Sam. 19:19.

27. Deut. 6:18; 12:28.

28. On the righteouness of God and Israel see G. von Rad, **Old Testament Theology,** I, Edinburgh: 1963), pp. 370-383.

29. Deut. 32:6, 15,18.

30. 1 Sam. 12:7.

31. Cf. on Retributive Justice and Criminal Law: Brandt, **Ethical Theory,** p.480 ff.

32. On equality see G.L. Abernethy (ed.), **The Idea of Equality,** (Richmond, VA: 1959).

33. Cf. Ex. 12:49; Lev. 19:33-34; 25:35; Num. 9:14; 15:15-16; Deut. 24:17; 27:19.

34. Num. 35:31.

35. Cf. The rules of succession: Num. 26:52-56, and see my "Eigentum", **in TRE.**

36.   Cf. my **Law and Religion,** pp. 43 ff., 90 ff.

37.   On the concepts of universality and generality, as established by Kant's Categorical Imperative, see R.M. Hare, **Moral Thinking,** (Oxford: 1981), ch. 6; M.G. Singer, **Generalization in Ethics,** (New York: 1961); Ricken, Ethik, pp. 106-116; and Brandt, **Ethical Theory,** pp. 19-36, 221-225. On the national character of Biblical Ethics see C.D. Stoll "Partikularitaet und Universalitaet in der Ethik des AT", in Burkhardt, **Begruendung ethischer Normen,** pp.67-79; Kaiser, **OT Ethics,** pp. 34-35. On chosenness and universal human rights see David Polish, "Judaism and Human Rights", in **Journal of Ecumenical Studies,** 19, (1982), pp. 40-50; H.C. Brichto, "The Hebrew Bible on Human Rights", in D.S. Sidorsky (ed.), **Essays on Human Rights: Contemporary Issues and Jewish Perspectives,** (Philadelhia: JPS, 1979), pp. 215-233; and my **Law and Religion,** pp. 75-89. For an orthodox defence of particularism see Michael Wyschogrod, **The Body of Faith: Judaism as Corporeal Election,** (New York: Seabury, 1983).

38.   Am. 3:2; this refers to many expressions of chosenness in Deut.; Is. 14:1, 41:8-9, 44:1-2, 49:7; Ez. 20:5; Sach. 1:17, 2:16; Ps. 135:4.

39.   Ex. 19:5-6.

40.   Deut. 28:9-10.

41.   Ex. 32:26; Num. 3:13. Cf. Ex. 33:7-11, and my **"Al haShehinah",** in S. Abramson & B. Luria (eds.), **P. Sivan Volume,** (Jerusalem: 1988), pp. 151-154.

42.   Ex. 17:8-13; 18:1-12, Jethro being the exception proving the rule.

43.   Deut 33:2; Hab. 3:3. Cf. BT 'Avodah Zarah 2 b.

44.   Deut. 27:8; cf. M Sotah 7:5.

45.   Deut. 21:10-11.

46.   Jos. 9:3-27.

47.   Nahum Sarna, **Understanding Genesis,** (New York: 1966), pp. 144-146.

48.   Sarna, p. 144 ff.; Kaiser, **OT Ethics,** p. 12.

49.   Gen. 2:16-17; 9:1-5; cf. T 'Avodah Zarah 8(9):4; BT Sanhedrin 56 a-60 a.

50.   Lev. 18:1-30; Deut. 22:22; cf. BT Sanhedrin 57 b.

51.   Gen. 9:6; Ex. 20:13; 21:12. As a result of war and persecution, the rule was limited to protect only the lives of Jews (M. Sanhedrin 4: 5; 9:2).

52.   Ex. 23:4-5; Deut. 23:8-9.

53.   BT Bava Metsia 59 b.

54.   Gen. 9:5.

55.   Ps. 8:6.

56.   Ps. 145:9.

57.   Spero, **Morality,** p. 133.

58.   Ex. 22:20; Lev. 19:34; Deut. 10:19.

59.   Ex. 23:4-5.

60.   Prov. 25:21.

61.   Kaiser, **Toward OT Ethics,** p. 12.

62. Ex. 12:49.

63. Amos 1:3 - 2:6.

64. Amos 9:7.

65. Ex. 34:6.

66. Gen. 18:25; Spero, **Morality**, pp. 69-70.

67. Cf. Kaiser, **OT Ethics**, pp. 34-35, 266-269, 290-292.

68. Lev. 25:44-46; Gen. 9:25. Cf. Kaiser, pp. 288-290.

69. Gen. 15:13,16.

70. Deut. 9:5; and see Greenberg, **The Ethical**, p. 58 ff.

71. Gen. 9:25.

72. Cf. S. Heschel, "Feminism", in Cohen & Mendes-Flohr, **Contemporary**, pp. 255-259. See also Kaiser, **OT Ethics**, pp. 204-208, 285-288.

73. Num. 27.

7. CHOICE AND INTENTION IN THE BIBLE

(a) Freedom of Will

A central problem of ethics is the concept of human choice; whether it is real or a mere illusion, what it consists of, and to what degree it is free from the given situation of the person[1]. In this chapter we will discuss the biblical attitude concerning freedom of will. We will distinguish between freedom of will on the one hand, and responsibility on the other. Furthermore, we will examine the biblical sources for a trace of the concept of conscience, and finally, we will discuss the value of intention and inwardness.

The appeal of the Torah to the listeners made sense only if we are to assume that they were able to choose between compliance and refusal. God is said to have asked man to direct his will to the observance of the commandments[2], which meant that decisions should be made by man irrespectively of external forces. The choice between the alternatives was said to be most meaningful, to cause life and blessing or death and curse[3].

Freedom of will is the underlying idea of the trials which the Torah said certain persons had to undergo, to test whether they would be able to overcome their human weakness. Abraham's was the supreme test of faith, whether he would be willing to offer his son against all the odds[4]. In such a situation the person undergoing the test was all by himself, and no other factor was thought to have carried weight in the decision-making process.

At times however, a person's choice could be hampered by internal or external factors. One may have been acting under a mistaken assumption or under coercion, and should therefore not be responsible for the act. Although having committed an offence, he may have done so in good faith and actually be innocent, such as Abimelech regarding Sarah[5]. The responsibility for killing another human being could not extend to cases which were actually acts of God, i.e. where God had "let the victim fall into the hand of the person who caused the death"[6]. The question was, of course, how to define the boundary between human foresight or negligence on the one hand, and divine intervention on the other.

One of the factors limiting human freedom is an inherent tendency of man to follow biological urges. God was said to hold in mankind's favour the doctrine that "the inclination of man's heart is evil from his youth"[7]. Sin was therefore not only the result of individual choice, but of a structural weakness of human existence. This is partly God's own fault, so to speak, and could not be fully blamed on human beings.

The Bible, however, does not speak of a limit to human freedom of choice as a result of the original sin. The concept of individual responsibility gives every person the chance to do good and to repent after having failed. Divine assistance is acknowledged in every situation, including that of making moral decisions.

Mankind is called upon to defeat this weakness and to overcome the sinfull urge within them[8]. If one is instructed to fight and overcome a natural inclination, the assumption must be that it is possible to do so. The prophets speaking of national repentance took it for granted that the people could change their behaviour and use their free will[9]. Jeremiah and Ezekiel, on the other hand, did not ultimately believe in the possibility of repentance without divine intervention, and instead of human repentance, hoped for a miraculous change of heart on the part of the people[10].

This means that the Bible does not present an unequivocal view on the freedom of will and on the human and divine elements, respectively, which play a role in human decisions. The individual is called upon to obey God and to refrain from evil doings, but his power is sometimes limited by prior acts or events. Moreover, freedom of will was considered to be a divine gift, and therefore not to be taken for granted. This was especially so after continuous sinning, when repentance might have become impossible.

(b) Responsibility

The Torah imposed responsibility on people for the commission of offences, even though God had been involved in one way or other in the choice[11]. For instance, the Egyptians were held responsible for the oppression of the Israelites, although their policy met with the divine plan of salvation. God's prescience, and His making use of their own desires, did not relieve them of their responsibility[12]. God was even said to have hardened the heart of Pharaoh not to let the people out of slavery, and nonetheless to have punished him for what he did[13]. The same was said regarding Sichon, King of the Amorites[14].

The question must therefore be raised as to why the blame could be put upon Pharaoh and Sichon, if their choice had been limited[15]. In one of the suggested answers reference is made to the fact that at the first five plagues Pharaoh is described as having hardened his heart himself, so that the hardening caused by God in the later plagues was already part of the punishment[16].

Indeed, while the Torah in general embraces a retribution theory of punishment, in this case a utilitarian doctrine prevailes. Punishment in this context was meant as a deterrent, and designed to create a story to be narrated in future, of how God "had made sport" of Egypt[17]. This is therefore an exception, proving the rule of free choice. In general, however, it may be said that determinism cannot easily be reconciled with the theory of retributive justice[18].

Only two institutions of biblical law seem to be based on utilitarian rather than retributive concepts. The justification for killing a thief who was caught while breaking in at night is based on the right of self-defence, but also on the probability of violence against the owner of the home[19]. If it were purely for conceptual considerations, the killer should have been responsible for the act, though absolved from punishment.

Similarly, the rule concerning the stubborn and rebellious son provided for his execution in order to prevent him from attacking his parents[20]. There would have been no justification for such harsh punishment, but for the deterrent effect of the rule. These exceptions constitute legal parallels to the narratives mentioned above.

Responsibility is indeed greater than might be assumed by the idea of free choice. The causing of death, even unintentionally, had to be be atoned for by exile[21], and the commission of a sin through error required expiation[22]. Here the assumption seemed to be that the involuntary act was the result of a preceding decision of the transgressor, regarding which he had a choice and should have foreseen the consequences. This idea is also expressed in the ancient proverb quoted with approval: "Out of the wicked comes wickedness"[23], which means that by a person's general lifestyle he assumes responsibility even for involuntary acts.

(c) Conscience

Although the concept of conscience[24], like other abstract concepts was unknown, the idea of a **forum internum** was present and active. Biblical thought located human conscience in the heart and the kidney. A person should not be held responsible, it was said, if his conscience was clear: "Now Abimelech had not come near her; and he said: God, will you slay even a righteous nation? Did he not say himself to me that she was his sister, and she herself said that he was her brother. In the simplicity of my heart and the purity of my hands have I done this"[25].

On the other hand, a guilty conscience is described in the following: "And it came to pass that David's heart struck him, because he had cut off Saul's skirt"[26]. Likewise, Job affirmed that his heart had never reproached him[27]. In a prayer it is said: "I will bless God, who has given me counsel, in the night also my kidneys instruct me"[28].

Conscience played an important role in the relationship between human beings and God[29]. It was through the realization of one's guilt that the duty of offering arose[30], and that the opportunity was given for repentance[31]. Wisdom, therefore, called for the purification of the heart as the decisive act of life[32].

We have seen that the area of responsibility need not be identical with that of free action or decision. The monist anthropology of the Bible led to the location of moral feelings and of conscience in various organs of the body, as we have tried to show above. Furthermore, we are going to mention several texts concerning the value of inwardness and good intention, together with the need for good behaviour. This, too, is in line with the notion of unity of body and soul prevalent in biblical thought.

(d) Intention and Inwardness

The moral as well as legal character of the Torah finds expression in the various appeals to raise the intention and inwardness of the listener[33]. The last of the Ten Commandments prohibits certain desires and feelings of envy, which is a regulation of mere states of mind[34]. Hatred and grudge should not be felt vis-a-vis a kinsman; on the contrary, one should love him as one loves oneself[35]. Purity of heart and the elevation of one's intentions are the objects of various admonitions[36].

Among the motivations given in the Torah for the various commandments are obedience and service to God, as well as awe or love of Him[37]. These motivations provide a general direction for intention, and represent the idea of inwardness.

The question should be raised as to whether the moral quality of an act depends more upon the result achieved, or upon the intention of the actor. We have mentioned Abimelech's argument that he had committed a heinous offence in good faith, and that he should therefore be acquitted[38]. This seems to be a clear indication in favour of the need for an evaluation of the mental elements of a crime. On the other hand, we find a series of offensive acts justified by the good intention of the actor. Take for instance the heroic incest of Tamar[39], or the behaviour of Yael, where their good intentions justified their immoral means[40].

The opposite case would be an act leading to a desirable result, but lacking the proper intention. Thus, a person aiding his poor relative in order to impress the rest of the family could serve as a test case; which of the two prevails in the characterization of the act, the result or the intention? Unfortunately, the biblical sources do not touch upon this problem[41], and we must assume that the positive act does not lose its value by the negative intention.

Such behaviour would, however, probably be subject to the prophetic critique of external piety and cultic propriety, without corresponding inward intention and moral basis: "Since what I want is lovingkindness, not sacrifice; knowledge of God, not whole-offerings"[42], and, "to do justice and love kindness and walk humbly with your God"[43].

Summing up this chapter on the internal aspects of religious behavior, we may say that biblical faith reflects divine omnipotence as much as human responsibility. The former, sometimes, leaves little room for human choice, while the latter tends to extend its effects. Attempts are made to bridge this abyss and describe the interaction of God and man. Moreover, biblical religion made for the internalization of traditions and cults, which put the emphasis upon the mental aspects, i.e. volition, moral contemplation and states of mind. On the other hand, biblical this-worldliness and rejection of quietism explain the appreciation of the physical aspects and effects, sometimes even at the expense of intentionality.

1. On freedom of will see Brandt, **Ethical Theory**, pp. 506-528; Frankena, **Ethics**, pp. 73-78; Pieper, **Ethik**, pp. 93-98; Schrey, **Einfuehrung**, pp. 88-99; and Hoeffe, **Lexikon**, pp. 62-65, 280-281. On the doctrine in Jewish thought see D. Winston "Free Will", in Cohen & Mendes-Flohr, pp. 269-274; and L. Jacobs, A **Jewish˙ Theology** (New York:Behrman, 1973), pp. 77-80.

2. Deut. 10:12.

3. Deut. 30:19.

4. Gen. 22:1-19.

5. Gen. 20:5.

6. Ex. 21:13; cf. Code Chammurabi 249.

7. Gen. 8:21.

8. Gen. 4:7.

9. E.g. Hos. 14:2-3; Mal. 3:7.

10. Jer. 31:31-33; 32:39-40; Ez. 36:24-28.

11. On the concept of responsibility see J. Feinberg, **Doing and Deserving: Essays in the Theory of Responsibility**, (Princeton: 1970); Frankena, **Ethics**, pp. 71-78; E.H. Erikson, **Insight and Responsibility**, (New York: 1964); H. Jonas, **Das Prinzip Verantwortung**, (Frankfurt M.:Insel, 1979); Schrey, **Einfuehrung**, pp. 96-99; and Hoeffe, **Lexikon**, pp. 263-264.

12. Gen. 15:14.

13. Ex. 4:21; 7:3; 9:12; 10:1, 20.

14. Deut. 2:30.

15. Cf. Ex. Rabba 13:4.

16. Tanchuma Wa'era 3.

17. Ex. 10:1-2.

18. On the freedom of will see D. Winston, in Cohen & Mendes-Flohr.

19. Ex. 22:1.

20. Deut. 21:18-21.

21. Num. 35:22-25.

22. Lev. 4:27-31.

23. 1 Sam. 24:14.

24. On the concept of conscience see Wisdom of Solomon 17:10; Rom. 2:15; 1 Cor. 8:7-12; Thomas Aquinas, **Summa Theologia**, i.ii, 19:5-6; D.D. Raphael, **The Moral Sense** (1947); P. Toon, **Your Conscience as your Guide**, (Morehouse-Barlow, 1984); Schrey, **Einfuehrung**, pp. 107-118; A. Schoepf, in Hoeffe, **Lexikon**, pp. 87-88; and W. Hesse, in Stoeckle, **Woerterbuch**, pp. 114-120.

25. Gen. 20:4-5.

26. 2 Sam. 24:10; cf. 1 Kings 2:44.

27. Job 27:6. Cf. Sir. 14:1; 37:13-14.

28. Ps. 16:7. Cf BT Berakhot 61 a; Midrash Psalms ad loc.

29. Cf. Gen. 3:7-11; 4:10-12; 2 Sam. 12:13; Ps. 51:5.

30. Lev. 5: 17, 23; Num. 5:6 Cf. J. Milgrom, **Cult and Conscience: The ASHAM and the Priestly Doctrine of Repentance**, Leiden, Studies in Judaism in Late Antiquity 18, 1976.

31. Hos. 5:15.

32. Prov. 4:23.

33. On the role of intention see Brandt, **Ethical Theory**, pp. 462-465; Schrey, **Einfuehrung**, pp. 107-118; A. Schoepf, in Hoeffe **Lexikon**, pp. 84-85. On intention in biblical ethics see Kaiser, **OT Ethics**, pp. 7-10.

34. Ex. 20:13-14; Deut. 5:17. Cf. Kaiser, pp. 235-239.

35. Lev. 19:17-18.

36. Num. 15:39; Deut. 9:4; 15:7-10; 20:1; 23:8; Ps. 15:2; 24:3; 51:12; Prov. 4:23. Cf. Spero, **Morality**, p. 134 ff.

37.   Agus, The Vision, p. 7 ff.

38.   Gen. 20:5.

39.   Gen. 38:13-26.

40.   Jud. 5:24.

41.   In rabbinical doctrine such a case is called a mitsvah shelo lishmah; cf. BT Berakhot 17 a; Tossafot, s.v. ha'osseh.

42.   Hos. 6:6.

43.   Mic. 6:8.

8. THE LAWS

Turning now to the ethical ideas in the various parts of the Hebrew Bible, we should first examine the legal passages.

(a) The Decalogue

According to the accepted view, the legal provisions of the Bible do not need or permit any rational argument, and do not leave room for a moral philosophy. The only ground for the commandments is said to be the will of God, an idea which has already been discussed and rejected by Plato's **Euthyphron**[1], by the Muslim **Mu'tazilites**[2], and by Thomas Aquinas[3]. In the preceding chapters, we have tried to develop a theory of biblical ethics and wish to continue this argument with special regard for the literary formulations.

Among the legal collections included in the Torah, the Decalogue occupies a central position[4]. It represents the minimum conditions imposed upon the junior party to the covenant. Its formulation is moral, not legal; for although dealing with the most serious offences, it does not refer to any human sanction. Divine punishment is announced for the violation of the first commandment, and a promise of divine reward is attached to the fifth. The rest of the commandments, regulating inter-human relations, is presented as an appeal to the individual's conscience. This approach is deontological, rather than teleological.

The formulation fits into the framework of the **covenant**[5], which is a bilateral document describing the consensus of both parties. Only the first commandments deal with the duties of loyalty, as assumed by a political vassal towards his overlord. The rest is a framework of mandatory and prohibitive norms, to be observed both within the family and without. There is a movement from the idea of God to that of the fellow human being, from the covenant situation to general human responsibility, and from external, observable acts to the life of the soul.

After specifying the duty of loyalty toward the exclusive master, the text follows the order of moral development. The rule of the Sabbath represents the responsibility toward the universe, being a divine creation, and space for the realization of the divine kingdom. The duty of honouring one's parents is the basis of education and tradition, and links the individual listener to the covenant. Human existence is protected and made possible by the norms of social behaviour, and the last commandment leads the listener towards individual and spiritual perfection.

By the same token, the text moves from what is perceived as God's own words, to the address of Moses, speaking of God in the third person. According to the rabbinical interpretation, the listeners heard the first commandments from a divine voice, while the rest were transmitted by Moses[6]. The first part of the Decalogue is also based on the experience of the divine phenomenon and the theonomic approach, while the rest expresses the ethical commitment of the individual in the presence of God.

From the legal point of view, the covenant between God and Israel consists of an offer[7], and an acceptance[8]. This acceptance had to be repeated from time to time by a public reading of the terms of the covenant[9]. The covenant granted every individual member of the people a status of priesthood, so that all would be serving the rest of humanity[10]. The signs of this status were, inter alia, the tassles at the corners of their clothes[11].

The offer and the acceptance were expressed through the intervention of Moses as a mediator. The offer was made to him[12], as his role was to be permanent representative of God[13].

The moral character of the decalogue expresses itself in the mutual speech of the two parties. In consideration for the declaration of the people, God was said to have spoken the Ten Words[14]. Thus, the relationship between the otherwise unequal parties is somewhat balanced in the form described by Buber's **I and Thou**.

The listener is addressed in the singular, to emphasize his personal relationship with God[15]. He is called upon to practise **imitatio dei** by refraining from creative work on the Sabbath. The Ten Words are meant to be **internalized**, rather than merely observed by act or omission. The first verse asks for the personal recognition of God as the liberator from the slavery of Egypt, while the second prohibits the recognition of any other god.

The observance of the Sabbath is to take the form of sanctification and of dedication of the day to God. The listener is called upon to consider his regular work as having come to an end, although he may actually be in the middle of it. The element of internalization appears, therefore, not only in the last of the Ten Commandments, but also concerning the Sabbath, when one is asked to forget about mundane matters, as if all work had been finished during the six weekdays[16].

The positive formulation of the fifth commandment, likewise calls for an internalization of the respect due to parents, rather than for refraining from any disrespectful act. The last commandment as such, definitely addresses the inner life of the individual, and not only external behaviour.

Every householder of Israel is called upon to feel **responsible** for the weekly rest, not only of that of his family, but also that of his servants, of the stranger within his gates, and even of his animals. While the Sabbath was originally given a cosmic and metaphysical meaning, it thus became a reminder of one's moral and social responsibility. This idea was first expressed as an additional remark[17], and later included in the second version of the decalogue[18].

The responsibility for those under one's control also appears in the statement that God would visit the iniquities of the fathers upon their descendants and extend His grace to many generations to follow[19]. This means that a person must think of his children when weighing a decision, to determine whether his acts would benefit them.

Another point of ethical significance is the absence of any reference to God in the second five commandments. They seem to be addressed to all human beings, irrespective of their belief in God[20]. It is as if God wished these commandments to be evaluated in their own right, rather then by the authority behind them[21].

(b) The Judgments

Whereas the Decalogue addresses individual conscience, the collection of judgments following thereupon is basically a **social structure**, which, however, includes many moral appeals to the individual[22].

The first two passages, dealing with the freedom of servants, cannot be understood as legal provisions. The Hebrew servant was said to leave the house of his master at the end of six years, together with his wife. This meant that his wife had been together with him during the years of his service, probably with the right of support from the master for the children as well[23].

This support must have been based on the moral responsibility of the master for the needy family of his servant, with which he was expected to keep in contact. Even the provision that the servant was entitled to his freedom after having worked for six years does not mention any human sanction. This shows that it constituted an appeal to the conscience of the master, rather than a legal duty.

The freedom of the female servant was also connected with a moral concept. There was an expectation that a female servant would eventually marry the master or one of his sons. If this expectation was not met, the woman was entitled to her freedom without any obligation for the restitution of her price[24]. The breach of such an implied condition was a kind of "treason", which is a strong term to use for breach of a **bona fide** relationship.

While most of the judgments deal with sanctions, whether penal or pecuniary, the rules protecting the stranger have no human sanction, only an argument and a divine sanction[25]. The idea that the listeners themselves had experienced being strangers is a universalisation, or a kind of **golden rule.** This is typical for an ethical argument, rather than for a legal duty.

Similarly, the treatment of the poor debtor does not include any human sanction[26]. The creditor is asked to return the pledge at sunset, lest the debtor remain overnight without any sheets. This is an ethical argumentation.

Even the rules concerning the administration of justice are of moral rather than legal character[27]. They speak to the individual when functioning in a judicial body, but do not provide any legal sanction. These rules appeal to the conscience of the individual, and do not apply to an external forum.

The verses dealing with the property of one's adversary or enemy are truly ethical[28]. No legal draughtsman or judge could have provided for such cases; they are meant to present moral teaching, without any legal or utilitarian motivation[29].

The already formulated rule of the Sabbath is here given an ethical explanation, viz. to grant a day of rest to the animals, servants and labourers[30]. Instead of the legal sanction mentioned on another occasion[31], we have here a rational and moral argument.

(c) Rules of Holiness

Among the legal passages of the Priestly Torah, the passages concerning Holiness hold a central position[32]. There are different forms of holiness: Priests and Nazirites are called upon to keep this quality, to be different from the rest of the community[33].

But holiness is also a quality of every Israelite, making it necessary to refrain from the consumption of torn meat or of swarming things[34]. These forms of holiness follow from an elevated self-image, which demands that members of the chosen people act with discrimination in matters of food, as well as in other affairs.

The most comprehensive form of holiness is connected with the covenant of Mount Sinai, its object being the transformation of Israel into a kingdom of priests and a holy nation[35]. The covenant expresses the ideas of chosenness and of being a child of God[36], as well as the special duties resulting from this status.

According to a rabbinical definition, being holy means being **Pharisees**, i.e. withdrawing from sin by taking from the permissible sphere and adding to the forbidden[37]. This is in line with the Men of the Great Synagogue, who advised making a **fence around the law**[38], so as to be sure to avoid transgression. The holiness chapter itself provides a number of examples. The duty of honouring one's parents is extended to include the concept of awe and putting one's mother in the first place[39]. The time for the consumption of meat from the sacrifice and the use of the harvest are limited[40]. A number of commandments already known are given moral reasons[41], up to the peak of moral holiness[42]. Self control should be practised regarding sacrifices[43], use of the harvest[44], love of others[45], delay in the consumption of fruits[46], and in mourning[47].

The chapter of holiness uses this concept as a title for a series of commandments, some religious and some moral. The call to be holy because of the holiness of God, is based upon the idea of **imitatio dei,** which in turn follows from the concept of man being created **imago dei.** This idea is first found in the passage concerning God's rest on the Sabbath[48], and the Sabbath is mentioned again in the chapter of holiness as an example of **imitatio dei**[49].

The speaker does not command, but tries to convince the listener. Human beings can indeed be godlike and transcend the physical sphere of existence. He gives respect to the reason and autonomy of his audience, and bases the commandments upon a moral foundation. If the virtue of holiness is common to God and man, it has a value in and of itself, and is not a theonomic concept. In the spirit of Plato's **Euthyphron**, we may say that holiness does not consist of what God commanded, but that God commanded what suited His own as well as human holiness. The causal conjunction "for I am holy", elevates the statement from the level of theonomy to that of ethics.

Rational argumentation can also be found in the assertion that a person bears responsibility for the evil done by another if he himself did not rebuke the wrongdoer[50]. Before putting the blame upon others, says the text, ask yourself whether you have done everything possible to prevent the evil. Failing to do so is in itself an evil.

The moral concept of universalization appears in the explanation of the duty to love the stranger, with reference to one's own experience[51]. Use is made of a kind of **golden rule**, which reminds us of one formulation of Kant's **Categorical Imperative.**

The same universalization appears in the commandment to love your neighbour as yourself and to love the stranger as yourself[52]. The norm which you apply to yourself should be applied to all others as well.

The chapter of holiness presents the commandments in a deontological way, i.e. as following from the duty itself. In other parts of the Torah we find **eudaemonistic** reasons behind the commandments, but in this chapter these reasons are very seldom offered. For honouring one's father and mother a promise of longevity had been given in the Decalogue, but in this passage there is no such promise. Little is also said about punishments, which again points to the ethical approach of the speaker.

The concept of holiness is extended to all of Israel[53]. The rules about the consumption of the meat of sacrifices are formulated for the laymen, while the corresponding rules for the priest are given on another occasion[54].

Everyone is called upon to be holy, even in the most intimate sphere. In times of mourning he should refrain from cutting his skin, for such behaviour does not suit a member of the holy nation and a child of God[55]. The dietary rules apply to all of Israel, and distinguish between them and the rest of humanity[56]. Not only the priests, but everyone of the holy nation should have tassels at the corners of his clothing, to remind himself of the duty of holiness[57].

Likewise, the prophet Elijah was probably called holy because of his exemplary character, or because of his charisma[58]. More problematic is the meaning of the title **holy ones** in Ps. 34:10. Perhaps the poet envisioned the people in the Temple, who had prepared for their visit by observance of the rules of purity and spirituality[59].

(d) Deuteronomy

The integration of ethics in a collection of laws can also be traced in the **Second Torah** compiled by Moses prior to his death, i.e. in Deuteronomy. While the framework is a series of sermons, which are naturally in the line of ethical argumentation, it also comprises the laws[60]. This corpus constituted the normative part of the covenant of Moab[61]. But these passages also include many appeals to individual conscience, where human authority plays no role in the implementation.

We have already spoken of the liberation due to the Hebrew servant after six years of service, that it was a moral rather than a legal statute[62]. This explains the context, which is a series of appeals to conscience in favour of the disadvantaged[63]. It also explains the fact that the rule was not practised for a long time[64]. Both the remission of debts in the seventh year and the liberation of servants are forms of charity, and are not subject to legal sanction.

The admonition of judges to pursue justice, together with its reference to divine reward, likewise points to the moral character of the argument[65]. In contradistinction to this passage is the prohibition of idolatry, the legal character of which appears in procedural details[66], and the provisions constituting the supreme court, which are obviously forensic rules[67].

A moral appeal is to be found in the prohibition of removing landmarks[68], while the following rule, concerning false witnesses, is clearly a rule of law[69].

Examples of rules of morality include the duty to restore lost objects[70], the exemption of the mill from seizure in distress[71], the duty to restore a pledge at dawn[72], as well as the provisions in favour of employees[73] and of disadvantaged persons[74]. Likewise, the prohibition of false weights and measures appeals to the conscience of the listeners, rather than imposing public control or sanction[75]. An ethical argument can be found in the duty of fencing the roof to prevent injury[76], and perhaps in the rules protecting the different species[77], while the immediately following provisions concerning the slandering of a bride are legal rules[78].

In considering the various moral, legal and cultic provisions of the Pentateuch, we should finally look for formulations of norms representing the highest moral principles. In fact, such formulae are given in the Decalogue, contained in some of the rules of holiness and in the covenant between God and Israel.

While the Mosaic commandments are actually addressed to the people of the covenant, many of them have a **universal** appeal, as befitting ethical arguments. Take, for example, the idea of equality of strangers as well as natives before the law[79], which is a universal rule included in the Israelite Torah. By the same token, the conservation of the traditions of the Book of Genesis in the Pentateuch is an expression of the extension and appeal of the latter to other peoples as well as to Israel.

Although the Pentateuch is built on the assumption of a divine written law, this does not mean disregarding change of conditions or of moral sensibilities[80]. Written laws on stone tablets were part of the ancient tradition of the covenant[81], which included also warnings against adding to the law or subtracting from it[82] and for obedience to its text[83]. The fixation in writing was not a lapse from an earlier system of unwritten law to a regrettable legalism and literalism of the Deuteronomist. Rather it indicated the duty of absolute obedience to God, which demanded lovingkindness and personal morality.

Just as the law of inheritance could be changed upon the petition of the daughters of Zelophead[84], any other rule could be set aside, if need arose. According to Jewish understanding, the Torah demanded a constant openness for moral consideration and for legal change. The results of such changes were then called Oral Torah.

1.   Plato, **Euthyphron**, (Stuttgart: Reclam, 1978).

2.   Cf. **Encyclopedia of Islam**, s.v. mu'tazila.

3.   **Summa Theologica** 2.1.100.8 a 2; cf. A Verdross, **Abendlaendische Rechtsphilosophie**, 2nd ed., (Wien: Springer, 1963), p. 85, (rejecting the positivism of William of Ockham).

4.   Cf. H. Pehlke, "Zur Exegese des Dekalogs", in Burkhardt (ed.), **Begruendung**, pp. 49-66.

5.   Ex. 34:28.

6.   BT Makkot 23 b.

7.   Ex. 19:5.

8.   Ex. 19:8; 24:3,7. According to a view recorded in BT Sabbath 88 a, the agreement was actually voidable for having been reached under duress, since God was said to have left no choice for rejecting His offer. The validity of the covenant was therefore found in the submission to the law during the Babylonian exile, whereby the people willingly accepted the Torah. Such an acceptance was also expressed in the transformation of the Pentacost festival into the "Festival of the Delivery of Our Torah", and in the early custom of the reading of the decalogue in the Temple daily (M. Tamid 5:1). This reading was later discontinued, lest it be construed as exclusive of other passages of the Torah.

9.   Deut. 31:10-13. The submission to the "yoke of the divine kingdom" (M. Berakhot 2:2), expresses the need for individuals to repeat the acceptance twice daily. Originally, together with the reading of the "Shema'" one used to also recite the decalogue, which was included in the "Tefillin" and "Mezuzah" as well, as shown in the in the Papyrus Nash.

10.   Ex. 19:6.

11.   Num. 15:38.

12.   Ex. 19:7.

13.   Ex. 19:9; 20:19; Deut. 4:44.

14. Ex. 19:8-9.
15. God is portrayed as looking at every individual seperately, and speaking only to him, like the Icon (**Pantocrator**) in the cupola of the Byzantine churches (cf. Tanchuma Ex. 20:1).
16. Ex. 20:10; Mekhilta and Pesiqta Rabbati 33.
17. Ex. 23:12.
18. Deut. 5:15.
19. Ex. 20:4-5.
20. Pesiqta Rabbati 21.
21. Cf. the saying of R. Chiyah bar Abba on Jer. 9:11 quoted in JT Chagigah 1:7, 76 c.
22. Ex. 21-23.
23. Ex. 21:3.
24. Ex. 21:8.
25. Ex. 22:20-23; 23:9.
26. Ex. 22:24-26.
27. Ex. 23:1-3, 6-8.
28 Ex. 23:4-5.
29 Cf. Prov. 25:21-22.
30 Ex. 23:12.
31 Ex. 31:14-15.
32 Lev. 19.
33 Lev. 21:6; Num. 6:5.
34 Ex. 22:30; Lev. 11:44.
35 Ex. 19:6.
36 Deut. 14:1-2.
37 Sifra Lev. 19:2; Midrash Leqach Tov, ad loc.
38 M 'Avot 1:1.
39 Lev. 19:3.
40 Lev. 19:5-10.
41. Lev 19:13-14.
42. Lev. 19:18, 33-34.
43. Lev. 19:6-7.
44. Lev. 19:9-10.
45. Lev. 19:17-18, 34.
46. Lev. 19:23-25.
47. Lev. 19:28.
48. Gen. 2:2-3.
49. Gen. 2:9.
50. Lev. 19:17.
51 Lev. 19:34; cf. Ex. 22:20; 23:9; Deut. 24:18.

52   Lev. 19:18, 34.

53   As distinct from Lev. 21:1.

54   Lev. 7:16-18.

55   Deut. 14:2.

56   Lev. 20:27.

57   Num. 15:40.

58   2 Kings 4:9.

59   Cf. 1 Sam. 21:5 ff.; Ps. 15, 24.

60   Deut. 12-26.

61   Deut. 11:26-32; 26:16-28:25.

62   Deut. 15:12.

63   Deut. 15:1-18.

64   Cf. Jer. 34:12-16.

65   Deut. 16:18-20.

66   Deut. 17:2-7.

67   Deut. 17:8-13.

68   Deut. 19:14.

69   Deut. 19:15-21.

70   Deut. 22:1-3.

71   Deut. 24:6.

72   Deut. 24:10-13.

73   Deut. 24:14-15.

74   Deut. 24:17-22.

75   Deut. 25:13-16.

76   Deut. 22:8.

77   Deut. 22:9-12.

78   Deut. 22:13-19.

79   Lev. 18:26; 24:22.

80   Contra D. Patrick. **Old Testament Law.** Atlanta: Knox, 1985; cf. DI 13-14 (1986-88) 221-224.

81   Deut. 9:10; 10:2,4; 6:9; 11:20; 27:2-3.

82   Deut. 12:32.

83   Deut. 30:10.

84   Num. 27:1-11.

9. WISDOM LITERATURE

(a) Psalms

The sources of Israelite wisdom, probably dating from the time of King Solomon, included the first elements of biblical ethics. Egyptian models may have served the teachers of wisdom at the court of Jerusalem to develop a kind of moral discourse within religious tradition. Since the administration of justice was thought to belong to the realm of wisdom, judges were to be appointed from among the wise[1]. The same applied to other cultural activities, such as the composition of prayers and psalms, which drew upon the insights and traditions of wisdom[2].

In the following, we will attempt to present ideas of moral philosophy as included in the Psalms and other wisdom literature[3]. This attempt is based on the assumption that an Israelite ethical tradition existed, and was reflected in various literary and historical sources of early as well as later periods.

The writers of the Psalms found the standard of right and wrong in the divine law. The distinction between correct and false teaching was derived from divine precepts[4], which means that wisdom alone was not considered authoritative in legal decision making.

On the other hand, the righteous person was also described as meditating on wisdom, and as having the divine teaching in his heart[5]. The glory of God could be found in the observation of the heavens, as well as by studying the law[6], which follows from God's being perceived both as Creator and Lawgiver. In both cases, however, the insight does not follow from human feeling or reason alone, but from meditation upon, and contact with the divine.

Sometimes, psalmists spoke of certain virtues independently of divine teaching and commandments. Compassion is said to be the quality of the righteous[7]. This does not refer to obedience and theonomy, but to traits of character which are praiseworthy among all human beings. God is asked to do good to the good people and to those who are upright in their hearts, no mention being made of those who keep the commandments[8].

Humility is another virtue praised for its own sake, without reference to any divine rule demanding it[9]. The meek are promised possession of the land and wellbeing[10], and divine justice is said to be concerned with character, not with observance of laws.

The virtue of the king was declared to be integrity of heart[11]. Any person entering the Temple, according to the view of one psalmist, should ask himself whether he had walked blamelessly, had done what was right and spoken the truth in his heart[12], or whether he had clean hands and a pure heart[13]. The same virtues were required on doomsday, stated one of the prophets[14].

Those who put virtues, rather than duties, in the center of their system of belief, prayed for a new heart and a new spirit in order to be able to change[15]. The condition of one's heart and spirit was not a reference to one's behaviour or observance of the Torah, but to one's moral integrity.

Under these circumstances, people must have felt less moral freedom, than moral dependence upon divine guidance. Their prayers reflected the central role of character, but also a belief in determinism.

Other psalms speak of free will as the basis of one's moral status. The speaker asserted that he had chosen the way of faithfulness and set the divine judgments before him[16], or that he had chosen the divine precepts[17]. Here we have the recognition of theonomy and the centrality of Torah, together with the emphasis on human freedom.

(b) Proverbs

Even closer to the ethical approach is the Book of Proverbs. According to Kant's **Categorical Imperative,** a moral rule could be described as such only if it was capable of universalization. From this point of view, wisdom literature is in line with ethical discourse, appealing, as it does, to all human beings.

The Israelite equivalent of what we know as Mesopotamian and Egyptian wisdom traditions remained universalist and individualist. Although the speakers must have known the Torah of Moses and the concept of the chosen nation, the holiness of the land and the Temple, they chose to address their listeners in a rational way[18]. Their approach was individualist and utilitarian, rather than collectivist and dogmatic, and they appealed to humanity, not to Israel alone.

Their concept of wisdom was universal and autonomous vis-a-vis the belief in revelation and Torah. While it is true that the fear of God was also considered by them to be the beginning of wisdom[19], this did not refer to the commandments. The listener was called upon to seek wisdom, and through this wisdom, to understand the awe of God and the knowledge about Him[20]. Instead of speaking of theonomy, revelation and covenant, the wise emphasized the preexistence of wisdom[21].

When Torah was mentioned, the reference was to the teaching by parents and masters, not to that of Moses or the priests[22]. Perhaps the latter was meant when mentioning Torah together with Prophecy[23]. But even in this case, the argument was utilitarian rather than authoritarian.

The eclectic approach of the author stands out where he treats rules of law by adding teleological reasons for observance, and at the same time stressing divine reward and punishment[24]. Take, for example, the following sequence of admonitions: "Blessings on the head of the virtuous man", the intention of which is to divine reward, as expressly stated in the Greek and Latin versions, and "He walks secure whose ways are honourable, but he who follows crooked ways is soon discovered", i.e. a utilitarian argument[25].

Israelite wisdom, like its Egyptian models, developed a teaching of virtues and vices to be used as educational material. Cool spirit was said to be desirable, while hot temper was criticized[26]. The highest virtue, according to one formulation, was "a heart of healing", which is probably a description of a tranquil mind; the opposite was "envy", or passion in general[27].

(c) Job

The author of the Book of Job started from the prevalent concept of moral causality, i.e. the doctrine that good effected good and happiness, while evil caused evil and suffering, "For affliction does not come out of the dust, nor does trouble spring out of the ground"[28]. According to another formulation, "Can the rush shoot up without mire? Can the reed grass grow without water? Whilst it is yet in its greenness and not cut down, it withers before any other herb. So are the paths of all who forget God..."[29].

Piety was the condition of life, thought the author originally, and a person disregarding his duty towards God would necessarily face the consequences. However, this does not say that the opposite was also necessarily true, viz. that the righteous would enjoy a happy life.

Suffering might also be beneficial, for as it is stated: "Happy is the man whom God corrects. Therefore do not despise the chastening of the Almighty. For he makes sore and binds up, he wounds but his hands make whole"[30]. But Job cannot understand his suffering as a result of his own behaviour, because he is sure of his innocence[31]. He protests that "Till I die I will not put away my integrity from me. I hold fast my righteousness and I will not let it go"[32].

God's reply does not refer at all to Job's claim, but shows him that he has too little information to be able to criticize providence: "Will you put me in the wrong? Will you condemn me that you may be justified? Have you an arm like God, and can you thunder with a voice like his?"[33]. Job accepts this reprove, and this is his supreme test, similar to that of Abraham when he is asked to offer his son[34]. Instead of challenging God with the question of theodicy[35], the author concludes that one should humbly ask God for enlightenment[36].

Thus, the Book of Job is a treatise on **epistemology**, describing the limits of moral perception and the need for submission to faith in the divine. Wisdom does not explain the world, so that an answer to the riddles must be sought in religious experience: "The fear of God, that is wisdom; and to depart from evil is understanding"[37]. Therefore, Job finally finds consolation in the experience: "I have heard of You by way of hearsay, but now my eye sees You. Therefore, I dislike my words and I repent, seeing that I am dust and ashes"[38].

The author thereby describes the limits of human wisdom and the need for revelation. Wisdom may be used for the guidance of human beings, but not to define theodicy. **Deus semper major,** and could not be forced into any ethical system[39].

(d) Ecclesiastes

The thoughts collected in the Book of Ecclesiastes deal, even more than the preceding texts, with ethics, i.e. with the definition of the good, or with the goal of all human aspiration[40]. The author wishes to describe "what was good for human beings to do under heaven during the few days of their life"[41].

His first conclusion was utter pessimism: "All is in vain"[42]. Even wisdom itself cannot be considered as the highest good, since "in much wisdom is much vexation, and he who increases knowledge increases sorrow"[43]. While these thoughts express the idea of relativism[44], and create ambivalent feelings vis-a-vis all values, there are other passages in the book stressing the stability, and calling for the study, of wisdom.

There is, above all, the time factor[45]. Human beings should be aware of this factor in their dispositions and throughout their lives. Alas, even the wise themselves do not know the time of their death[46], which shows them to be subjects of time rather than its master.

Only God is said to be above time[47] (and space), which means that man must submit to His rule. Since God is seen as being behind all phenomena, and as being the setter of time, the wise are called upon to enjoy their work, for who can bring them to see what will be after them?[48]. This idea of **carpe diem** includes "eating and drinking and finding enjoyment in all the toil with which one toils under the sun the few days of one's life, which God has given one, for this is one's lot"[49].

The ethical teaching of the Book of Ecclesiastes therefore calls upon people to make use of the opportunities given to them by God, and to submit to their lot, or to destiny[50]. Ecclesiastes, as well as Job, present the particular insight of Jewish wisdom, viz. that human categories of thought could not be applied to metaphysics, and that theology was a dubious undertaking. Furthermore, Ecclesiastes points to the limits of all ethics, vis-a-vis other factors of human life and of the world[51].

1.   Deut. 1:13-15; 16:19.

2.   Cf. J. Reindl, "Weisheitliche Bearbeitungen von Psalmen", VT, 32, (1981), pp. 333-356.

3.   Cf. W. Richter, **Recht und Ethos. Versuch einer Ortung des weisheitlichen Mahnspruchs,** (Muenchen: 1966).

4.   Ps. 119:104.

5.   Ps. 37:30-31.

6.   Ps. 19.

7.   Ps. 37:21, 26; 112:5.

8.   Ps. 125:4.

9.   Ps. 131:1.

10.   Ps. 37:11.

11.   Ps. 101:2.

12.   Ps. 15:2.

13.   Ps. 24:4.

14.   Is. 33:15.

15.   Ps. 51:12.

16.   Ps. 119:30.

17.   Ps. 119:173.

18.   W. Zimmerli, "Zur Struktur der alttestamentlichen Weisheit", ZAW NF, 10, (1933), pp. 177-204.

19.   Prov. 1:7; cf. Ps. 111:10; Job 28:28.

20.   Prov. 2:4.

21.   Prov. 8:22-31.

22.   Cf. Prov. 1:8; 3:1.

23.   Cf. Prov. 29:18.

24.   See Kaufman, **Toledot**, 2, p. 580; G. von Rad, **Theologie**, i, 5th ed., (1966), p. 449.

25.   Prov. 10:6 vis-a-vis 9; cf. to the latter the alternative formulation see Prov. 28:18, where the reference could also be to divine punishment.

26.   Prov. 14:29; 15:18; 17:27; 22:24; 29:22.

27.   Prov. 14:30; cf. Zeph. 1:18.

28.   Job 5:6.

29.   Job 8:11-13.

30.   Job 5:17-18.

31.   Job 9:21.

32.   Job 27:5-6.

33.   Job 40:8-9.

34.   Job 40:3-5; 42;1-6.

35.   Job 38:3.

36.   Job 42:4.

37.   Job 28:28.

38.   Job 42:5-6.

39.   On the correlation of ethics and religion see W.M. Bartley, **Morality and Religion**, (London: 1970); Schrey, **Einfuehrung**, pp. 22-34; and M. Forschner, "Religion", in Hoeffe, **Lexikon**.

40.   Aristotle, **Nicomachean Ethics**, 1:1, 1094 a 2-3.

41.   Eccl. 2:3.

42.   Eccl. 1:2.

43.   Eccl. 1:18.

44.   On ethical relativism see Frankena, **Ethics**, p.109; Brandt, **Ethical Theory**, pp. 271-294; and Hoeffe, **Lexikon**, pp. 205-207.

45.   Eccl. 3:1-8, 17; 8:6.

46.   Eccl. 9:11.

47.   Eccl. 3:14.

48.   Eccl. 3:22.

49.   Eccl. 5:17; cf. 9:7-9.

50.   Cf. also G. Fohrer, **Geschichte der israelitischen Religion**, (Berlin: deGruyter, 1969), p. 377; and R. Rendtorff, **Das AT: Eine Einfuehrung** (Neukirchen, 1985), pp. 278-280.

51.   On the limits of ethics cf. Pieper, **Ethik**, pp. 105-107; Schrey, **Einfuehrung**, p. 162.

10. THE PROPHETS

The primacy of morals in the relations of human beings towards God was first proclaimed by the literary prophets, although later this idea also appears in certain passages of Psalms and Proverbs. While the Torah called for the observance of both rituals and morals, it was the prophets who declared the former to be worthless without the latter[1]. This insight may have been reached by studying moral passages of the Torah[2], as a reflection upon Egyptian or Mesopotamian wisdom traditions[3], or as a result of their own personal experience and inspiration.

(a) Amos

Take for example the case of Amos, whose prophecy was probably the first to be recorded. While his listeners were sure of their unique status as the chosen people of their God, Amos taught them to understand themselves as part of humanity, and to **universalize** the ideas which they had thought to exist only in their own tradition.

The idea of chosenness should not be used to claim any privilege, but to bear more responsibility: "Hear this word that God has spoken against you, O people of Israel, against the whole family which I brought up out of the land of Egypt: You only have I known of all the families of the earth; therefore I will punish you for all your iniquities"[4]. Moreover, the whole concept of chosenness should be understood as a relative one, as seen from the point of view of Israel. Other people could equally see themselves as chosen: "Are you not like the Ethiopians to me, O people of Israel? says God. Did I not bring up Israel from the land of Egypt, and the Philistines from Caphtor and the Syrians from Kir?"[5].

This meant that the test of **generality** was applied to the concept, which then led the prophet to reinterpret it in a rational way. As a result of this tendency of universalization, the prophet applied his standards of behaviour to other nations as well as to Israel. He even applied it to the behaviour of one nation towards another, without any direct connection to Israel. Ergo, he criticized the cruelty of the people of Gaza, although none of the listeners were actually involved: "Thus says God: For three transgressions of Gaza, and for four, I will not cause it to return; because they carried into exile a whole people to deliver them up to Edom. So I will send a fire upon the wall of Gaza, and it shall devour her strongholds"[6].

Ethical rationalization and a call for transcendence beyond theonomy can be found in Amos' equation of **God** and **Good**. On the one hand, the prophet called for exclusiveness in the worship of God, and on the other hand he used the same term to call for exclusiveness in the dedication to the good: "For thus says God to the house of Israel: Seek me and live; but do not seek Bethel, and do not cross into Gilgal or cross over to Beer-sheba". A little later he continues: "Seek good and not evil, that you may live... Hate evil and love good, and establish justice in the gate"[7]. The latter concepts do not depend on revelation, but enjoy the same authority, in the eyes of the speaker, as the will of God. Therefore, according to Amos, ethical concepts should be respected for their own authority[8].

Amos describes the social injustice of the northern kingdom, which would ultimately bring about its own destruction[9]. There is hardly any reference to religious sin or disloyalty to God, probably because the prophet felt the extraordinary need for moral instruction.

(b) Hosea

The same approach may be traced in the prophecy of Hosea. He deplored the absence of certain virtues, as well as the absence of the knowledge of God: "There is no truthfulness nor lovingkindness, and no knowledge of God in the land"[10]. Similarly, the prophet rendered the word of God: "For I desire lovingkindness and not sacrifice, the knowledge of God, rather than burnt offerings"[11]. In both cases, the former concepts exist as equal to, and independent of, the theonomic principle of knowing God.

In the former speech, the prophet also connected the knowledge of God with the knowledge of God's Torah[12]. Indeed, the knowledge of God is linked with following His will: "...because they have broken my covenant, and transgressed my Torah. But they cry to me, My God, we Israel know you. Israel has spurned the good..."[13]. The good is again somehow equal to, but not identical with, Torah or knowledge of God, otherwise there would be no point in this further lamentation. Thus, we have in Hosea's view, two religious concepts: knowledge and Torah; and three moral ones: truthfulness, lovingkindness and the good.

While Samuel had demanded obedience to the will of God[14], and Amos had stressed the importance of law and justice, it was Hosea who called for more than that, namely the need for lovingkindness[15].

(c) Isaiah

In the speeches of Isaiah, justice and righteousness are divine virtues and attributes, which means that they are more than theonomic orders: "But the God of hosts is exalted in justice, and the holy God shows himself holy in righteousness"[16]. Justice and righteousness are seen as general principles, binding upon God, as well as upon human beings.

In contradistinction to these virtues, valuable in themselves, the prophet's demand of the people was that they refrain from rejecting the Torah of the God of hosts, and from despising the word of the Holy One of Israel[17]. Isaiah blamed the people for having disregarded the Torah, not for having violated any moral principle. On another occasion he accused the people of being unwilling to listen to God's Torah[18].

But Isaiah, when blaming his listeners, also referred to moral principles. Before accusing them of the rejection of Torah, he reproached them for calling evil good and good evil[19], and on another occasion he demanded: "Wash yourselves; make yourselves clean; remove the evil of your doings from before my eyes; cease to do evil, learn to do good; seek justice, relieve the oppressed, defend the fatherless, plead for the widow"[20].

On doomsday, according to Isaiah, a moral test would be applied to determine whether a person would or would not be saved: "He who walks righteously and speaks uprightly; he who despises the gain of oppressions; who shakes his hands, lest they hold a bribe; who stops his ears from hearing of bloodshed; and shuts his eyes from looking upon evil"[21].

Isaiah likewise touched upon the problem of determinism. On the one hand he emphasized the free choice of man, and on the other he spoke of God's intervention, "to make the heart of the people fat, their ears heavy and their eyes shut, lest they be seeing with their eyes, and hearing with their ears, and understanding with their heart, return and be healed"[22]. However, in other cases divine providence did not affect human freedom of choice.

Thus, the prophet distinguished between the objective execution of the divine will, and the subjective consciousness of human beings, which perceive their acts as resulting from human decisions: "O Ashur, the rod of my anger, staff of my indignation! I do send him against an ungodly nation... But he does not mean so, neither does his heart think so, but it is in his heart to destroy..."[23]. God is described as being able to use the free will of the Assyrian king to carry out parts of His own plan. We may imagine that the king could have decided differently, and God would then have had to find a different way to execute His will[24].

Like his predecessors, Isaiah declared morality to be a **conditio sine qua non** to cult and prayer[25], although in his view the theonomic argument in favour of moral norms prevailed over the ethical one[26].

(d) Micah

For Micah, on the other hand, the good was not only a theonomic idea, but had some independent existence of its own. He could therefore say: "He has showed you, O man, what is good and what does God require of you; but to do justice, and to love kindness, and to walk humbly with your God"[27]. Not only had the preceding question assumed the existence of a moral beside the religious norm, but the answer, quoted above, includes the general human ideal of justice and lovingkindness, besides the particular ideal of religious tradition, here called "walking humbly with your God".

(e) Jeremiah

A distinction between the formalistic obedience of Torah and the real knowledge of the way of God is drawn by Jeremiah: "They are foolish, for they do not know the way of God[28], the judgment of their God". The prophet could not have thought that the people simply did not know of the commandment prohibiting a false oath, but he blamed them for giving a legalistic interpretation to the commandment. He went on to deplore their ignorance of the most elementary knowledge: "The stork in the heaven knows her appointed times, and the turtle and the swallow and the crane observe the time of their coming; but my people do not know God's judgment. How do you say: 'We are wise, and God's Torah is with us'?"[29].

The people claimed that they knew Torah, but they actually misinterpreted it. In order to correctly understand the Torah simple knowledge is not enough; a moral attitude is needed. Therefore in the future, the prophet said, a new covenant with God would become necessary: "But this is the covenant which I will make with the house of Israel after those days, says God, I will put my Torah in their interior and I will write it on their heart; and I will be their God and they will be my people"[30].

This prophecy was an expression of Jeremiah's loss of confidence in the ability of the people to repent. He told his listeners that, left to themselves, they had no chance to prevent the catastrophe[31]; they were like clay in the potter's hand and could not take their destiny into their own hands[32].

Jeremiah emphasized the moral rules of the law rather than the cultic ones: "Add your burnt offerings to your sacrifices, and eat the flesh. For in the day that I brought them out of the land of Egypt, I did not speak to your fathers or command them concerning burnt offerings and sacrifices. But this command I gave them, 'Obey my voice, and I will be your God, and you shall be my people; and walk in all the way that I command you, that it may be well with you'"[33]. Again, the prophet criticized the religious traditions of the people for its failing to make them notice that the central meaning of devotion is to God, rather than devotion to the Temple.

Because of his evaluation of their moral standard, the prophet also explained the estrangement between God and the people as a result of falsehood: "Wherever you sit, you are deceived; because of their deceiving, they refuse to acknowledge Me, says God"[34]. Had the people been directed by the pursuit of truth, they would never have failed in establishing the right relationship with God.

Jeremiah's moral sensitivity and his fight for truth even led him to raise the question of theodicy, and to express doubts regarding God's justice[35]. He could do this not only on the grounds of his own personal experience, but also as a result of his ethical thinking and independence.

(f) Ezekiel

A similar meaning should be ascribed to the prophecy of Ezekiel: "And I gave them my statutes and taught them my judgments, which man should do and live by them. I also gave them my Sabbaths... but the house of Israel rebelled against me in the wilderness; they did not walk in my statutes and they rejected my judgments, which man should do to live by them, and they greatly profaned my Sabbaths... I gave them also statutes that were not good and judgments whereby they should not live. And I polluted them in their own gifts in that they set apart all that opens the womb, that I might destroy them, to the end that they might know that I am God"[36].

Since there always existed the danger of misinterpretation, even divine laws could turn into statutes that were not good and judgments whereby they should not live. There needed to be a special intervention on the part of God to make Torah beneficial: "And I will give you a new heart and I will put a new spirit within you; and will take away the stony heart out of your flesh. And I will put my spirit within you and cause you to walk in my statutes and you shall keep my judgments and do them".[37]

This does not mean that Ezekiel and the other prophets derived all moral ideas only from the will of God. The very possibility that divine laws could be not good, calls for the differentiation of theology and ethics, and for the critical insight of human beings, even vis-a-vis the laws of God[38].

1.   Cf. Kaufman, **Toledot**, 1, pp. 31-34.

2.   Cf. Eichrodt, **Theologie**, ii, 4th ed., (1961), p.230.

3.   Cf. N.W. Porteous, "The Basis of Ethical Teaching of the Prophets", in H. Rowley (ed.), **Studies in OT Prophecy presented to Th. Robinson**, (Edinburgh: 1950), (=N.W. Porteous: **Living the Mystery**, (Oxford: 1967), pp. 47-60). ·

4.   Amos 3:2.

5.   Amos 9:7.

6.   Amos 1:6-7.

7.   Amos 5:4-5, 14-15.

8.   See also Hans Walter Wolff, **Amos geistige Heimat**, (Neukirchen, 1964).

9.   Y. Kaufman, **Toledot**, 3, p. 78.

10.   Hos. 4:1.

11.   Hos. 6:6.

12.   Hos. 4:6.

13.   Hos. 8:1-3.

14.   1 Sam. 15:22.

15.   Y. Kaufman, **Toledot**, 3, p. 146.

16.   Is. 5:16.

17.   Is. 5:24.

18.   Is. 30:9.

19.   Is. 5:20.

20.   Is. 1:16-17.

21.   Is. 33:15.

22.   Is. 6:10.

23.   Is. 10:5-7.

24.   See F. Hesse, **Das Verstockungsproblem im Alten Testament**, (BZAW 74, 1955); John Barton, "Ethics in Isaiah", **JThS**, 32, (1981) pp. 1-18.

25.   Is. 1:15.

26.   Y. Kaufman, **Toledot**, 3, p. 192 ff.

27.   Mic. 6:8.

28.   Jer. 5:4.

29.   Jer. 8:7-8.

30.   Jer. 31:32; cf. 32:39-40.

31.   Jer. 10:23.

32. Jer. 18:5 ff.

33. Jer. 7:21-23.

34. Jer. 9:5.

35. Jer. 12:1-2.

36. Ez. 20:11-12, 25-26. Cf. my 'Erkhey Mishpat, p. 103.

37. Ez. 36:26-27.

38. Contra Kaufman, Toledot, 2, p. 590.

11. BIBLICAL HISTORIOGRAPHY

(a) Moral Principles

In this chapter we will examine Biblical historiography, particularly in relation to law and ethics. The concept of history appears in the Song of Moses: "Remember the Days of Old, consider the years of many generations..."[1], and a special warning is given to the people, charging them with telling the things of the past to their descendants[2]. This means that history is considered to be an important component of education, and that historical consciousness is needed in order to have a proper attitude towards God.

Biblical historiography was concerned mainly with God and salvation. Its object was the moral meaning of events, the extent of human freedom, the response to the divine offer, and finally, God's choice between corrective justice and graciousness.

The emphasis of the historical writers was upon the religious aspect of the Torah, particularly human loyalty towards God, so that sometimes little was said about moral responsibility to fellow human beings[3]. A wrong committed against another person was answerable vis-a-vis God[4], which means that it followed from theonomy and not from ethical thought. History was understood from the perspective of the covenant, i.e. as a drama with only two personae: God and Israel.

Moreover, the historical books of the Bible do not present a systematic body of theology or of ethical principles, but may be found to contain some norms and structures of correct behaviour. These norms and structures may, however, provide material for the eventual formulation of a moral theory, guiding the listener and reader in their relationship with God.

History is also the medium for transmitting many of the moral principles of everyday life. Time and again the listener was to realize that the people of the past had had a free choice as to whether to follow the will of God or not, that their fate had depended upon their deeds, and that the opportunity to repent had been theirs.

In many instances the idea was expressed that there existed a moral causality, bringing the effect of a person's guilt upon his own head, as well as determining future acts by earlier choices.

Biblical historiography fulfilled an important criterion of ethical thought, namely that of universalization, in putting the events of one generation into a historical context, and the history of the people within a universal framework, beginning with the creation of the world. While other nations would concentrate on their specific past alone, Israel knew of its place among the other nations as well as of a time prior to its own existence. Moreover, biblical historiography expressed strong self-criticism, in addition to the freedom to transcend its own national interest.

Israel perceived God as a God of justice, who thereby put Himself on a par with His people. History was the chain of divine **tsedakot** (acts of equity toward Israel)[5]. This was a model for human beings to use in relating to each other equitably[6]. It was also to be related via history, of how the king was as much restricted by the law as any of his subjects.

While the historical writings describe the value of the individual in his relationship with God and fellowman, there is also a constant reference to the responsibility of the individual for his kinsmen and for the other members of the covenant. Many events of Israel's history are described by the authors of the historical books as resulting from the negative traits of their leaders[7]. Obviously the reader is invited to accept the historiographer's thesis concerning the link between character and destiny.

A description of David's remorse[8], for example, had the exemplary meaning of emphasizing the value of conscientiousness. Time and again biblical historiography stressed the value of the good intention[9], but the author was also aware of the possibility that a person might be motivated by a divine provocation or temptation[10]. Such a person would then bear the responsibility for his actions, even if they were procured by an act of God.

(b) The Covenant

The central idea of the historiographers is indeed the correlation of divine action with that of humankind through the covenants made with Noach, Abraham and Israel. History is perceived as the realization of these covenants, which were dependent upon either obedience or rebellion on the part of the human partners.

Although the covenant was between unequal parties, the very fact that God was ready to encounter man in this form was recognition of a certain equality. This meant, firstly, the mutual choice of each partner to become a party to the covenant, and secondly, that both sides freely consented to the agreement. God was described as having acquired the people of Israel as His own people[11], and as their father who had begotten them[12].

The result of this relationship was the constant hope to be treated by God according to the rules of family solidarity. God was expected to redeem Israel, and to bring them to His own heritage[13]. The redemption out of the slavery into "God's tribal heritage" was another ethical reflection in the historiography of Israel[14].

Needless to say, these concepts were thought to have imposed a responsibility upon the people. They were supposed to justify the relationship and to act as stewards of the heritage. The land was not to be transferred to them forever, for it belonged to God, and the people were like strangers and sojourners with its real owner, (especially if they did not behave like God's own people)[15].

From the beginning, the human partner to the covenant was under an obligation to observe certain rules: the prohibition of eating from the Tree of Knowledge and Adam's stewardship in the Garden of Eden, the Noachide commandments before and after the flood, the commandments given to the patriarchs, and finally, the revealed laws of Israel - all these were the human obligations of the covenants. The covenant with Abraham, for example, was made with the expectation that Abraham would "command his children and his house after him to observe the way of God to do equity and justice"[16].

Historiography also wished to reply to the moral question of how God related to the rest of mankind, who were equally God's creatures. The answer is choice or election, which means that it was a result of God's freedom of choice. God was said to have chosen Aaron as his priest[17], and not other Israelites or Levites, and Moses as his servant and spokesman, to the exclusion of the rest[18]. Likewise, God was described as having chosen Israel as his people out of his love for them, which did not need any justification[19].

The corresponding choice on the part of Israel was the corollary to God's choice. It was implied in their promise to obey God's words[20], and was reiterated through their participation in the celebration of the covenant. This choice was expressed by the answer of Amen, following the curses against violators of the covenant[21]. The people were also asked to choose between God and the gods of other traditions, just as God chose between them and other nations[22]. Although the covenant was celebrated on special occasions, the choice was to take the form of a continuous commitment, and would be made void by an adverse act. If, at a later time the people chose to worship other gods, declared the author of the book of Judges, they would thereby repudiate the covenant and would have to face God's reaction[23].

This reaction, however, was not automatic and legalistic, rather part of a father's power of correction which also expressed his compassion. The child could expect to be reinstated in his chosenness if he repented and asked the father for forgiveness. Biblical historiography developed a special pattern of such action and reaction, of justice and mercy, as well as of the ungoing dialogue between God and Man[24].

(c) Divine Grace

Moral considerations transcend the realm of legal obligation, and include the showing of grace and loving-kindness. The divine realization of the covenant, in any given situation, was said to be conditional and dependent upon the fulfillment of the people's commitment. The promises for the future, till the end of days, were always seen as conditional. However, just as God's freedom allowed for forgiveness at any given moment, the promises for the distant future could also be realized, in spite of the unworthiness of Israel, merely as a result of divine grace[25].

Thus, the prayer put into the mouth of King David included a statement that God had established his people Israel, and had become their God forever[26]. The same idea appeared in a royal psalm, viz. that God made an oath to David, and that in truth he would not turn back from it. David's children were to rule forever, and their capital, Zion, would forever be God's habitation[27]. In times of crisis, the author of the biblical history declared, God would preserve David's dynasty[28].

Vis-a-vis the danger of the Assyrian empire threatening the future of Judah, the historiographer stressed the divine grace. Out of Jerusalem a remnant would come forth, and God would defend this city and save it, both for His own sake and for the sake of His servant David[29].

The ethical idea behind the notion of divine grace was, of course, that love could serve to overcome evil. This idea follows from the description of God's way with Israel, and is part of **imitatio dei**. Thus, biblical historiography was actually less concerned with the historical facts than with the moral relations between God and the people.

The same can perhaps be said regarding all Holy Scriptures. Religion was never really distinguished from morality, the latter being considered of the essence of man's duties to God. Beside the central role played by justice, the reader of the Bible notices the importance of love and respect both vis-a-vis God and human beings. The message is moralistic as much as theological.

1.   Deut. 32:7.

2.   Ex. 10:2; Deut. 4:9.

3.   Kaufman, **Toledot**, 1, p. 27.

4.   1 Sam. 2:25.

5.   Jud. 5:11; 1 Sam. 12:7; Mic. 6:5; Ps. 103:6; Dan. 9:12.

6.   Gen. 30:33; 31:36; 38:26; 1 Sam. 24:18; 26:23.

7.   E.g. Jud. 9:56-57; 2 Chron. 26:16-21.

8.   1 Sam. 24:5.

9.   E.g. 1 Kings 15:14; 2 Kings 20:3.

10.   2 Sam. 24:1; 1 Kings 22:21.

11.   Ex. 15:16; Ps. 74:2.

12.   Deut. 32:6.

13.   Ex. 15:13,17. Cf. the concept **'achuzah** - Jos. 22:19; and **nachalah** - 1 Sam. 26:19; 2
      Sam. 14:16; Jer. 2:7; 16:18; 50:11; Ps. 68:10; 79:1.

14.   Ps. 74:2.

15.   Lev. 25:23.

16.   Gen. 18:19.

17.   Num. 16:5, 7.

18.   Num. 12: 6-7; Ps. 106:23.

19.   Deut. 7:6-8.

20.   Ex. 19:8; 24:3,7.

21.   Deut. 27:11-26.

22.   Jos. 24:15,22.

23.   Jud. 5:8; 10:14.

24.   Jud. 2:7-23; 10:6-16; 1 Sam. 7:3-4; 12:8-11; 1 Kings 8:33-34.

25.   See   Jorge   Mejia,   "The   Aim   of   the   Deuteronomistic   Historian: A
      Reappraisal", **Proc. 6th World Congress of Jewish Studies**, vol. 1,
      (1977), pp. 291-298.

26.   2 Sam. 7:24.

27.   Ps. 132.

28.   1 Kings 11:36; 2 Kings 8:19.

29.   2 Kings 19:30-31, 34.

B. POSTBIBLICAL ETHICS

12. JEWISH HELLENISM AND SECTS

(a) Letter of Aristeas

The author of the Letter of Aristeas, who was probably a Jew living at the end of the second century B.C.E. in Alexandria, aimed at reconciling Jewish legal tradition with Greek ethics[1]. He quotes the High Priest Elazar telling the Egyptian king Ptolemy II (285-247 B.C.E.), that "the good life consisted in observing the laws, and this aim was achieved by hearing much more than by reading"[2]. In other words, the Jewish tradition was parallel to the Hellenistic one, and the law was the realization of ethical theory. Hearing must have symbolized submission to the law[3], which, in the author's view, was preferable to the reading of philosophical and ethical writers.

The dietary laws were explained as a means of protecting the particularity of the Jewish people, but also "that through the whole of our lives we may also practise justice to all mankind, remembering the all-sovereign God" (**Letter**, v.168). Thus, an ethical interpretation is offered to justify the dietary laws, and ethical limitations are imposed upon them.

Another idea derived from ethics is that of the **golden mean**. The delegates were said to be well qualified "with the middle way as their commendable ideal" (122). This idea could have been adopted from the thought found in Ecclesiastes 7:16-18, but was probably a reflection of Greek philosophy[4], and of the ideas of Roman society[5]. The same principle was later accepted in the school of the Rabbis[6], and included in the code of Maimonides[7].

The author of the **Letter** also referred to the concept of **imitatio dei**. In reply to the question as to how the king could keep his rule to the end without offence, the advice was given: "You would administer it best by imitating the eternal goodness of God. By using long-suffering, and treatment of those who merit (punishment) more leniently than they deserve, you will convert them to repentance" (188).

This advice was based on a preference of morals over law, and it rejected the Stoic attitude, which did not recommend pity. Just as God was said to show mercy to the sinner, the king and probably also the judge, should have pity. This statement is all the more remarkable, as it contradicts the notion of justice and equality. Even among the rabbis this position was debated[8], and the administration of a big country must have felt such advice to be a real novelty.

(b) Ben Sira

About 170 BCE, Ben Sira presented his system of morality in the style of **Proverbs** and the other books of biblical wisdom. However, while his predecessors had believed in the freedom of will and had called upon every listener to become righteous, he emphasized the **chosenness** of some human beings and the **inequality** of mankind. Following biblical metaphors, he says: "Likewise, also all men are made from the clay, and Adam was created of earth, in His great wisdom God distinguished them, and differentiated their ways. Some He blessed and exalted, and others He hallowed and brought nigh to Himself. Some He cursed and abased and overthrew them from their place"[9].

This is a justification of the Jewish tradition vis-a-vis Hellenist universalism. The author uses the medium of wisdom, appealing to everyone alike, but he is also a spokesman of Judaism and of its claim for uniqueness. It is possible that his view is somehow connected with the belief in **predestination**, which was prevalent among the Essenes[10].

(c) Philo of Alexandria

According to Philo of Alexandria (20 BCE - 50 CE), the Patriarchs had lived lives of virtue based on the law of nature. "They listened to no voice or instruction but their own: they gladly accepted conformity with nature, holding that nature itself was, as indeed it is, the most venerable of statutes..."[11]. The treatise on Abraham, therefore, describes him as "one who obeyed the law, some will say, but rather, as our discourse has shown, himself a law and an unwritten statute"[12].

This was part of Philo's system of interpreting the Torah in terms of Greek philosophy, and of justifying the law of Moses vis-a-vis ethical thought. By establishing the continuity between the lives of the Patriarchs and the positive law of Moses, Philo hoped to prove his thesis that the Torah was identical with the law of nature or with ethics. The purpose of the commandments, according to his interpretation, was a life of virtue and conformity to nature. This had been the goal of the Patriarchs, and had not been changed through legislation in the time of Moses.

The law of nature is quoted in order to criticize the positive laws of the Greeks, which were often in conflict with the laws of the Bible[13]. Since the law of Moses was identical with the law of nature, its application extended to the whole world[14]. Hence, according to Philo, instead of accepting the criticism of the Hellenists, the reader should use biblical law as a measure of criticism of the Gentile culture.

(d) Manual of Discipline

Likewise, the **Manual of Discipline** of the Qumran community (1st cent.CE) makes use of various concepts of Greek ethics, among them truth, righteousness and justice[15]. Additional virtues include "a spirit of humility, patience, abundant charity, unending goodness, understanding and intelligence; (a spirit of) mighty wisdom which trusts in all the deeds of God and leans on his great lovingkindness; a spirit of discernment in every purpose, of zeal for just laws, of holy intent with steadfastness of heart, of great charity towards all the sons of truth, of admirable purity which detests all unclean idols, of humble conduct sprung from an understanding of all things, and of faithful concealment of the mysteries of God"[16].

The Essenes believed in the predestination of the righteous and the sinners[17]. Nevertheless they justified divine reward of the former and punishment of the latter[18]. In sectarian thinking, the universe represents a constant struggle between the forces of light and those of darkness, the sect itself forming part of the forces of light[19]. But the struggle between good and evil is to be found within every human being[20]. This enabled the sect to develop its ethical system.

(e) The Fourth Book of Maccabees

This sermon on the value of reason (1st cent. CE) is devoted to one of the virtues, as illustrated by Jewish suffering. The martyr for sanctification of God's Name is described as a stoic overcoming tyranny by endurance. The author considers Jewish tradition as the true realization of Greek ethics, and thereby presents a synthesis between Judaism and philosophy[21].

(f) 4 Ezra

In his description of afterlife, the author (about 100 CE) speaks of the good people, who "have striven much and painfully to overcome the innate evil thought, that it might not lead them astray from life unto death"[22]. The assumption is made that everybody has the freedom to choose a life of virtue.

(g) Flavius Josephus

In his apologetics of Judaism composed around 96 C.E., this Jewish historian writes about Moses: "And the reason why our lawgiver in his legislation far exceeded all other legislators in usefulness to all, is that he did not make religion a part of virtue, but had the insight to make the various virtues part of religion; I mean justice, fortitude, self-control and the mutual harmony of all things of the members of the community with one another. All our actions and studies and words have a connection with piety towards God, for our lawgiver has left none of these things indefinite or undetermined"[23].

Thus, "the virtues", or Greek ethics in general, are not alien to Judaism, but are included in its system of religion. The Torah of Moses is not limited to law and religion, but includes ethics as well. This could be taken as a reference to the wisdom of Moses as well as to divine revelation. The former would be in line with the usual discourse on virtues, namely that Moses was a philosopher as well as lawgiver. Ascribing the virtues to divine revelation, on the other hand, would mean that there is no Jewish ethics connected with piety, but only a system of piety prescribing certain virtues.

1.   E. Bickermann, **Studies in Jewish and Christian History**, (Leiden: Brill, 1976), 1, pp. 123-136; M. Hadas, **Aristeas to Philocrates**, (New York: Ktav, 1973), p. 54.

2.   127, trans. R.J.H. Shutt, in J.H. Charlesworth (ed.), **The OT Pseudepigrapha**, (New York: 1983).

3.   Cf. Pereq Qinyan Torah, M 'Avot 6:5 **"shemi'at ha'osen"**.

4.   Aristotle, **Nic Ethics**, 2:6.

5.   Horatius Flaccus, **Odes**, 2:10:5.

6.   Talmud E.I. Chagigah 2:1, 77a.

7.   **Mishneh Torah**, Hilkhot De'ot 1:4.

8.   Mishnah Ketubot 9:2.

9.   Ben Sira 33:10-12.

10.   See infra.

11.   **On Abraham** 1:5-6, transl. F.H. Colson, (Cambridge, Mass.: Harvard UP); **Loeb Classical Library**, vol. 6, p. 7.

12.   **On Abraham** 46: 276; Colson, p. 135.

13.   **On Joseph** 30; Colson p. 156.

14.   **Life of Moses** 2:9,51; Colson, p. 472-5.

15.   1:1, transl. G. Vermes, **The Dead Sea Scrolls in English,** (Penguin Books, 1962).

16.   Opus cit. 4:2 ff.

17.   **Hymns Scroll** 15:12-20; **Sect Canon** 5:1.

18.   J. Maier & K. Schubert, **Die Qumran-Essener,** (Muenchen: UTB, 1982), p. 57.

19.   Maier & Schubert, p. 57.

20.   **Sect Canon** 3:18; 4:23; Maier & Schubert, p. 61.

21.   M. Hadas, **The Third and Fourth Books of Maccabees,** (New York, 1953).

22.   4 Ezra 7:92.

23.   **Against Apion,** 2. 170-171.

C. RABBINICAL ETHICS

13. HALAKHIC MORALITY

(a) Legal and Moral Halakhot

The common opinion about Halakhah, as a legal or even legalistic system of norms, is in need of correction and differentiation. A considerable part of Halakhah is not intended to be enforced by external authority, but is left to the conscience of the individual. In this chapter we will present a great number of rules which apply **in foro interno,** to use the term of Canon lawyers, and these rules are as much part of Halakhah as those enforceable by rabbinical courts. The legal part of Halakhah makes sense only together with the system of individual moral responsibility.

According to the rule of Halakhah, a person may be entitled to a certain act or to have a certain remedy, but at the same time he may be called upon to relinquish this right in favour of another party. Such a duty is called by a number of terms, such as **lifnim mishurat hadin** (keeping within one's legal domain)[1], **derekh tovim** (the way of good people)[2], **middat chassidim** (the rule of the pious)[3], and **din Shamayim** (the rule of Heaven)[4].

The element of **shurat hadin,** the first concept described above, may be illustrated by the case of the border-line of a piece of land, which is legally the limit within which the owner may build. If, however, he restrains himself in favour of his neighbour, by not building close to the border-line, he thereby acts according to the first principle of morals. Later on, the same concept came to include any act beyond the course of duty, e.g. renouncing a legal right in favour of another person, and even leniency in sentencing a convicted criminal[5].

The interesting aspect in the last concept, **din Shamayim,** is the reference to Heaven, i.e. to God, with regard to the moral duty; as if the legal duty was not considered to be based on the revelation at Sinai. The reason for this is probably that the latter was also the concern of the human court, while the moral rule was the concern of God alone. Likewise, a distinction was made between duties required by law, and behaviour which extended beyond them to satisfy requirements of Heaven[6]. Again morality is seen as the special concern of God, while legal duties are in the jurisdiction of the courts.

Another expression of the parallelism of law and morals within Halakhah is the fact that rabbinical tradition distinguishes between positive or mandatory commandments on the one hand, and negative or prohibitive commandments on the other. An omission of the former was not punishable (by flogging), but was left to the transgressor's conscience[7]. Even a prohibitive rule of the Torah was exempt from regular sanction, viz. flogging, if it could be corrected by a positive commandment[8]. Among the prohibitions of the Torah, those concerning speech rather than physical action were exempt from punishment as well[9].

Likewise, rabbinical systematics declared any positive commandment for which the Torah gave a promise of special reward for its observance, to be beyond the jurisdiction of a human court[10]. The assumption was made that such a reference to divine sanction excluded the matter from human adjudication.

It is true, however, that when a person consistently refused to observe a positive commandment, he could be forced to do so by the court through a kind of contempt of court procedure. The court could give an order for indeterminate flogging until the person fulfilled his duty[11]. Yet the original moral character of these rules did not change, in spite of the possibility of disciplinary action. Indeed, it was said that the effect of the guilty conscience was more effective than that of flogging[12].

Sometimes, a certain action was considered legitimate, but the possibility of misinterpretation and of suspicion demanded that the person "remove himself from ugliness and from what is similar to it"[13]. This moral principle was designed to amend the legal norm, which did not reveal the same degree of sensitivity. A similar formulation consists of the demand that a person not only refrain from transgression, but also from committing any act "similar to a transgression"[14].

Sometimes Halakhic sources merely criticized certain forms of behaviour without granting legal relief against them. Such a stand belongs to the realm of morals, rather than of law. Take for instance the following rule: "He who asked his colleague to go and negotiate a match for him, i.e. betrothing a certain woman on his behalf, and the agent went and performed the betrothal ceremony, however not on behalf of the principal, but on his own behalf... the act of the colleague is effective on his own behalf, which means that the woman is his and not the principal's. However, the colleague has acted fraudulently"[15]. Indeed, according to strict law, an agent could repudiate the agency at any time and act as a principal for his own benefit. This **lacuna** of the law is then filled by a moral concept, viz. that every person is supposed to act in good faith.

Another category of Halakhah is that of matters "left to the heart", which is equivalent to matters tried **in foro interno**. Since no sanction was provided for these matters, where necessary Scripture added the precept "to fear God", which is a religious sanction[16]. In the strict sense of morality, however, a matter which causes divine reward or punishment does not belong in the category of morals, but may be seen as part of religious law, subject to divine sanction.

(b) Change of Borderline

Now that we have found moral standards to exist beside the legal rules of Halakhah, we must examine their correlation in the history of Halakhah. First, we must keep in mind that Halakhah in general could function as a legal system only by authority of the state. Lacking recognition, Halakhah became a system of morality and entirely lost its legal character. Take, for example, the abolition of Jewish criminal jurisdiction by the Roman administration, even before the destruction of the Temple. As a result, most of the rules of the tractate Sanhedrin became social conventions of the rabbis and their followers, and were no longer law. This was a decisive step towards the privatization of Halakhah, and a considerable displacement of the borderline between law and morals.

While the strong system of self-government of the Jewish community provided an effective system of sanction for religious, moral and legal norms of Halakhah, the political emancipation of the Jews in Europe and America made these sanctions ineffective. Halakhah thereby became a matter of morals and religion, and lost its legal character. Only in Eastern countries and in the State of Israel part of Halakhah preserved its legal character. This was certainly the most important change in the borderline between Jewish law and morality.

Another factor to be considered in the understanding of this borderline is the rule established by legal anthropologists, that early law is usually flexible and in accordance with the norms of morality. Only in the second stage do legal systems tend to become rigid and formal, and it is at this level that equity or moral considerations are drawn in. The last stage, which is that of modern law, enables the law itself to correct its shortcomings through legislation[17]. According to this model, we can describe Halakhah as being in the second stage, and therefore in need of a kind of equity or moral complementary.

The borderline between halakhic law and morality was indeed flexible, and permitted the transformation of moral into legal rules[18]. Often a **lacuna** of the law was filled by reference to a moral duty, as we have seen above. In other cases, moral and religious pressure was imposed to change the behaviour of a person, and this was done by means of a curse. For instance the Halakhah of contracts states: "If a purchaser had paid the price, but not yet taken possession of the merchandise, the seller could still retract, but one used to say that He who had inflicted punishment upon the generation of the Great Flood would also inflict punishment upon the party going back on his word"[19]. In a traditional and closed community, such a curse almost amounted to legal sanction, demonstrating the legalization of a moral concept.

Another version, closer to the original appeal to a person's conscience, is the proclamation that such a person had become untrustworthy[20]. Originally, this may have been the opinion of a moralist, but very soon it probably became a rule of evidence, e.g. that you could not trust such a person as a witness[21]. At this stage the proclamation had therefore become a legal sanction.

Similarly, the first steps in the employment of labourers were not originally of legal consequences, so that each party could retract. When it was felt that both the employer and the employee should have kept their word and one party reneged, it was said that the person willing to abide by the informal agreement had a cause for complaint[22]. This meant that he could not bring an action in a rabbinical court, but he could complain and publicize his grievance, thereby putting pressure upon the other party.

The original moral meaning of this concept appears in the rule that "one should not complain, lest one commit other sins"[23]. Hence, there was need for a cause for any complaint, and once such a cause was recognized and publicized, it became a kind of legal norm.

The transformation of a moral duty into a legal one sometimes took the form of accepting the duty as a binding norm of the brotherhood of the Sages, which was similar to that of the Pious, the **Chaverim**, or the Community of Qumran[24]. An act or a forbearance was either agreeable or disagreeable to the membership, and thereby became as a law for those who cared for their membership.

The following is an example of such a duty: "He who pays his debts in spite of the legal remission of debts in the seventh year, is agreeable to the sages... He who keeps his word is agreeable to the sages"[25]. Originally, remission of debts was the rule according to the Deuteronomic provision. At a certain stage, during the Second Commonwealth, it was felt that according to moral concepts the debtor should not, if possible, make use of the remission. This then became the rule among the Sages, was mentioned when the Deuteronomic rule was discussed, and prompted the change of the biblical law. Hillel's **prosboul**, the lending for a pledge, the depositing of the bill in court, and finally, the simple stipulation contracting out of the Deuteronomic remission - all these were techniques used to change the legal situation[26].

A negative formulation runs as follows: "He who disposes of his property, disregarding his children, his will is effective, but he is disagreeable to the Sages"[27]. Likewise, there was a saying that "he who goes back on his word is not agreeable to the Sages"[28]. This, too, was a kind of public censure, which was almost a legal sanction[29]. All these positive and negative opinions originally amounted to a code of honour of the rabbinical elite, like that of the pietists[30], and eventually became incorporated in the sources of Halakhah as general rules of law.

The moral character of such duties can be traced in a parallel term, the **path of the good people**, which called for behaviour beyond the ordinary standard. If a rabbi had an argument with his employee, when adjudicating the case his rabbinical colleague asked him to be generous[31]. According to one reading, this was declared to be a legal norm for people in the category of the defendant. According to another reading, though it was not a legal rule, being derived from Scripture outside of Torah, it was nevertheless enforced against the defendant. For our purposes this constitutes transformation of a moral into a legal rule[32].

The same process is reflected in a parallel concept, which does not address the elite, but everyone. It is one's duty to do what is **just and good** in the sight of God[33], which was interpreted as vesting the right of preemption with the neighbour of the owner of land who wishes to sell. The seller of land or a building had to offer it to his neighbour at the market price, so as to give him the opportunity for expansion. Preemption has no basis in the Torah, except for the general call for just and good behaviour. Once it had been derived from this term of morality, however, the institution was discussed in the Halakhic sources and subsequently became part of the system[34].

The change from moral to legal norm took place regarding charity[35], child support[36], support of parents[37], and the general duty to put one's property at the disposal of others. The latter obligation is based on the general concept of **Sodomite behaviour**[38], i.e. of abusing one's rights to the detriment of others. There is an assumption that property is limited by various obligations towards others, and should be put at their disposal as long as no loss is caused to the owner[39]. All these rules, originally derived from moral precepts, were eventually transformed into legal standards[40].

The law of torts in particular, reflects the process of increased liability by transformation from moral to legal rules. In various instances, the law did not impose responsibility upon a tortfeasor originally, but a critical remark was added: "He is acquitted under human law, but still liable under the law of Heaven"[41]. Here again, the ordinary law of torts, though based on revelation, was thought to be less of divine concern than the moral code complementing it. At the stage reached in the Mishnah, the moral comment had become part of religious law itself.

We have already mentioned the parallel development in the law of agency, where the concept of fraudulent behaviour played a similar role in the development of legal responsibility[42]. Even the unstructured call for keeping inside one's legal domain, which was meant to be interpreted by the individual according to the situation, later became a kind of legal norm[43].

Certain categories of rabbinic legislation are named after their moral origin. Take for instance the series of law reforms based on the concept that "her ways are pleasant and all her paths lead to peace"[44]. This verse of Proverbs, originally referring to wisdom, was interpreted with reference to Torah, as justification for those innovations which had become necessary to promote the said values. All these rules originally deviated from strict Halakhah. They were taken from moral concepts, and finally became themselves part of the legal system.

Since so many concepts derived from morals became part of the law, the illusion arose that there was no real distinction between law and morals in rabbinical thought, and that every rule had to be derived from Torah itself. The truth is just the opposite: the presence of moral concepts in the Halakhah is due to the active role taken by the rabbis themselves in the development of the Halakhah, by bringing in their own moral insights at various stages of the discussions. Eventually, these insights were included in the Halakhic sources, and even became rules of law.

(c) Noachide Commandments and derekh 'erets

In two cases at least, Halakhah refers to parallel systems of behaviour control, which are more or less part of morality. These systems are the collection called the **Noachide Commandments,** and the body of rules called **Derekh 'Erets.** The former, though formulated as a series of laws, is actually derived from ethical consideration of what should be the demand of

Non-Jews living under a Jewish system of law[45]. They are a form of laws of nature, applying to all human beings by virtue of being descendants of first man (Adam), or of Noach, the first man after the Great Flood. They have been interpreted as a "theological-juridical theory", showing "by the Kantian notion of the a **priori** conditions of experience that the Torah specified and ultimately particularized what humankind already had in general"[46].

Rabbinical sources trace these basic commandments in Genesis, which could, of course, be a mere **asmakhta** (memotechnic device). They could actually be taken as the sum of elementary religious and moral responsibilities, without which there would be no justification for human existence. However, at least one of the commandments, the prohibition of killing, is expressly ascribed to divine revelation, and the same act of revelation could have included additional commandments.

Maimonides assumed that the **Noachide Commandments** had two parallel sources. One was recorded in the Scripture, reflecting a revelation to Adam and to Noach, the other was wisdom, i.e. ethical reasoning. The first source had actually been given to mankind in general, but at present is recorded only in the Torah of Moses, and should be quoted by giving recognition to the latter. The second source, obviously, is independent of the Torah and appeals directly to every human being[47].

According to Maimonides, obedience to the **Noachide Commandments** as a result of ethical discourse was insufficient, as it was lacking in piety and recognition for the function of Torah, even for the Non-Jewish world. This would mean that human perfection depended on direct contact with God, not on ethical and rational thought alone, that it demanded recognition of the Sinai Covenant, and that obedience to theonomy was higher up in the hierarchy of human perfection than human autonomy[48].

The central role of revelation in the regulation of human behaviour led to the idea that positive Halakhah prevailed over the **Noachide Commandments**. The Torah given at Sinai was thought to have become emancipated from the earlier system. The people of Israel were no longer included within the concept of **Noachides** (or general humanity), but were said to derive their particular status from the sanctification of their patriarch Abraham[49].

Moreover, the most important of the **Noachide Commandments** was amended, so to speak, with regard to Jews. According to Halakhah, a Jew was no longer liable for capital punishment by a Jewish court if he had killed a Non-Jew[50], while members of other nations were culpable for the killing of any human being.

However, this regression vis-a-vis the former recognition of the chief human right[51], was criticized around 200 C.E. in the rabbinical academy: "Before the promulgation of the Torah, killing of any human being was punishable. Is it conceivable that the Torah would mitigate instead of aggravate the rule?"[52]. In conclusion, the killing of Gentiles was declared to be outside the ordinary jurisdiction, but subject to divine punishment. Again, the positive law of the Torah was put into opposition with the Law of God, the latter being in line with the **Noachide Commandments** and with the universalization of rules demanded by ethics.

While a general presumption existed in rabbinical jurisprudence that "nothing could be permitted to Israelites that was prohibited to Gentiles", various distinctions were made to grant exceptions to this presumption[53]. This was firstly a result of the state of war in which Judaism existed during the formative period of rabbinic thought, and secondly, an emphasis on positive law over ethical speculation. According to the original presumption, Halakhah was indeed subject to moral criticism, however, rabbinical scholasticism evaded these points of outside evaluation by establishing halakhic autonomy and positivism. In a sense, this process is parallel to the change from the universalist attitude of the first part of Genesis to the particularist approach of the rest of the Torah.

The other reference of Halakhah to an independent system of norms is that of **derekh 'erets,** literally - the way of nature. This system is said to have been in force for twenty-six generation prior to the giving of Torah, or in other words, since the creation of mankind. But instead of assuming that the system was amended by the Torah, at least with respect to its application to Israelites, the idea was adopted that **derekh 'erets** was a precondition of Torah[54]. There is no reference to any revelation connected with this source of behavioural control, though some of its rules are traced in Scripture.

The interesting phenomenon is the recognition given to it, not only as a guidance **praeter legem** but even **contra legem.** For instance, Maimonides advises the readers of his practice not always to make use of strict law. One should not divorce a sick wife to save further medical expenses, as strict Halakhah allowed. In this case Maimonides relies upon **derekh 'erets** as a balance to Halakhah, and we would call this a moral norm above and beyond the law described in the code[55].

Rabbinical rejection of **ascesis** and its affirmation of life, even in violation of the Sabbath and other commandments, seems to be derived from this concept. To serve God and overcome sin one should engage not only in Torah but also in **derekh 'erets,** which in this context means worldly activities as well[56]. Thus a man should first build a house and plant an orchard before taking a wife, in order to provide the material basis for his family[57]. Likewise, in line with **derekh 'erets**, one is supposed to limit consumption of meat[58].

According to one school of thought, keeping a voluntary fast or refraining from enjoyment of this world was thought to be sinful, however others considerd some asceticism to be a step towards holiness[59]. The former probably relied on the concept of **derekh 'erets**, though another proof text was quoted. The latter probably believed holiness to transcend the way of nature, and used asceticism as a balance to excessive self-preservation.

While the impact of the **Noachide Commandments** upon Halakhah was at best indirect, the rules of **derekh 'erets** were easily applied to Jews as well as to the rest of mankind. Perhaps the former constituted a threat to the halakhic system, especially after Pauline criticism of Halakhah, and therefore had to be removed from the norms of Judaism. On the other hand, **derekh 'erets** was felt to be less threatening to the integrity of Halakhah, and therefore Halakhah tended to refer to it.

(d) Morality independent of Halakhah

The question arises as to whether Halakhah left room for an autonomous ethics outside of those concepts which were already formulated and recognized by the classical sources. According to what Abraham Joshua Heschel called **Pan-Halakhism**, everything is included in Halakhah and no freedom is given to ethics[60]. This situation is similar to that of the latest phase of English **Equity**, existing only in the judge's breast as a closed list, and being for all purposes a part of the law.

According to the formulation of A. Lichtenstein, Halakhah is both a moral as well as a legal system, and therefore contains the answer to any problem[61]. As a result, a moral decision must be based on a text or tradition of Halakhah itself, and nothing could be created by the conscience of the individual. In other words, the term ethics should actually not be used, since it all boils down to an interpretation of authoritarian texts or traditions.

While it is true that this positivism, or formalism[62], is mitigated by a willingness to tolerate moral intuition either by way of **imitatio dei** or by the new concept of **da'at Torah**[63], it will always be subject to the halakhic sources already in existence[64]. This willingness, however, constitutes a kind of paradox, for these undefined concepts really contradict the said positivism. In any event, this attitude leaves no room for human ethics outside of Halakhah in its extended sense. A norm derived from **imitatio dei** or from **da'at Torah** would still be the result of hermeneutics, not of individual conscience.

A positive role for human ethics outside of Halakhah is offered by Seymour Siegel as a major criterion of Conservative Judaism. According to his view, Halakhah must be confronted with the moral feeling of human beings, and where necessary, amended or abrogated[65]. In other words, Halakhah is not an unchangeable norm, but has to be examined time and again in view of the conscience of the individual concerned[66].

Indeed, many of the innovations in Halakhah, whether by way of **taqqanah** (legislation), **perush** (interpretation) or **hora'at sha'ah** (exceptional adjudication) - are the results of such discrepancies between tradition and moral criticism.

Take, for instance, the innovations to avoid humiliation of the poor, which had to be introduced by those whose greater sensitivity than that of their predecessors demanded such action[67]. No biblical or rabbinical authority was quoted, the need for the change being derived from ethical insight alone.

Another example is the rule against the observance of a commandment while making use of a stolen object, like a palm twig for the Festival of Tabernacles[68]. Although this could be derived from a strict reading of the passage in Scripture, it was probably first developed by ethical discourse, and then supported by exegesis.

Many other amendments of Jewish law were results of this process, i.e. of the moral critique of the Halakhah. Hillel's **prosboul**, for instance, reflected his insight that the observance of the law would not assist the poor, which should actually be the paramount goal of biblical remission of debts. In this case, as well as in many others, the moral idea was eventually incorporated in the law and thereby lost its voluntary and moral character.

Moral evaluation of Halakhah is part of the rationalism which is essential to its decision making process. Rabbinical consciousness was aware of this element, calling it **sevarah** (logical inference). Ergo, the duty of thanksgiving before consuming food was ascribed to this category, the underlying idea being commutative justice of human beings towards God, the owner of all[69]. Another example of this is the absolute value of human life, which except in self-defence must never be taken, even to maintain one's own life. A person should rather relinquish his life than kill an innocent human being, for "how do you know that your blood is redder than his?"[70]. This rule was derived from the ethical concept of equality and justice, existing outside and independently of Halakhah.

Although Halakhah was said to have rejected the opinions of R. Meir[71], it accepted his view respecting the last will of a deceased person[72]. This must have been the result of the moral responsibility felt towards that person, even after his death and in contradiction to formal Halakhah. This responsibility is called **mitswah**, though it actually violates express provisions of the Torah[73], and has no scriptural basis. All of these cases, therefore, exemplify the function of ethics outside of Halakhah.

The reference to **derekh 'erets** by Maimonides[74], which we have seen as an implied criticism of positive Halakhah, is another example for the independence of judgment vis-a-vis halakhic authority. These cases must not be seen as exceptions or as parts of a closed list, but as guidelines for the moral responsibility of the individual to disregard the law if it violates his ethical principles.

1.   Mekhilta deR. Ishmael ad Ex. 18:20; cf. S. Berman in **JJS**, 26, (1975), pp. 86-104, and 28, (1977), pp. 181-183; S. Shilo, in **ILR**, 13, (1978), pp. 359-390. On this and the following moral concepts cf. I. Herzog "Moral Rights and Duties in Jewish Law", in **Studies in Jewish Jurisprudence**, Vol.2, (New York: Hermon, 1972); Federbush, **Hamusar**, pp. 60-72; M. Silberg, **Talmudic Law**, pp. 93-130; E. Berkovits, **Halakhah Kochah veTafqidah**, Jerusalem 1981, pp. 84-104; Spero, **Morality**, pp. 166-200; Jacobs, **Tree**, pp. 182-192; A. Kirschenbaum, "Categories of Morality in Jewish Law", in **Melanges a la memoire M.H.Prevost,** Paris: Presses Universitaires de France, 1982; and my **Introduction,** p. 29 ff.

2.   Prov. 2:20; BT Bava Metsia 83 a; JT Bava Metsia 6:7, 11 a.

3.   BT Bava Qama 30 a, 50 b, 80 a, cf. my **Mimishnat Chasidim,** and **Introd.**

4.   M Bava Qama 6:4; T Shevu'ot 3:1; BT Bava Qama 55 b; cf. L. Jacobs, **Tree of Life**, p. 182 f.

5.   BT Berakot 7 a.

6.   BT Bava Metsia 37 a; cf. Federbush, p. 141.

7.   BT Makkot 13 b; Federbush,p. 98.

8.   M Makkot 3:4.

9.   BT Makkot 15 a; Federbush, p. 100.

10.   E.g. Ex. 20:12; Deut. 22:7; cf. JT Bava Batra 1:11, 15 a end; BT Chullin 110 b; see Federbush, p. 101; S. Pines, **Musar haMiqra vehaTalmud,** (Jerusalem: Mosad Harav Kook, 1948), p. 29 f.

11.   JT Nazir 4:3, 53 b top; BT Ketubot 86 a, Nazir 23 a, Sabbath 40 b; cf. Federbush, pp. 86, 101 ff.

12. BT Berakhot 7 a.

13. Tos. Yevamot 4:7; 'Avot deR. Nathan, B, 2:1; BT Chullin 44 b.

14. Derekh 'Erets Zuta 2:8; cf. 1:12. Such a rule was an individualization of the general rule of **making a fence around the law**, applying to the legislature: M 'Avot 1:1.

15. M Qiddushin 3:1; BT Qiddushin 58 b; cf. Jacobs, **Tree of Life** p. 184.

16. Sifra ad Lev. 19:32.

17. Cf. G.W. Paton, **A Textbook of Jurisprudence**, 4th ed., (Oxford: UP, 1972), pp. 48-65.

18. Cf. Federbush, pp. 70-95; Spero, pp. 182-188.

19. M Bava Metsia 4:2.

20. BT Bava Metsia 49 a.

21. Like the other cases of incapacity to testify: M Sanhedrin 3:3.

22. M Bava Metsia 6:1; cf. Federbush, p. 136.

23. Derekh 'Erets Zuta 1:15. This rule was developed by 19th century R. Israel Lipkin of Salant, the founder of the Moralist Movement. He emphasised that even for complaint there was need for special justification.

24. Cf. M Demai 2:2-3.

25. M Shevi'it 10:9; cf. Federbush, p. 136, and my **MiMishnat Chasidim**.

26. M Shevi'it 10:2-3; cf. my **Introd.**

27. M Bava Batra 8:5; this norm may be connected with the story of Hyrkanos who had disinherited his son Eliezer and later regretted it (Gen. Rabba 41 (42):1). See also ET., s.v. **eyn ru'ach chakhamim nochah.**

28. BT Bava Metsia 48 a; cf. BT Bava Qama 94 b.

29. Cf. Rashi BT Bava Metsia 48 a sub voce **'anu 'eyn lanu.**

30. See my **Mimishnat Chasidim.**

31. BT Bava Metsia 83 a.

32. See my review of Urbach, **The Sages**, in **Kiryat Sefer**, 46, (1971), pp. 15-22.

33. Deut. 6:18; cf. Federbush, p. 126.

34. Bt Bava Metsia 108 a; cf. Federbush, p. 85; Silberg, **Talmudic Law**; Urbach: **The Sages**, ch. 13.

35. BT Bava Batra 8 a.

36. BT Ketubot 65 a, 69 a.

37. JT Qiddushin 1:7, 61 c.

38. Cf. S. Shilo, in **ILR**, 15, (1980), pp. 49-78.

39. Bt Ketubot 103 a; cf. Federbush, p. 91; and my "Eigentum", in TRE.

40. Federbush, pp. 76-95.

41. M Bava Qama 6:4; cf. L. Jacobs, **Tree of Life**, p. 182 f.

42. BT Qiddushin 58 b; cf. Jacobs, p. 184.

43. Cf. Mordekhai, Bava Metsia 257, contra R. Asher ben Yechiel, Bava Metsia 24 b. Cf. Tel Aviv Rabbinical Court Case 5637/21, **Rabbinical Courts Judgments**, 5, pp. 132-153; S.

Shiloh, "Lifnim miShurat haDin", ILR 13 (1978), pp. 359-390; S. Berman, "Lifnim mishurat hadin", JJS 26 (1975), pp. 86-104; 28, (1977), pp. 59-73.

44.   Cf. ET s.v. **'evah, darkhey no'am** and **darkhey shalom**; my "'al hashalom", in **Levav Shalem**, S. Bacharach Memorial, (Jerusalem: 1971), pp. 63-67; I. Englard, "The Interaction etc.", JLA 7 (1988), p. 123.

45.   T 'Avodah Zarah 8:4; Seder 'Olam 5; BT Sanhedrin 56 a.

46.   D. Novak, **The Image of the Non-Jew in Judaism**, Toronto Studies in Theology 14, (New York): Mellen, 1983).

47.   Maimonides, **Mishneh Torah**, Melakhim 8:11.

48.   See Spinoza, **The Theological-Political Tractate**, ch.5; A. Lichtenstein, **The Seven Laws of Noah**, (New York: 1981); S.S. Schwarzschild, "Do Noachides have to believe in Revelation?", JQR 52-53, (1962), 297-308, 30-65; D. Hartman, **Maimonides; Torah and Philosophic Quest** (Philadelphia: JPS, 1976) n. 62; I. Twersky, **Introduction to the Code of Maimonides** (New Haven: Yale, 1980) p. 455; M. Fox, "Maimonides and Aquinas on Natural Law", DI 3 (1972) pp. 5-36; M. Levine, "The Role of Reason in the Ethics of Maimonides", **Journal of Religious Ethics**, 14, (1986), pp. 279-295; J.I. Dienstag, "Natural Law in Maimonidean Thought", JLA 6 (1987) 64-77; O. Leaman, "Maimonides and Natural Law" JLA 6 (1987) 78-93; J.D. Bleich, "Judaism and Natural Law", JLA 7 (1988), pp. 5-42. See also **infra**.

49.   BT Nedarim 31 a.

50.   M Sanhedrin 5:1; Mekhilta, Neziqin 4, s.v. **wekhi yazid**. Note that under the Roman administration the Rabbinical court had lost its jurisdiction of criminal cases, especially where the victim had been Non Jewish.

51.   Cf. Leon Roth, "Moralization and Demoralization in Jewish Ethics", **Judaism**, 11, (1962), pp. 291-302.

52.   Mekhilta, **loc. cit.**

53.   BT Sanhedrin 59 ab.

54.   Lev. Rabba 9:3; cf. ET s.v. **derekh 'erets**; Jacobs, **Tree**, pp. 193-199; Ch. Z. Reines, **Massot uMechqarim be Mussar uveMishpat Israel**, (Jerusalem: 1972), pp. 130-131.

55.   Maimonides: **Mishneh Torah**, 'Ishut 14:17.

56.   M 'Avot 2:2; BT Berakhot 32 b Rashi.

57.   BT Sotah 44 a.

58.   BT Chullin 84 a.

59.   BT Ta'anit 11 a.

60.   A.J. Heschel, **God in Search of Man**, (New York: 1955), p. 328.

61.   "Does Jewish Tradition Recognize an Ethic Independent of Halakhah?, in Kellner, p. 106. See also M. Fox, **The Philosophical Foundations of Jewish Ethics: Some Initial Reflections**. Second Annual Feinberg Memorial Lecture, University of Cincinnati; and in N. Rakover, **Maimonides as Codifier**, (Jerusalem, 1987).

62. The term chosen by D. Bleich in his presentation to the 9th World Congress of Jewish Studies 1985, C, pp. 55-62. See also his rejection of Natural Law in "Judaism and Natural Law", **JLA** 7 (1988), pp. 5-42.

63. Bleich, in **Proc. 9th World Congress.**

64. This is similar to the view of W.S. Wurzburger, "Law as the Basis of a Moral Society", **Tradition** 19 (1981) pp. 42-54.

65. S. Siegel **Conservative Judaism and Jewish Law,** (New York: 1977), pp. 124-132.

66. Cf. D. Novak, "Natural Law, Halakhah and the Covenant", **JLA**, 7, (1988), pp. 43-67, showing the legitimacy of this concept in Jewish thought.

67. M Ta'anit 4:8; BT Mo'ed Qatan 27 a; BT Ketubot 8 b.

68. M Sukkah 3:1; JT Sukkah 3:1, 53 c; BT Sukkah 30 a.

69. BT Berakhot 35 a. See Berkovits, **Not in Heaven.**

70. BT. Sanhedrin 74 a; Maimonides, **Mishneh Torah,** Yesodey Hatorah 5:7.

71. BT 'Eruvin 13 b.

72. BT Gittin 15 a.

73. E.g. rules of burial, mourning and property of converts; cf. E. T., s.v. 'avelut, p. 60, **bet haqevarot,** p. 260 b, **ger,** p. 282, and **halanat hamet,** p. 442.

74. **Mishneh Torah,** 'Ishut 14:17.

14. HALAKHAH AND AUTONOMY

(a) The Problem

One of the central problems of theology as such must be raised prior to the understanding of Halakhah: is there an inherent contradiction between autonomy and theonomy, or can the two be reconciled with each other? According to Kant, autonomy is the only ethical basis of moral systems[1], and modern psychology and pedagogy teach us that the moral development of every human being should lead him from heteronomy to autonomy.

On the other hand, the basis of religious systems is theonomy. Halakhah derives the norms of behaviour from revelation and asks for obedience. The goal of human beings, according to rabbinic thought, is to serve God, not to realize their own will and potential[2]. According to the formulation of R. Chanina at the beginning of the third century C.E., "He who is under the legal obligation and fulfills the divine commandment is more virtuous than he who does the same thing without being commanded"[3]. While a volunteer certainly has merit, he nevertheless lacks the element of being obedient, which is obviously essential in the service of God[4].

The depreciation of voluntarism may have been an expression of anxiety vis-a-vis Gentile Christians observing some of the commandments, e.g. the Sabbath or the study of Torah[5]. There was a danger that their example would be followed by certain Jews, which led R. Chanina to emphasize the higher value of Jewish over Gentile observance of these commandments.

Likewise, according to the interpretation given by the **Tosafists** during the 12th century, "the person under the duty has greater difficulties to observe the commandment and he constantly negates his own inclination to observe the commandment of his Creator". The volunteer, on the other hand, has the easier task. He, so to speak, "knows he has bread in the basket and therefore does not feel hungry, but can stop the observance at any moment"[6].

The true realization of Halakhah, according to this view, demands a duty, so that a person keeping a commandment without being obligated to do so cannot reach the eqivalent status. There were, of course, those who held according to the opposite view, viz. that a person fulfilling a commandment without being under obligation was of a higher rank than the one who simply discharged a duty[7].

The positive attitude toward the volunteer must have been behind the saying of R. Meir during the second century C.E., that a Non-Jew who studied Torah was as virtuous as the Jewish High Priest[8]. This must have been the personal experience of R. Meir with Christian scholars of the Bible with whom he had had contact. On the other hand, during the third century R. Jochanan declared such scholars to be guilty of violating Deut. 33:4, viz. that the Torah was the heritage of the Community of Jacob[9]. The rabbi must have felt threatened by Christian claims to be **Verus Israel**, and therefore thought that the study of Torah should be left to those to whom it was a duty.

The problem, obviously, was not whether a Gentile should study Torah, but whether a Jew might help him in this endeavor. As we know, throughout Jewish history many rabbis maintained contact with Non-Jews on exegetical queries. Nevertheless, the view may have been shared by those rabbis as well, that the true meaning of Scripture remained reserved to those willing to submit to the **yoke of the commandments**.

According to a view expressed in the academy of 'Erets Israel during the fourth century C.E., one must not interpret the divine measures, such as the rule concerning the bird's nest (Deut. 22:6), as measures of compassion. They should rather be seen as legal norms, "to show that the Israelites are God's servants and keepers of His commandments and of His strict laws, even where the Satan or the Non-Jews argued against them and claimed they were superfluous"[10].

This view, too, can be interpreted as a reaction to an exaggerated rationalization of the commandments[11]. There is always a danger that such rationalization might lead to the rejection of an irrational commandment, so one should refrain from this method altogether.

In the same vein, a saying of R. Elazar ben 'Azaryah rejected the total internalization of divine commandments. It is undesirable to make their observance an autonomous decision instead of an act of obedience: "Do not say you detested wearing mixed species of cloth, eating pork or having illicit sex. Rather say, you would do it but for the prohibition made by your Father in Heaven, because this is the way to belong to God and to accept His kingdom"[12].

This attitude, of keeping at a distance from the divine will, conflicts with the attitude tolerating ethical evaluation of revealed norms. Indeed, many rabbinical statements are in line with such ethical voluntarism, but other statements show an attitude of greater identification of human and divine will[13]. The goal of Torah could be seen in making the will of God one's own, which means that autonomy would be expressed even within theonomy.

The antithesis of the notion of autonomy is Kierkegaard's interpretation of Abraham's offering of Isaac as the "teleological suspension of the ethical" in the name of the absolute. While ethics is generalizing and rational, God might address a special command to a person in violation of both. Theonomy could therefore suspend an ethical norm and go against autonomy.

Among Orthodox Jewish thinkers this model is often used to define the halakhic point of view vis-a-vis humanism, or vis-a-vis the ideas of Reform and Conservative Judaism[14]. However, the whole idea of the offering of Isaac is its exceptional character. It is because of the rationality of biblical faith that there was room for this supreme test of faith. If every rule of Halakhah was to be interpreted as a closed system without reference to human values, Abraham would have been well prepared for the commandment, and this incident would not be seen as the example of faith that it is.

While admitting that there might be exceptions, we must therefore assume that biblical theonomy in general relies on human understanding and conscience for the interpretation of the divine commandment. The Torah, not being in heaven, does not for a moment suspend human reason and responsibility[15]. The possibility should therefore exist to derive the concept of autonomy from that of rationality.

Liberal thinkers, such as Moritz Lazarus, have always tried to trace elements of autonomy in rabbinical sources in order to reconcile Jewish theonomy with Kantian autonomy[16]. Hermann Cohen rejected this attempt[17], and E.E. Urbach followed his lead[18]. Nevertheless, a new examination of the sources might change this either-or approach, and show that rabbinical theonomy allows human autonomy to function as a way of serving God and doing His will.

A reconciliation between autonomy and theonomy could indeed be found, if the theonomic system would refer its believers not only to the divine will, but to their own responsibility. If such a system would ask the person to make independent decisions and thereby follow the divine will, it would combine theonomy with autonomy. This concept could be found in any system of theonomy, **a fortiori** in that of rabbinical thought, which delegated authority of legal interpretation to human beings, even against Scripture itself.

The rabbinical doctrine of the Oral Law is based on the delegation of responsibility from God to man. According to the system of the Pharisees and the Rabbis, Scripture by itself made no sense without the creative participation of human beings. Scriptural formulations on the exact date of certain festivals remained equivocal, the final decision being left to the sages. Likewise, Scripture did not define which acts were prohibited on festivals and which were permissible; this authority was delegated to the sages as well[19]. Hence, rabbinical theonomy relied on the assistance of human reason.

Moreover, the doctrine of the plural senses of Torah, gives human beings a say in divine law[20]. Revelation is incomplete without the different perceptions of the attendants. The meaning of Torah is determined not by the objective truth about the word of the divine legislator, but by the discourse of the listeners. If every word can be understood in five, seventy or six hundred thousand different ways, the say is actually given to the people, and what the majority of the academy decided, not what God actually said, is the law. Hence, we have a delegation of power from theonomy to human adjudication.

Most clearly, such a delegation of authority takes place in cases of **reshut** (discretion), as distinct from cases of **mitswah** (commandment). Take, for instance, the rule of redemption in favour of the needy next-of-kin: "If your brother becomes poor and sells part of his property, then his next-of-kin shall come and redeem what his brother has sold" (Lev. 25:25). According to a tradition ascribed to R. Joshua, the next-of-kin is under a duty to redeem the property, while R. Eliezer is quoted as saying that redemption is optional, i.e. within his discretion[21]. This means that Halakhah left the exact measure of family solidarity up to individual responsibility and to ethical reasoning. Ethical discourse would therefore be needed to determine one's behaviour in this major part of social life, and this by a kind of referral expressed by Halakhah.

Another example is the rule of the killer leaving the city of refuge: "But if the killer shall at any time go beyond the bounds of his city of refuge to which he fled, and the avenger of blood finds him outside the bounds of his city of refuge, and the avenger of blood kills the killer, he shall not be guilty of blood" (Num. 35:26-27). According to a view ascribed to R. Akiva, the avenger of blood had the discretion as to whether to kill the killer or not, while R. Jose the Galilean was quoted as saying that there was a religious duty of avenging the blood of the next-of-kin under such circumstances[22].

In both cases the controversy related to tribal solidarity under changed conditions, whether it was still obligatory or had become optional only. Taking the second view would mean that the duty had been removed from the legal to the moral sphere. This would then be a referral from theonomy to autonomy.

(b) Concepts of Autonomy

Perhaps the most significant expression of theonomy is the concept of **'ol malkhut shamayim** (the yoke of the divine kingdom) and of **'ol mitswot** (the yoke of the commandments). The term indeed signifies the heteronomic character of faith and commandments. But these yokes are not imposed from above, rather they need express assent on the part of every individual, twice a day. This is the rabbinical interpretation of the reading of **shema'**[23]. The so-called yoke is really an agreement in which the individual becomes a party. It is another form of the **I-Thou** relationship described by Martin Buber[24].

The recital of the **shema'** is seen as a dialogue between the word of God and the reader. Having read the first sentence with the Holy Name, the reader responds by a blessing of "the Name, the Glory of the Kingdom, for ever and ever", which constitutes his submission to the yoke of the divine kingdom[25]. Again, we see theonomy as dependant upon human autonomy.

Likewise, a maxim ascribed to R. Elazar ben Tsadoq, according to what seems to be the correct reading, comes out in favour of autonomy: "Act with the intention to the acts and speak about them to their own end"[26]. While this reading calls for an intention directed to the act, rather than to the commanding authority, another reading calls for the intention to serve God. The former version reads **lishmam** (for their own intention), not **leshem shamayim** (with the intention toward Heaven)[27]. The observance of a divine commandment, say of supporting the poor, should be accompanied by the intention of helping a human being, not by wishing to serve God or acquiring merits.

This is the same idea as that of the Light of Torah. God is quoted as having expressed satisfaction at the observance of the commandments, even without any thought about Him: He wished that the people would rather leave Him and keep His Torah, than **vice versa,** for in any event the light of Torah would bring them back to do good[28]. The value of Torah is seen in its contents, rather than in its divine origin and authority. Such an attitude is based on a human-centered assessment, and points in the direction of autonomy.

A similar tendency is apparent in the identification of Wisdom and Torah, which had started with the interpretation of the term in the Book of Proverbs[29]. Therefore it could even be said: "A person declared he had acquired wisdom but not studied Torah, and he therefore expressed his apprehension about his status there (probably in the future world). In reply,

God is described as promising on oath that Wisdom and Torah were equally valuable. He who feared God and observed the words of Torah, had Wisdom and Torah in his heart"[30]. Thus, even an unlearned person had a share in the study of theonomic sources, because by observing the commandments and having experience, he **ipso facto** had Torah. This is of course a human-centered thesis, extending the authority of religious sources to include the intuition of the unlearned.

Torah was seen as an instrument rather than as an end in itself. According to a tradition ascribed to R. Simon, the Torah was given to serve the people of Israel, Israel was not created to observe the Torah[31]. This is a clear antithesis to the over-emphasis of the theonomic elements. Take, for instance, the saying that "the world was created **bizekhut hatorah**" (because of the Torah, in order to make Torah possible)[32]. If man was not created to keep the Torah, but the Torah for man, one cannot be satisfied with voluntarism and positivism. The meaning of Torah must then be found beyond it, in the moral improvement of man.

Likewise, the Sabbath was given to Israel, but Israel was not given to the Sabbath[33], which means that the preservation of life is more important than the observance of the Sabbath. A person observing the Sabbath is also described as making Sabbath[34], an emphasis upon the creative participation of man in the divine institution.

Observance of Torah can be the result of human autonomy if we assume that God wanted the people to take responsibility and make decisions as to the forms of His worship. This seems to be the idea of the following teaching: "For it is a statute of Israel, a judgment of the God of Jacob - if it were not a statute adopted by Israel, it would not have been a judgment of God of Jacob"[35]. Here the people have a veto over divine legislation, so to speak. Like a constitutional monarch, God is said to refer to His subjects before making His commands. Divine legislation therefore is a bilateral, rather than a unilateral process. But if the people participate in the decision making, there is room for autonomy within the theonomy of Jewish thought.

The latter idea is applied in the festival calendar. The declaration of the new month and the intercalation is effective, even though mistaken. God is said to bow to the human decision, and to make His festivals dependent upon the will of men[36]. The direct function of this idea was prevention of sectarianism, but it also demonstrated the possibility of autonomy within theonomy.

Another application of this idea is the rule that no rabbinical ordinance should be imposed against the will of the people. If God was described as bowing to human decision, a **fortiori** the decision of any human authority should follow the will of the people. Indeed, decisions regarding the calendar were made with the proviso that consent would be forthcoming[37]. Hence the proviso was imposed on all decisions of legislative effect as a bureaucratic principle in the Babylonian tradition, and as a democratic one in the tradition of 'Erets Israel[38].

Study allows the sage not only to identify himself with Torah, but to become a Master of the Torah, a title which should actually be reserved for God alone[39]. Such a title stresses the creative share given to human beings in the development of Halakhah. Instead of considering Torah as a verbatim teaching of God, the title hints at the choices given to the sages and the degree of autonomy granted to them[40].

Human autonomy expresses itself in the greater authority which is given to rabbinical interpretation than to Scripture, and in the rule that where the Oral Law differed from a provision of the text, the former is to be followed. Likewise, greater honour is awarded to the sage than to the Scroll of the Law, for the sage sometimes deviated from the text, and it is his view which prevails[41].

Divine revelation was said to have remained open-ended to allow for different views, such as the controversies of the Schools of Shammai and Hillel[42]. It could even be said that God Himself had used ambiguous language to allow for various interpretations according to the reasons and needs of different people[43]. In practice, the majority rule decided, but this did not mean that the view of the minority, or even of a single scholar, was considered to be wrong. All such opinions were preserved in the Halakhah tradition, and in due course the minority view could become authoritative.

The famous story about the 'Akhnai Oven, with its rejection of supernatural or prophetic elements in the interpretation of the law, is another assertion of human autonomy[44]. God himself yielded to the views of human beings over His own, so to speak. This is a clear rejection of sectarian dogmatics and fundamentalism, such as represented by the Temple Scroll and by Christianity[45]. According to the Rabbis, there was no fixed meaning of the divine Torah, hence there should be no bitter quarrel over theological or legal questions. Various interpretation of Scripture were possible and even desirable, which meant that the matter was left in the hands of human authority. Theonomy was expressed by the intention to obey and serve God, but autonomy was the guideline for both the interpretation and administration of Torah.

(c) Criticism

The real test, as to whether human autonomy can be recognized by protagonists of theonomy, is the possibility to criticize sacred institutions and texts. Autonomy does not fit into a system of fundamentalism, but may play a role in a system of theonomy. The rabbis, for example, were aware of the necessity to read and reread the Torah in a critical way. Wherever such reading led to the conclusion that the situation had changed, and that the law no longer fulfilled its task, there was need for a **taqqanah** (a rabbinical amendment to repair the fracture in biblical law).

The most famous example is Hillel's **prosboul** mentioned above, but there are many other examples of rabbinical innovations both **praeter** and **contra legem**[46]. Each rabbinical innovation resulted from the insight that a change was required, just in order to preserve the spirit of the law. No such assessment of the practical results of Torah would be possible without reliance on human judgment, and the decision could not be understood without the assumption of autonomy.

Another critical evaluation of divine law was ascribed to R. Simon, who **darish ta'ama diqra** (interpreted the text with reference to its reason). According to his method of interpretation, there was no justification for the rule of the rebellious son. "Why should he be executed for having eaten a quantity of meat and drunk a measure of wine? This case should therefore not be understood as an actual ruling, it never happened in the past nor will it happen in the future, but was meant as a theoretical paradigm"[47].

His critical attitude should be seen against the background of other views, justifying the rule in spite of the conflict with moral sensitivity. According to one of his colleagues, the rule had a teleological reason, while another claimed that it was to be understood in the spirit of voluntarism and positivism, as a test of obedience[48].

Likewise, R. Simon was said to have criticized the attribution of collective punishment to God, and to have preferred a more moral interpretation[49]. According to his conscience, punishment, even in the heinous case of the cult of **Moloch**, was unjustifyable but for the individual guilt of the accused. The same argument was raised regarding other passages of the Torah[50].

A critical attitude towards divine law was also ascribed to the Daughters of Zelophead when claiming the inheritance of their father: "When they had heard that the land should be allotted to the tribes, as represented by male heirs only, they assembled for consultation. They said that divine compassion must be superior to that of human beings. The latter had more pity for males than for females, but God was merciful to all His creatures"[51].

Although in the passage regarding the discrimination of female heirs God Himself speaks to Moses[52], the rabbinical interpretation dared to criticize this discrimination and to relate this argument back to the daughters of Zelophead. Moses is impliedly accused of having misrepresented the will of God. This is an extreme example of human criticism levelled at the contents of revelation. The new version of the law is shown as full justification of a humanist and rational approach to the law[53]. Here, God Himself is described as having authorized human beings to engage actively in the formulation of divine law. Such an idea could only develop within a framework of autonomian ethics.

On several occasions Moses is described as having criticized the word of God, and instead of being punished, to have been followed by God. Such homilies could only mean that the word of God demands active and critical response on the part of the human listeners, as if God had purposly given an incomplete formulation in order to give man a chance to become a partner in His law.

The first example relates to the concept of individual responsibility. The statement that God visited the iniquities of ascendants and descendant upon each other[54], was felt to contradict the law of individual responsibility[55]. The first attempt to harmonize both doctrines was made in the Decalogue[56], but one of the rabbis still felt an explanation to be necessary: "This is one of three arguments offered by Moses to the Holy One, Blessed be He, to which God replied that Moses had become God's teacher... When God had told Moses that He visited the iniquities of the ascendants upon descendants, said Moses: Master of the Universe, many evildoers engendered righteous children, should the latter therefore be affected by the sins of the former?... Is it fair to let the righteous suffer for the sins of their parents? Whereupon the Holy One, Blessed be He, declared that Moses was His teacher and made an oath that He would take back His word and confirm the view of Moses. Therefore, the text said that ascendants and descendants should not be executed for each other's offences. Then God was said to have made an oath that the doctrine would be recorded in the name of Moses, as indeed shown in 2 Kings 14:6"[57].

In a second example, Moses is shown as having violated the divine law of waging war against the Amorites, because in his view, sending messengers of peace was preferable to waging war. Again, God is said to have accepted the teaching of Moses, and to have changed the Torah accordingly[58].

This second example is especially instructive, since it shows Moses in an already well-known situation of violating the divine command. Was he not severely punished for not having spoken to the rock, but having struck it? The listener to the homily therefore expects a similar punishment, or at least a rebuke, when Moses sends messengers of peace instead of waging war. And this is exactly the right background to show the listener the importance of Moses' opposition to the divine commandment. God had purposly given a bad commandment, so to speak, to enable Moses to correct it and become a partner in the Torah.

A third example exemplifies the subjective character of human ethics and its place within the system of theonomy. This is a corollary to Kierkegaard's suspension of ethics by the divine commandment. A person might be prevented from obeying the general commandment of God because of an individual demand of his conscience. Moses is said to have been reluctant in the execution of the divine commandment of waging war against Midian, because of his own moral feeling: "The Holy One, Blessed be He, had ordered Moses to take the revenge for the people of Israel... which meant he should have done so himself. How could Moses, then, send the others instead? This was so because Moses had grown up in the land of Midian, and had said to himself, it would be unjust to harm his benefactors: Do not throw a stone into the cistern from which you have drunk"[59].

All these stories cannot be explained as mere pieces of philosophical discourse. A rabbi delivering a sermon to his audience, and this is the framework within which rabbinical homilies evolved, addresses the behaviour and beliefs of his listeners. The stories about Moses are meant to teach that everybody may question authority. If Moses was expected to stand up to God when his conscience demanded it, then the listener should be active in the study of Torah, by replying and questioning his teacher[60]. The stories, therefore, express the autonomy necessary for the study of Torah, which is similar to the attitude of moral philosophers.

We have seen that criticism was needed to reform and improve the law. In other cases, however, criticism did not lead to practical results. The speaker may have faced too much opposition on the part of his audience, or he himself may not have been an activist. Let us describe this phenomenon by way of two such cases.

In a homily on the **mamzer**, the child born of an adulterous or consanguinous union, the rabbi used the verse Ecclesiastes 4:1: "'Behold the tears of the oppressed who have no comforter, who suffer from the power of their oppressors without having a comforter' - this refers to the rule of **mamzerim** (Deut.23:1). If their parents had committed an offence, why should the wretched offspring be afflicted? The oppressors are the Great Synedrion using the authority of the Torah to deprive this offspring from connubium. They have no comforter, therefore God declares He will comfort them. In this world they would be afflicted by their disqualification, but in the future they would be like pure gold"[61]. In spite of his strong criticism, the author did not dare to declare the law of **mamzer** to have lapsed. A solution would only be given in the future by divine intervention, or perhaps through human interpretation or legislation[62].

Likewise, human criticism of divine law was mentioned in a homily on warfare against Amalek, but the speaker came to the conclusion that no such criticism was permissible. King Saul had spared the life of Agag, King of Amalek, and of the Amalekite flocks[63]. According to the author of the homily, Saul had justified this omission: "R. Huna and R. Banyah said, Saul argued against his Creator regarding the annihilation of Amalek. His argument was that the guilt of the men should not have been visited upon the women, upon the children and upon the lifestock. Thereupon a divine voice was heard: 'Do not overdo righteousness'(Eccl. 7:16). Our sages said, Saul had argued against the offering of the heifer (Deut. 21:1-9), why was the animal killed for the guilt of man, and in reply to this argument the divine voice was heard. R. Simon ben Laqish said that he who had pity where he should be cruel would end up being cruel where he should have had pity. Saul indeed was cruel vis-a-vis the Priests of Nob, whom he accused of treason (1 Sam. 22:18-19)"[64].

While the arguments put into the mouth of King Saul reflect the idea of human autonomy, the conclusion drawn by the author of the homily is in line with voluntarism and heteronomy. The question must have been under discussion between rationalists and positivists, between those who, like R. Simon, looked for the purpose of the commandments, and those who emphasized absolute submission to the will of God[65]. There seems to be a connection between these homilies and the rationalist or irrationalist attitude toward the commandments[66]. While the former speakers demanded an ethical and critical study of Torah, the latter rejected such a human-centered attitude.

The last two cases referred to the moral criticism of the Torah and to the illegitimacy of human argument against God. Much greater freedom was given for criticism of rabbinical views and practices. Rabbinical tradition had indeed employed a great number of legal devices in order to maintain the theory that biblical law was still followed without change. In the view of one critic, "the store of the Sons of Chanun were destroyed three years prior to the destruction of the Temple because their owners had applied legal devices to avoid the duty of tithing"[67].

These devices were introduced by learned people, probably with the implied consent of the academy. Our criticism must have originated among pietists who were dissatisfied by such legalism. Again, such criticism was expressed on subjective grounds and within the framework of moral discourse. It shows the value of rational and ethical argument against what otherwise was declared halakhically permissible.

Another rabbi explained the destruction of Jerusalem as the result of the strict application of Torah, without due regard for ethical considerations. According to the **lectio difficilior,** the rabbis were to be blamed for having passed judgment according to strict law[68]. The ethical idea of justice is considered as sometimes being in conflict with the law of Torah, and in such cases the judge should make his decision according to his conscience. This is again an assertion of human autonomy.

In both the latter homilies, the speakers criticized rabbinical legalism, which could be done only on the ground of subjective moral feelings. This rejection of judgment, only according to Halakhah, denies the claim for Halakhic autonomy and positivism. Such homilies are therefore expressions of ethical criticism and human autommomy.

1   I. Kant, **Grundlegung zur Metaphysik der Sitten,** (Stuttgart: Reclam, 1961), p. 1.

2   Cf. Y. Leibowitz "Commandments", in Cohen & Mendes Flohr, pp. 67-80; Leibovitz, **Yahadut,** pp. 28, 72-82, 310-313, 344-345; likewise, M. Fox, "Maimonides and Aquinas on Natural Law", **DI** 3 (1972) p. xxi, declares that Judaism rejected the idea of natural law and ethics. Cf. also I. England, " The Interaction of Morality and Jewish Law", **JLA** 7 (1988) pp. 114-124.

3   BT Qiddushin 31 a; cf. I. Heinemann, **Ta'amey haMitswot beSifrut Israel** (Jerusalem: 1942), pp. 23-25; and Urbach. **The Sages,** ch. 13.

4   Englard quates Maimonides in this context, Hilhot Melakhim 8:11, where the degree of piety in limited to those Noachides observing their commandments because of the Sinaitic revelation. However, for the purpose of the theonomy, it would have sufficed to demand observance of Noachide commandments as a divine revelation to mankind, which means that Maimonides actually had the supremacy of Israel's Torah in mind.

5   Cf. BT Sanhedrin 58 b, 59 a. While this was the attitude taken around the middle of the 3rd century, a positive attitude towards Christian study of Torah and observance of some commandments was expressed in the 2nd century: BT Bava Qama 38 a, Sanhedrin 59 a, 'Avodah Zarah 3 a. See also Urbach, **The Sages,** ch. 16.

6   Tosafot Qiddushin 31 a, s.v. **gadol;** Tosafot 'Avodah Zarah 3 a, s.v. **gadoL**

7   Ibid. the original view of R. Joseph before he heard this rule.

8   BT Bava Qama 38 a.

9   BT Sanhedrin 59 a.

10   Rashi ad BT Berachot 33 b. See also infra ch. 15 (a) and 21 (b).

11   Cf. BT Bava Metsia 115 a; Heinemann, pp. 29-30.

12   Sifra Qedoshim 11:22, ad Lev 20:26; cf. M 'Avot 2:4. See also infra ch. 21 (b).

13   M 'Avot 2:4; Derekh 'Erets Zuta 1:10.

14   Such as Leibovitz, Soloveitchik, Lichtenstein, Fox, Bleich and Kirschenbaum.

15   BT Bava Metsia 59 b.

16   Lazarus, **Ethik;** cf. I, Guttmann, **Dat umadda,** (Jerusalem: 1955), p. 218; and E. Fackenhein, **Encounters between Judaism and Modern Philosophy,** (New York: 1973), p.31.

17   Cohen, **Juedische Schriften,** (Berlin: 1924), iii, pp. 1-35.

18   Urbach, **The Sages,** p. 315.

19   Cf. "Scripture delegated the authority to the Sages", BT Chagigah 18 a; **Tanur shel 'Akhnai,** BT Bava Metsia 59 b; see also I. Englard in **Shenaton haMishpat Ha'Ivri,** 1 (1974) p. 45 ff.

20   BT Berakhot 58 a; cf. my **'Erkhey Mishpat,** 138.

21   BT Qiddushin 21 a.

22   M Makkot 2:7.

23   M Berakhot 2:2.

24   Buber, **Ich und Du,** (Leipzig: 1923).

25   This interpretation was given by my wife in answer to my question, as to how the reading of the **shema'** came to mean acceptance of the **yoke of the Kingdom.**

26   Sifre Deut. 48; BT Nedarim 62 a; Derekh 'Erets Zuta 2:5.

27   Cf. M 'Avot 2:12.

28   Lamentations Rabba, Petichta 2 quoting Jer. 9:11.

29   Cf. rabbinical interpretations of the term and the desription of **wisdom** in Scripture and cf. BT Qiddushin 49 b, top.

30   Deut. Rabba 11:6; cf. Rom. 2:15; Heb 8:10, 10:16.

31   Eccl. Rabba 1:9, ad Eccl. 1:4. The functional character of Torah was recently stressed by Mordekhai Kaplan.

32   Gen. Rabba 1:1; Rashi ad Gen. 1:1.

33   BT Yoma 85 b.

34   Ex. 31:16; Yalqut Shim'oni ad loc., 1:409.

35   Ps. 81:5; JT Rosh Hashanah 1:3, 57 b.

36   M Rosh Hashanah 2:9.

37   T Sanhedrin 2:13.

38   BT Bava Batra 60 b; BT 'Avodah Zarah 36 a; JT Sabbath 1:7, 3 d; 'Avodah Zarah 2:9, 41 d; E.T., s.v. **'eyn gozerin gezerah.**

39   BT 'Avodah Zarah 19 a; cf. Urbach, **The Sages,** ch. 13.

40   Cf. my **'Erkhey Mishpat,** pp. 34-40.

41 BT Makkot 22 b.

42 T. Sotah 7:12; BT 'Eruvin 13 b.

43 JT Sanhedrin 4:2, 22 a; Soferim 16:5.

44 BT Bava Metsia 59 b.

45 Cf. my "The Temple Scroll and the Codification of Jewish Law", JLA 2 (1979) pp. 33-44.

46 Cf. Moses A. Bloch, **Sefer Sha'arey haTaqqanot**; Die Institutionen des Judentums. Krakow 1879-1894; and my **Introduction**, pp. 23-26.

47 Deut. 21:18-21; BT Sanhedrin 71 a.

48 Cf. T. Sanhedrin 11:6; JT Sanhedrin 8:1, 26 a; Sifre Deut. 220; BT Sanhedrin 72 b.

49 Sifra Lev. 20:5.

50 Cf. Mekhilta, Pascha 13 ad Ex. 12:26; Yevamot 79 a; Sanhedrin 44 a.

51 Sifra Num. 133 ad Num. 133 ad Num. 27:1.

52 Num. 26:52-57.

53 Num. 27:6-11.

54 Ex. 34:7; Num. 14:18.

55 Deut. 24:16.

56 By the addition of the qualification **lesone'ay** (to those who reject me): Ex. 20:5; Deut. 5:9.

57 Num. Rabba 19:33, 55 b ad Num. 21:17; cf. BT Berakhot 7 a; Sanhedrin 27 b. See also BT Makkot 24 a, where the vicarious liability of ascendants and descendants is ascribed to Moses and the correction is credited to Ezekiel. Both versions are meant to encourage the listeners of the homily towards independence of judgment and criticism even vis-a-vis the highest authority.

58 Deut. Rabba 5:13, ad Deut 20:10; see my **'Erkhey Mishpat**, p. 38f.

59 Num. 31:2, 6; Num. Rabba 22:4, 60 c; Tanchuma, ed. Buber, ad loc.

60 Qinyan Torah ('Avot 6):6.

61 Zech. 4:2; Lev. Rabba 32:8 ad Lev. 24:10.

62 Cf. Jacobs, **Tree**, pp. 257-275.

63 1 Sam. 15:9.

64 Eccl. Rabba 7:33, ad. Eccl. 7:16.

65 Cf. my **'Erkhey Mishpat**, p.39.

66 Cf. Cf. I. Heinemann, ch. 3; Urbach, **The Sages**, ch. 13.

67 JT Pe'ah 1:6, 16 c; BT Bava Metsia 88 a.

68 BT Bava Metsia 30 b. According to a "corrected" version, the rabbis were not to be blamed, but the parties insisting on their rights rather than agreeing to a compromise.

15. RABBINICAL ONTOLOGY AND POSITIVISM

(a) Imitatio Dei

While most thinkers of Halakhah emphasize its objective and positive character, we may also be able to trace certain elements in rabbinical thought which allow for an ontological interpretation of Torah and Halakhah. Developing such an interpretation of Judaism could enable us to reconcile the positivism of Jewish law with the ontological approach of ethics. In a sense, we would like to maintain the view that the concept of Natural Law can be reconciled with that of revelation[1], only that by using the term ontological we wish to include theological and metaphysical elements as well.

For instance, if we accept the concept of **imitatio dei**[2], we derive the norms of our behaviour not from the arbitrary will of the supreme authority, in the way of ethical voluntarists, but from our concept of God: "Just as He is merciful, you shall be merciful"[3]. Jewish theology thereby enables us to develop an ethical system, having philosophical sources of information besides those of Torah and Halakhah.

The concept of **imitatio dei** is actually at the basis of the law of Torah. The Creator is shown to have observed the Sabbath before calling upon Israel to do so, and He is presented as being holy, before the same quality is demanded of the people. In the narratives included in the Torah, God is depicted carrying out various acts of benevolence, which provide the basis for the commandment to "walk in His ways and to hold fast to Him" (Deut. 8:6).

The problem with this method is two-fold. Our concepts of God are sometimes inconsistent, and God himself, being free, transcends any contradictions and paradoxes. He appears not only as merciful and forgiving, but also as punishing and taking revenge. Sometimes He is described as consistent and unchanging, while on other occasions He seems to regret His decisions. According to a daring formulation, God Himself prays that His attribute of compassion will overcome His attribute of justice[4].

The question therefore arises as to how a consistent ethics can evolve out of **imitatio dei**. Moreover, the fact that God appears as legislator vis-a-vis mankind, not only as the One who reveals His own character, limits the inferences which could be drawn from God's attributes.

Indeed, being legislator as well, God need not be bound by His own attributes, and could have demanded from man something contradicting His own ways. While Plato's **Euthyphron** mentions only the either-or scenario; either the gods command what is good in any event, or they define what is good and demand compliance with their will, there may actually be a third option; sometimes God may demand what follows from the good and from His benevolence, and on other occasions He may demand obedience to His will as a test of faith.

The concept of **imitatio dei** could be understood as one source of information concerning the will of God, besides the other sources, such as Torah and Halakhah. We may assume that in general Halakhah should be interpreted in light of **imitatio dei**, unless there were a direct call, like that for the offering of Isaac. In ordinary cases, we would reject any rule of Halakhah which conflicts with justice and compassion, even if the claim is made that such a rule is the will of God. We should keep in mind that the offering had to be demanded by God Himself, while the revocation of the command could take place through a messenger.

Ontology, according to this line of thought, would be a kind of **check and balance** to positive Halakhah, not an alternative. The danger of subjectivity could be met, as we are going to describe below.

However, many speakers of Halakhic Judaism actually express fear of anarchy and subjectivity, leading them to an attitude of ethical voluntarism and positivism[5]. They rely on one view, for example, that the commandment regarding the bird's nest (Deut. 22:6), should not be interpreted as a result of divine compassion, but as a positive law[6]. The leader in prayer is to refrain from references to the moral meaning of Torah, because this might set conditions to the observance of certain commandments, give precedence to Agadah over Halakhah, and justify new and subjective interpretations.

The reasoning that the divine laws are not the emanation of divine compassion, but **gezerot** (arbitrary rules of law), which should not be questioned, emphasizes their formal and authoritarian character. According to this view, even a rule of reason must be transformed into a test of faith, like the tests of Abraham and Job. We are not supposed to understand decisions of divine providence, which are also called by the term **gezerot**[7]. Hence, the opposition to moral discourse concerning the commandments seems to follow from the opposition to questions of theodicy.

Needless to say, this is just one view, while the authors of the Aramaic **Targumim**[8] and most commentators and moralists differ from this ethical voluntarism[9].

Moral norms cannot be derived from God's attributes alone, or from nature and reason. They must also take into consideration spiritual experience, human faith and sources of law. Because of this variety of sources, everyone has a certain leeway as to which of the sources to follow in a particular case.

(b) Man in the Image of God (imago dei)

According to the view of Ben Azzai, the foundation of all commandments is the teaching that man was created in the image of God[10]. By putting at the basis of Torah not a commandment, like that of love, but the principles of creation and **equality**, he adopted an ethical approach. Ben Azzai thereby stated that every human being is entitled to the dignity and treatment due to a creature of God, and that they should all behave in a way befitting such a creature. This is an idea similar to Kant's categorical imperative, viz. that every person should be treated as an end, not as a means.

Moreover, the commandment of loving the other like oneself does not provide **human dignity** to everyone. Only the statement about humanity being created in the divine image prevents us from saying "just as our own dignity has sometimes suffered in the past, the dignity of our fellow should also sometimes suffer. Therefore we should know that our fellow is in the image of God"[11].

This moral consideration is of direct consequence, not only to individual behaviour, but to the interpretation of Halakhah. According to a Halakhic rule, "the dignity of beings is important enough to overrule a norm of the Torah"[12]. The simple sense of this saying gives preference to the concept of human dignity over any divine law. It was, however, considered to be too far-reaching, so that the preference for employing this concept was limited to rabbinical laws. Perhaps we should say that the dignity due to human beings by others must reign supreme, even over religious duties, while the individual entitled to human dignity should think of God first.

Another consequence of the **image** concept is the insight that the life of human beings is beyond evaluation, and that every individual is a world by himself[13]. Here, the moral concepts of creation and of imago dei are truly **universal**, while the concept of loving the other like yourself, mentioned above, led some rabbis to a particularist interpretation[14].

Still, within the framework of the Jewish people, the concept of human dignity prevailed. Every member of the people is entitled to the greatest respect, being a descendant of Abraham, Isaac and Jacob[15], and being a descendant of kings[16].

Likewise, every person's soul is seen as a deposit given to him or her in purity, to be kept pure and restored to God at will[17]. At the awakening one should therefore thank God for the soul which is pure, created by God, taken back and to be restored by Him in the future[18]. This is an appeal by way of **noblesse oblige**, moral behaviour actually being the ontological need of the human soul.

A beautiful homily compares the soul to a princess married to a commoner. Even if he provided her with the finest delicacies of the world, it would not be enough, because she is a princess. All that we do for our soul is inadequate, because the soul is divine[19].

The characteristic of human beings is their **moral freedom,** which is perhaps the most important element of the imago dei. Obedience to the divine will counts because it is not prescribed by nature. Only he who can do otherwise becomes a true servant of God and closer to Him than the angels. This is somewhat parallel to the unleavened bread. It has to be prepared out of dough which could ferment, and must be prevented from doing so by human intervention[20]. Only the possibility of sin gives meaning to obedience and service, and only free individuals can serve God adequately.

As a result of the idea of **imago dei,** a mundane matter like washing oneself can become an act of worship[21]. The law is thereby supplemented by the moral of intentions. The Jewish marriage ceremony includes a reference to the divine likeness of human beings, which is to set the tone in conjugal relations[22]. Contraception, abortion, and needless to say killing, are seen as acts of aggression against the **divine image,** which also means against God[23]. Respect for the dead is grounded in the same idea of **image**[24].

On the other hand, human beings are not only **imago dei** but also a category of their own, and their limitations should not be overlooked. The rule concerning the marriage of the captive woman (Deut. 21:10-14), was understood as a compromise with the evil inclination, rather than as an ideal[25]. Since the Torah is addressed to human beings, not to angels, there is an assumption that sometimes **de minimis non curat lex** (the law does not care for trifles)[26]. Likewise, a series of mitigating rules was applied to the law out of consideration for human needs and frailty[27].

Thus, the presumption was established that human beings cared for their dead relatives[28], and for their property[29], and the Halakhah had to reckon with that fact. Similarly, nobody was to testify regarding himself or anything in which he had an interest, the for it was thought that he would have difficulties being objective and truthful[30].

Hence, moral considerations about the divinity, as well as the humanity of every individual, were taken into consideration in Halakhic discourse. This illustrates the legitimacy and necessity of ethics for a reasonable interpretation of Torah.

(c) **Reason**

Halakhah claims to be based on reason, which is another element of ontology, and an alternative to halakhic positivism and voluntarism. The function of reason is called by a number of names, which we will now explain one by one.

First of all, **lo bashamayim hi** (the Torah is no longer in heaven), but is subject to rational discussion among the sages. The study relates to the traditions transmitted by human beings and examined by **sevara** (reason). This is done, inter alia, by those who are **medammim** (applying the principle of analogy), or **lemedim** (learning one thing from another), i.e. extending the rules already known to cover new questions. Another logical discourse is **higgayon** (thought or speech), the deeper insight of advanced scholars.

Logic, especially the inference **ab minore ad maius** or **a fortiori**, is called **din** (adjudication), not only in the forensic, but also in the academic discussion. Finally, the reason of a given argument or rule is also called **ta'am or ta'ama** (taste, sense), describing the favourable acceptance of such an argument or rule by the audience.

The first principle was expressed in the previously mentioned story concerning the 'Akhnai Oven, where R. Eliezer represented the prophetic and irrational element in the halakhic process, while R. Joshua and the rest of the sages insisted on human autonomy and rationalism[31].

Inference by way of **sevara** was the complement to the study of sources, **gemara**, and represented the individual, as distinct from the common opinion in Halakhah. If a matter was brought up in the academy, one would ask whether it was part of the sources or a logical conclusion, as some of the rabbis specialised in the one or the other[32].

The rule that the onus of proof is upon the plaintiff is based on reason rather than on Scripture, viz. on the experience that the patient seeks out the physician, not the reverse[33]. Another rule of reason is the principle of equality of the value of life, which prohibits the taking of another person's life to save one's own (except in cases of self-defence)[34]. Literary sources are superfluous as long as the solution can be reached by way of reason[35].

A saying of R. Jochanan shows the process of Torah as being a direct continuation of rational discourse: "If the Torah had not been given, we would still be able to derive the value of modesty from the observation of cats, the evil of stealing from the observation of ants and the need for marital fidelity from the observation of doves"[36].

Urbach discusses this saying with regard to the issue of autonomy vis-a-vis heteronomy, making the comment that the inference from nature was justified only before the Torah. Meanwhile, he says, this source of moral norms has become redundant and cannot be quoted in favour of autonomy[37]. In our opinion, if this were so, then there would be no sense in including such a statement in a homily. We should rather look for some lasting importance of this idea, even within the theonomic framework. Rules of Torah and Halakhah should therefore be interpreted in light of their natural law background and not be allowed to conflict with nature and reason.

In this case, the term for reasoning by way of induction is **lemedim** (we conclude from observation). A similar form of reasoning, viz. the extension of a rule of Scripture by using analogy, is called **medammin** (we declare the similarity). This method is behind most of the rabbinical discourse, though sometimes it is deemed to be insufficient to justify an innovation[38].

Obviously, the use of this method must be limited to the rational parts of Halakhah, but no rational application of logics would make sense in irrational institutions. Therefore, it was held that **eyn medammin biterefot** (the method of analogy is inapplicable regarding the rules of ritual slaughtering).

Logical thinking and hermeneutics is also called **higgayon**, and some of the rabbis largely relied on this method, both for the exegesis of Scripture and for the solution of halakhic questions. Traditionalists, like R. Eliezer ben Hyrkanos, warned parents from teaching it their children, and even mature students were advised to study tradition before engaging in **higgayon**[39].

Induction and analogical discourse is often called **din** (adjudication), and represents the ontological basis of Halakhah. Accordingly, certain commandments could be seen as logically independent from the text: **devarim she'ilmale nikhtevu din hu' sheyikatevu** (matters which should have been written, even if they were not)[40]. There is a part of Torah not only identical with, but relying on human reason. Revelation is therefore not meant to be a confrontational and dichotomic phenomenon vis-a-vis ethics, rather the continuation of insights of ethics already known, and should be interpreted and applied accordingly.

The term **din,** or **shurat hadin,** has already been explained in connection with the idea of **lifnim mishurat hadin** (superogation). But the former term also describes the generality of the law, as distinct from individualized and flexible solutions[41]. Moreover, it refers to a norm based on the scriptural concept, vis-a-vis its rabbinical amendment based on utilitarian consideration[42].

As mentioned above, another term for reason, as used in the rabbinical discourse, is **ta'am** (taste, sense). Some of the teachers used the Sense of Scripture as an hermeneutical principle[43], which was based on the legitimacy of rational thought and even allowed for a critical evaluation of the norms themselves[44].

Only exceptional rules were mentioned as **hilkheta bela' ta'ma**[45], meaning rules without rational grounding, while the ordinary rule was expected to be rational. The teacher should give reasons for the norms[46], and a judgment[47] creditor or debtor was entitled to reasoned judgment. But again, some of the rabbis did not accept reason as legal authority, especially if its conclusions conflicted with other rules[48].

In rejection of irrational and prophetic claims, however, R. Joshua and the rest of his colleagues insisted on the value of reason as a source of Halakhah. Rejecting the conservatism of R. Eliezer, they claimed that the time of prophecy had passed, and that all authority must evolve out of rational discourse[49].

The norms of Torah could therefore be ascertained by reason, not only by tradition and revelation. The Patriarchs could be said to have followed the rules of the Torah before they had been revealed by God, and this they could have done only by virtue of their reason and conscience[50].

Accordingly, Moses was perceived not as a mere mediator of the divine message to the people, but as its interpreter and administrator: "When God finished speaking to him (Ex. 31:18), how could Moses have learned the totality of Torah, of which it was said that its measure was larger than the earth (Job 11:9)? We must therefore assume that Moses had been taught by God the principles (the rest being his own interpretation)"[51].

A rule of merely positive law, in contradistinction to rules derived also from reason, is called **chiddush** (innovation), which means that it is the positive creation of the legislator. Such a rule should be given a strict interpretation and not be extended by analogy[52]. This is similar to the rule against the application of analogy in matters of ritual slaughtering.

Certain solutions were deemed to be unacceptable because of their strange character and senselessness in the eyes of the uninitiated[53]. This was another contribution of reason and ethical discourse to the development of Halakhah. On the other hand, Torah extends beyond the limits of human reason. It also includes rules "which are criticized by Non-Jews and by the evil inclination, such as the prohibition of pork, mixed species, levirate, purification of lepers, the red heifer and the killed ram. In these commandments Scripture emphasizes divine authority and the need to submit to it"[54]. Obviously, rational criticism stood a greater chance vis-a-vis rabbinical statements than the Torah itself.

There was always the counter-argument about the danger of subjectivism, which sometimes led to the rejection of reason altogether. However, the fact that Torah had to be studied together with others[55], and that the student should seek to learn from a number of teachers[56], provided relief. Even if we assume that concepts like reason and justice tend to be controversial, rabbinical pragmatism already provided an answer: "The judge takes into account what his eyes see", even if others would have seen the matter differently[57].

1.   Contrary to the views of Y. Leibowitz, **Yahadut**, p. 26 f.; M. Fox, "Maimonides and Aquinas on Natural Law", DI 5 (1972) p. 5 ff.; and recently J.D. Bleich, "Judaism and Natural Law", JLA 7 (1988), pp. 5-42; and in line with D. Novak, "Natural Law, Halakhah and the Covenant", JLA 7 (1988) pp. 43-67. See also my **'Erkhey Mishpat**, pp. 57-65.

2.   Cf. S. Rosenberg, "Ethics", in Cohen & Mendes Flohr, p. 201; Spero, **Morality**, pp. 35, 85; and David S. Shapiro, **Studies in Jewish Thought**, 1, (New York: 1975), pp. 122-144.

3.   Sifra ad Lev. 19:2; Sifre Deut. 49 ad Deut. 11:22; Midrash Tanna'im ad Deut. 13:5; BT Sabbath 133 b, Sotah 14 a.

4.   BT Berakhot 7 a.

5.   E.g. Leibowitz, Fox. Lichtenstein, Bleich and Kirschenbaum.

6.   M Berakhot 5:3; JT Berakhot 5:3; 9 c; BT Berakhot 33 b. See supra ch. 14 (a) and infra ch. 21 (b).

7.   Cf. BT Yoma 67 b.

8.   Targum (Quasi) Jonathan and so-called Jerusalem Targum ad Lev. 22:28; Lev. Rabba 27:11, s.v. **shor 'o seh.**

9.   Cf. Heinemann, **Ta'amey haMitswot**, p. 12 ff.

10.   Sifra Lev. 19:18. On this concept see Alexander Altmann, "Homo Imago Dei' in Jewish and Christian Theology", **Journal of Religion**, 48, (1968) pp. 235-259.

11.   Gen. Rabba 24:7.

12.   BT Berakhot 19 b; JT Berakhot 3:1, 6 a.

13.   M Sanhedrin 4:5.

14.   L. Roth, "Moralization and Demoralization", **Judaism** 11 (1962).

15.   M Bava Metsia 7:1.

16.   BT Bava Metsia 113 b.

17.   BT Nidah 30 b; cf. Urbach, **The Sages**, ch. 10, note 10.

18.   BT Berakhot 60 b.

19.   Lev. Rabba 4:2 ad Lev. 4:2; Spero, **Morality**, p. 85.

20.   BT Pesachim 35 a.

21.   BT Shabbat 50 b; Lev. Rabba 34; 'Avot deR. Nathan 30.

22.   BT Ketubbot 8 a.

23.   Mekhilta, **bachodesh** 8, ad Ex. 20:13.

24.   Deut. 21:23; BT Mo'ed Qatan 15 b.

25.   BT Qiddushin 21 b; cf. BT Chullin 17 a; Jacobs, **Tree**, p. 44.

26.   BT Berakhot 25 b.

27.   Jacobs, **Tree**, pp. 44-50.

28.   Cf. ET, s.v. **'adam bahul 'al meto**.

29.   Cf. ET, s.v. **'adam bahul 'al mammono**.

30.   ET, s.v. **'adam qarov 'etsel 'atsmo, 'en 'adam mesim 'atsmo rasha', 'en 'adam ro'eh chovah le'atsmo**.

31.   BT Bava Metsia 59 b; and supra.

32.   BT Bava Batra 77 a; Yoma 33 a. On **sevara** see also Berkovits, **Not in Heaven**.

33.   BT Bava Qama 46 b; Spero, **Morality**, p. 279; cf. BT Ketubot 22 a.

34.   BT Pesachim 25 b; Spero, p. 279.

35.   BT Ketubot 22 a.

36.   BT 'Eruvin 100 b; cf. L. Jacobs, "The Relationship between Religion and Ethics in Jewish Thought", in Kellner, p. 46.

37.   Urbach, **The Sages**, ch. 13; and see S. Leiman, "Critique of Louis Jacobs", in Kellner, p. 58 f.

38.   BT Gittin 19 a.

39.   BT Berakhot 28 b; 'Avodah Zarah 19 a.

40.   Sifra ad Lev. 18:4; BT Yoma 67 b. This concept was developed by R. Sa'adyah ben Josef in his **'Emunot veDe'ot** and translated **Mitswot Sikhliyot**; cf. Fox, **Ethics**, pp. 174-187.

41.   Cf. T Terumot 2: 1-3; Pesachim 4(3):7.

42.   M Gittin 4:4.

43.   E.g. R. Shimon, cf. Sifre Deut. 159, 281 ad Deut. 17:17, 24:17; BT Sanhedrin 21 a; Bava Metsia 115 a.

44.   Cf. supra.

45.   BT Gittin 14 a.

46.   BT Niddah 24 b.

47.   BT Sanhedrin 31 b.

48. Thus the colleagues of R. Simon, Cf. BT Berakhot 23 b, as to the use of **ta'ama** or of **qal wachomer**.

49. BT Bava Metsia 59 b; Bava Batra 12 a; Ex Rabba 28:6, ad Ex. 20:1; Tanchuma Yitro 11, quoted by E.E, Urbach, **The Halakhah**, ch. 15.

50. Gen. 26:5; M & JT Qiddushin 4 end; BT Qiddushin 82 a; Gen Rabba 61:1; 95:3, ad Gen. 25:1; 46:28; Lev. Rabba 2:10, ad Lev. 1:2.

51. Tanchuma Ki Tissa 16.

52. JT Terumot 7:1, 44 c; BT Sanhedrin 27 a.

53. M Parah 3:3; cf. R. Levi ben Chaviv, Responsa, 8, p. 75; L. Jacobs, **Theology in the Responsa**, (London: 1975), pp. 142-144, (see also pp. 305-306).

54. Sifra ad Lev. 18:4; BT Yoma 67 b.

55. BT Berakhot 63 b.

56. BT 'Avodah Zarah 19 a.

57. BT Sanhedrin 6 b, end; cf. J. Roth, The Halakhic Process: A Systemic Analysis, (New York: JTS, 1986), p. 83 ff.; and my review in **Conservative Judaism**, 41 (1989) p. 79 ff. and p. 82.

16. HALAKHIC DEONTOLOGY AND TELEOLOGY

(a) Deontology

The concept deontology is derived from the Greek **deon** (duty). It has the meaning of an ethical system based on duty rather than on utility or any other goal. In such a system, an act or a forbearance is morally correct by its own moral value or derivation, not by the pleasure, happiness or wisdom thereby produced.

While Scripture and rabbinical thought often refer to reward and punishment in this or in the future world, some teachers emphasize that the duty of the commandment is decisive, not its results[1]. In this chapter, we will therefore examine whether the deontological approach is indeed rooted in rabbinical tradition, or implanted from Western philosophy.

An important idea in line with deontological ethics is that of 'ahavat hashem (the love of God). In a comment on this concept it was said that a Jew should not study so that he could eventually earn the title of Rabbi, become a member of the academy, live long or merit a future life. His only motivation should be the love of God, which might, however, earn him these honours in the end[2].

Although love is not exactly the same as duty, this homily can be understood as a rejection of the common tendency of having reward and punishment in mind, and as an affirmation of the deontological rather than the teleological approach. It does not say whether one should merely disregard reward and punishment while fulfilling the commandment. It may even imply that one should see reward and punishment as a myth, instrumental for the motivation of those who are unable to consider simply the commandment itself.

The alternative and deontological approach would be basing the observance of the commandments on **yir'at hashem** (the fear, awe or reverence of God). A saying ascribed to Antigonos of Sokho (2nd century B.C.E.), calls upon the listener not to be like the servant for remuneration, but like one willing to serve without remuneration, for whom the fear of Heaven is guiding[3]. Although this particular saying seems to reflect Greek thought, the motivation by fear or by love of God is, obviously, Jewish. We may therefore indeed speak of a Jewish deontological approach.

The study of Torah and the performance of the commandments should also take place with the motivation of **lishmah** (for the sake of the Torah or the commandment)[4]. According to the formulation of R. Elazar, "do everything **leshem pe'ulatam** (with the intention to the act), and speak of every matter **lishmam** (for its own sake)"[5]. This means that no thought should be directed towards reward or punishment, and it corresponds with the demand to love the commandment and not the reward[6]. A similar remark is ascribed to Rava, that "the commandments were not given for enjoyment"[7].

However, if the reading is correct, this means that the intention should be directed towards the act itself rather than towards God. The alternative formulation contains a reference to God: "And all your acts should be directed towards Heaven"[8]. While the latter formula reflects the theonomic character of Torah, the former goes beyond this concept towards deontological ethics.

Although a person could observe a commandment with ulterior motives, this is accepted as a first step only, and in the hope that he will eventually come to observe the commandment for its own sake[9]. This is considered a plausible outcome because the act in itself is believed be of educational value, and to lead to a deeper identification with its spritual meaning.

Even though reward and punishment is often mentioned in connection with the commandments, the true observance of the commandments should be **be'emunah** (with faith)[10], or **betom** (in its totality)[11]. Both are states of mind, alternative to the more prevalent thought about **mattan sekharan** (their reward), and rejecting the preference given to certain commandments. It is said that reward is often delayed and uncertain, in order to teach us to equally respect both small as well as great commandments.

Another term pointing in the direction of deontology is the description of observance as **latset yedey chovato** (to exit one's duty), which means that a person had fulfilled a commandment[12]. Originally, this must have meant that the person was held captive by his duty as long as he had not carried it out.

Likewise, the rule demanding restoration of lost property to the owner was considered as so overwhelming that the text simply says that you **cannot** close your eyes, meaning that you may not do so[13]. The idea is that the person addressed by the rule so identifies himself with it, that the rule becomes part of his nature. We should remember the alternative view, quoted above, viz. that one should not say that he detests pork or certain forms of sex, rather that our Father in Heaven has prohibited them[14].

The true deontological approach does not permit the theonomic basis of the commandments, which is implied by their being commandments. This is perhaps clearest where Halakhah mentions rules of morality which are independent of any divine basis.

For instance, take a rule such as: "Do not waste the water of your cistern, if another person needs it"[15], which in itself is used as a basis of certain Halakhot. Or consider the rules: "Do not use another person's property (without his express permission)"[16], and "He who uses another person's property against the direction of the owner, is like a thief"[17]. We have already mentioned the rhetorical question: "Why do you think your blood is redder than that of the other fellow?"[18]. All of these statements were brought into the academy on the ground of reason and experience, their value lay in the contents and, to use the rabbinic term, they could be traced in **derekh 'erets** and not in theonomy.

(b) Volunteering and Duty

A paradoxical conclusion of deontology is the evaluation of a volunteer as being below the person doing his duty[19]. This evaluation, because it is paradoxical, expresses the deontological character of Halakhic thought. Even if we assume that it reflects the reaction to Pauline appreciation of Gentile voluntarism as well, rabbinical appreciation of the legal duty has meaning by itself. The justification of the act is its normative basis, not the inclination or moral intuition of the person performing it.

The problem of deontology affected Jewish women who, according to Halakhah, were exempt from the study of Torah and the observance of timely commandments. In fact, women did not volunteer to fulfill some of these commandments, but actually submitted to the duty of observing them. The expression of this intention was the recital of the blessing to God, that He had sanctified them and commanded them to observe these commandments. A posteriori the rabbis of Franco-German Communities, during the 11th and 12th centuries, agreed to this clear change in the halakhic status of women[20], and to the possibility of changing from voluntarism to equality of duty.

The same happened during the present century regarding the participation of women in the study of Torah. Though excluded by Halakhah from this most important activity[21], women have taken upon themselves this duty, and have thereby practically done away with this form of discrimination[22].

To come back to our topic, this ultimately means that a synthesis can be found between the status of volunteer and that of being duty bound. The duty can be created not only by imposition from above, but also by submission from below. The real difference between the volunteer and the person doing his or her duty is not in the objective application of the rule, but in the subjective commitment to the rule. The volunteer is the one acting without such a commitment, while he who does his duty is the one whose acts follow from his deontology.

(c) Teleology

Obviously, Halakhah is a system regulating social and individual behaviour. Its aim is the perfection of the individual Jew, the creation of a Kingdom of Priests and a Holy Nation[23], and the realization of the covenant between God and Israel. In this sense, all Halakhah is a means to an end and does not fit the purely deontological idea[24].

The observance of the commandments is meant to lead to a state of being close to God, and to guide the Jew on an infinite ladder of perfection[25]. While it is true that God Himself can never be reached, there is definitely progress in the stages of closeness. Even if we accept the idea that all is meant to be an expression of obedience to God and of service to Him, the concept of divine benevolence leads one to seek a positive goal in the commandments. Rabbinical spokesmen would not have said that "most of the **mitswot** have no instrumental or utilitarian value and cannot be construed as helping a person fulfill his earthly or spiritual needs"[26].

On the contrary, the Rabbis perceived the commandments and the Halakhah defining them as a divine device for the benefit of Israel. According to the formulation of R. Chananyah ben 'Aqashyah, "God wanted to give Israel an opportunity of **zekhut** (merit, reward), therefore He gave them so many commandments"[27]. The only difference between rational and irrational commandments is in human cognition, not in divine intention[28]. This does not mean that the commandments have thereby turned into a service to man, but that God in His benevolence prescribed a self-rewarding kind of service. The dichotomy between the divine and human goals of the commandments finds its solution in the divine ability to bridge the opposites[29].

Thus, the commandments addressed to the individual were interpreted according to their purpose. "The commandments were given only in order to test (or refine) the people. For it makes no difference to God whether the slaughtering of animals is performed in one form or another"[30]. The goal could also be found beyond this world: "This world is the lobby of the future world. Prepare yourself in the lobby, so that you may enter the palace"[31].

According to another formulation, the aim of all commandments is the promotion of peace in society[32]. In other words, the observance of the rule is not directed to the act itself, neither is it meant to effect the individual, rather to the good of society.

In particular, the dignity of human beings is a protected value of Halakhah. According to a statement in its original formulation, the dignity of man prevails over other biblical commandments[33]. During the discussion in the academy, however, this was held to be too far-reaching. The dignity of man was therefore held to prevail only over rabbinical commandments. Nevertheless, the meaning of this rule must have been to justify the consideration of the result when there was a conflict of duties.

Likewise, according to the feeling of Rabbi Aqiva, the rules of seclusion during the days of menstruation would lead to quarrels between spouses and to a divorce. He therefore suggested a lenient interpretation permitting the use of cosmetics by the wife during this time[34].

The reason given for a number of norms is the need to avoid the humiliation of sinners[35] or of poor people[36]. The justification of the norm was thus not in the act per se, but in its effect upon others[37].

1.   Cf. Y. Leibowitz, "Commandments" and S. Rosenberg, "Ethics", both in Cohen & Mendes Flohr, pp. 67-80, 195-202.

2.   Sifre Deut, 41, 48, referring to Deut. 11:13, 22; BT Nedarim 62 a.

3.   M 'Avot 1:3.

4.   R. Elazar, BT Sukkah 49 b; cf. N. Lamm, **The Study of Torah Lishmah in the Works of R. Hayyim of Volozhin.** New York 1966.

5.   Sifra Deut. 48; BT Nedarim 62 a; cf. M. Higger, **Massekhtot Ze'irot,** (New York); Bloch), p. 131.

6.   BT 'Avodah Zarah 19 a.

7.   BT Rosh Hashanah 28 a.

8.   M 'Avot 2:12; cf. Derekh 'Erets Zuta 2.

9.   Rav, BT Nazir 23 b.

10.   JT Pe'ah 1:1, 15 d.

11.   Deut. Rabba 6:2.

12.   Cf. Rabban Gamliel, M Pesachim 10:5.

13. Targum ad Deut. 22:3.
14. Sifra ad Lev. 20:26.
15. BT Yevamot 11 b.
16. BT Bava Metsia 117 b.
17. M Bava Qama 9:4; BT Bava Qama 100 b; Bava Metsia 78 b; T Megillah 1:5.
18. BT Pesachim 25 b.
19. BT Qiddushin 31 a; cf. supra ch. 14 (a).
20. Tosafot Qiddushin 31 a, s.v. **dela**.
21. Cf. my discussion of Y. Leibowitz's position in my **Dat haNetsach**.
22. Cf. Maimonides, **Mishneh Torah,** Hilkhot Talmud Torah 1:13.
23. Ex. 19:6.
24. The Rabbis of the second century C.E. had come into contact with the hedonism of Epicurus and rejected this teaching, without necessarily rejecting teleological thinking in general: cf. my **Law and Religion**, p. 36.
25. Contra Leibowitz, Yahadut, pp. 13-36; Leibowitz, "Commandments", in Cohen & Mendes Flohr, p. 70; cf. Isadore Twersky, **Studies in Jewish Law and Philosophy**, (New York: 1982), pp. 52-75; and Miriam Galston, "The Purpose of the Law according to Maimonides", **JQR** 69 (1978), pp. 27-51.
26. Thus Leibowitz, op.cit.
27. BT Makkot 23 b.
28. Cf. I. Heinemann, **Ta'amey haMitswot**, vol.1, p. 14 ff.
29. Leibowitz, p. 71.
30. Gen. Rabba 44:1.
31. M 'Avot 4:16.
32. BT Gittin 59 b. Cf. my "'al hashalom", **Levav Shalem**, [S. Bacharach Memorial Vol.], (Jerusalem: 1971), pp. 63-67.
33. BT Berakhot 19 b.
34. Sifra Lev. 15:33; BT Sabbat 64 b; Avot dR. Nathan 2(3).
35. JT Qiddushin 4:1; 65 d; BT Sotah 32 b.
36. M Ta'anit 4:8; BT Pesachim 82 a, Ketubot 8 b, 54 a, Mo'ed Qatan 27 a.
37. Cf. my **'Erkhey Mishpat**, pp. 150-154, and **Law and Religion**, pp. 35-42.

17. RABBINICAL JUSTICE, GENERALITY AND UNIVERSALITY

(a) Situation Ethics

The aim of Halakhah is certainly to realize justice in the world, which includes the demand for a general and universal law, as well as for equality of treatment for everyone[1]. Sometimes, however, a situation may be too complex to be regulated by one general norm. There may be need for an individualization of the rule, according to the particular case under consideration. In other situations, individuals or groups may be so different from each other that the law would have to differentiate the norms applying to them, and not treat equally the unequal.

In this chapter we will, therefore, first discuss solutions defying generality in order to meet the special needs of the situation. Then we will deal with three forms of differentiation among classes of people, which Halakhah seems to have reconciled with its concept of justice: Non-Jews, Women, and Impediments.

Halakhic sources sometimes reflect a difficulty in the formulation of general norms, and a tendency to leave the decision to the person concerned. In these cases, recognition is given to the uniqueness of the situation, which should be taken as the sole guideline in the decision. Although Jewish law is based on the assumption of generality and universalism, it does not attempt to subsume all given situations under general norms. The divine will must be assumed to be unequivocal even in the most exceptional circumstances, but this does not necessarily indicate to the human beings concerned how to handle the case. Theonomy, in such situations, means referral to the parties concerned, or to human authority, to dispose of the problem by human decision[2].

Such a situation emerges in the case where "two boats met on a river and it was impossible for both to proceed without risk, so that they had to agree on the priority of passage, or two camels ascending the pass of Beth Choron, and it was impossible for both to proceed without risk, so that they had to agree likewise. The empty one should give way to the one with cargo, the one near to its destination should give way to the one still at a distance. If both had equal load or equal distance, they should compromize and arrange some payment in return for the right of prior passage"[3].

In such an exceptional situation the parties cannot expect an authoritarian solution from above, but must work out their own answer. This is a true example of the coexistence of ethics and theonomous concepts, and of the existential responsibility of individuals vis-a-vis law or religion.

Solutions of this kind were later collected, quoted and became precedents for similar situations. Thus, rabbinic law included a provision about "two parties holding a piece of cloth, each of them claiming that he had found it and that it belonged to him, each of them should make an oath to the other that he owned not less than half the cloth, and the cloth should be divided"[4]. Even in matters of torts, where no evidence was forthcoming, compromise was suggested by some authorities[5], while others decided in favour of the defendant[6].

As a result of this attitude, some of the rabbis preferred to dispose of all litigation by referring the parties to mediation[7]. This was often an expression of weakness on the part of the judges, but in other cases it was based on the insight that conflicts are solved better by the parties themselves, than by an authoritarian solution imposed from above.

Another situational solution, suggested instead of the ordinary administration of Halakhic justice, was **shudda dedayyaney**, or **shuchda dedayyaney** (judicial discretion)[8]. It was a reaction to the rigid system of evidence adopted by Halakhah, allowing for an individual solution based on the circumstances[9].

It was applied only in cases where the facts could not be determined. For example, when conflicting titles existed to the same property, or when two equally possible interpretations of a will stood against each other. This discretionary power was, in the tradition of 'Erets Israel, called **shuchda dedayyane** (bribe of the judge, an occasion for drawing a personal advantage from the legal process), and the Babylonian equivalent was **shudda dedayyane** (the throwing of object of contention to one of the litigants), both meaning the favour or discretion of the judges[10].

In such situations, rabbinical law accepted the modern concept of judicial evaluation of the evidence. Today, whether to believe a witness or not, depends upon the judge's emotion and is not subject to the right of appeal. While in general Halakhah laid down a theory of evidence, instead of authorizing the free evaluation of the evidence by the judge, in these exceptional cases it conferred full discretion upon the court.

Quite problematic is another situational answer, viz. **kol de'alim** gevar (the stronger prevails)[11]. It is based on the insight that in spite of the many rules, there can be unprovided for situations where the parties revert to using their own resources to protect their rights. Together with the concepts of blood-vengeance and of taking the law into one's own hands, this solution points to the danger of too rigid a legal system, and serves as a kind of safety valve.

The question must be raised as to whether these exceptions fit within the framework of general and universal rules, whether they permit one to foresee the law, and whether justice is realized by them. None of the solutions mentioned was based on Scripture or rabbinical authority, nevertheless they seem to have met with the consensus of the parties concerned. Though not being general and universal, they may have worked for pacification, and thereby have been justified as a lesser evil.

(b) The Nations

Although Jewish thought perceived of all human beings as created in the image of God, and thereby adopted a generalizing and universalizing attitude towards mankind, rabbinical morals limited many of the biblical commandments to fellow Jews[12]. This is a moral regression vis-a-vis the univeral character of the story of creation[13], and constitutes a reaction to the war situation, as well as to Anti-Judaism and Anti-Semitism. Jews were indeed isolated in their concept of covenant and chosenness, especially after having suffered for their loyalty towards God and His revealed Torah.

Another factor hampering the maintenance of universalism was the belief in chosenness. Rabbinical Judaism insisted on the value of Torah and commandments as special privileges granted to the Jewish people, and as imposing a special responsibility on their part.

The meaning of every commandment is expressed in a blessing preceding the act, mentioning the special sanctification of Israel. The value of the festivals and of the Torah in general was likewise described in the formula of their blessings, also mentioning the special election of the Jewish people. While the rules of holiness required refraining from taking revenge and bearing a grudge vis-a-vis the fellow Israelite, rabbinical interpretation permitted both against others[14].

The reason for this regression was also to prevent too close contact with Gentiles, lest it lead to religious assimilation and to inter-religion marriages[15]. The Rabbis lacked a basic trust of non-Jews, Gentiles being involved in foreign cult and constituting a threat to the Jewish religion[16]. The rabbis warned their followers to beware of Non-Jews, that they were apt to kill them, and would not hesitate to break sexual taboos[17]. Likewise, the possession of a Gentile did not support his claim of right in rabbinical law, the Gentile being suspected of illegal taking[18].

According to the rabbinical view, God had once offered all nations to join the covenant of Sinai and to share in the Torah, but each had expressed reservations and rejected parts of the law[19]. This was obviously a case of apologetics against the argument of unjustified particularism and discrimination.

Halakhic generalizations and prejudices became the subject of Christian-Jewish polemics. If the Rabbis interpreted biblical commandments speaking of one's fellow as excluding others, Christians emphasized the extended meaning of the terms[20].

However, Jews in the diaspora were unable to maintain such a negative relationship with their Gentile neighbours, so a presumption was created that they were no real idolators[21]. According to some views, a Jew should even join with Gentiles in their prayer, if there was nothing offensive in its contents[22].

Some voices were raised in favor of the universalization of moral law. Against the exclusive interpretation of the law, calling for the acquittal of the killer if the victim was a stranger, the argument was made: "Before the promulgation of the Torah such killing was punishable (under the Noachide law); could the promulgation of the Torah have meant a lowering of the moral standard?"[23]. In other words, the argument went that Jewish law and ethics had to incorporate whatever was morally preferable in human tradition, because the Torah was meant as an additional, not alternative system of norms[24]. Unfortunately, this attitude was not adopted by the majority.

In any event, the rabbis were not only ready to accept converts and to recognize them as full Jews, but also to appreciate the merits of righteous gentiles observing the **Noachide Commandments**[25]. While it is true that there were also single voices against proselytes[26], the fact that the gates into Judaism were kept open, in spite of the danger for the people involved and in spite of formal difficulties[27], is a strong indication of universalism.

The double standard of the Halakhah regarding the in-group and the out-group[28] could be overcome, either through common experience in a democratic society in the diaspora, or through the inclusion of other nationals in the State of Israel. Thus, the distinction between the two groups becomes outdated through the concepts of citizenship and human rights. Participation of Halakhic scholars in policy discussions, and a broadening of the horizons of traditionalists is bound to bring about a more differentiated Halakhah and do away with the notion of friend-foe.

Judaism, even with its negative opinion of Gentiles and its belief in chosenness, is still more universalist than the so-called universal religions, Christianity and Islam. Universalism depends on the insight of pluralism, and these religions have not yet realized this insight to the extent that it has been part of Judaism.

(c) Sex Differentiation

Another problem reflecting on generality and universality is the Halakhic attitude towards women[29]. While the discrimination of foreigners could perhaps be justified because they have the possibility to convert to Judaism, no such contingency to earn the privileged status is granted to women. Indeed, one of the sages interpreted the initiative of the Daughters of Zelophead as the result of the insight that men (the intention being rabbis), have less pity on women than God[30].

Halakhah was formulated by and for men, and did not draw women into its framework. Wives, daughters and single women were objects of the rules, but never seen as participants in the **minyan** of Israel and in the study of Halakhah. The model of the Halakhah regarding the status of women is the restriction of the rabbinic rule of phylacteries to men, and the exemption of women from this precept[31]. Hence, the central commandment of studying Torah and the commandments linked to a certain time of day were applied to men only. As a result of this exemption, women were given a lower standing than that of men[32].

Men were said to be obliged to be fruitful and multiply, but according to the authoritative opinion, this duty was not extended to women[33]. While this exemption could be justified for the particular case of a barren wife after 10 years of marriage, there was no justification for the reliance on this exemption to set aside a wife's claim for a divorce.

Women, according to the Halakhah, do not count in the quorum of the congregation, they are not admitted for judicial or other public function and are incapable of testifying. A great number of legal presumptions disfavouring women are applied by Halakhists **iuris et de iure**, and are the cause of injustice[34].

The participation of women in the political process of the State of Israel and their involvement in the study of Halakhah will eventually bring about changes in these areas. Jewish society, including the rabbis, is in the process of including both sexes and listening to feminist grievances. The generalization of Halakhah beyond the limits of andro-centrism will eventually be the result.

(d) Impediments

Another framework of Halakhah opposing the generality and universality of the law is the great number of no fault impediments, especially the impediment of **adulterini**, of children from consanguinous unions and of their descendants[35]. These rules follow from the responsibility of the Jewish man in the choice of his wife, a responsibility towards both God and his future descendants. By avoiding a spouse affected by such an impediment, he submitts to the idea of holiness, shows obedience to God and provides the necessary conditions for building a successful Jewish family.

However, the disregard of the person tainted by the rule, and his deprivation of a fair chance to marry within the faith, is an example of particularism, which does not suit the rules of morality, viz. generalization and universalisation of rights and duties.

As already stated, the injustice was felt, but there was not enough courage to change the law. Although doubts had been raised long ago as to the purity of pedigree of most people[36], the rules of impediments were nevertheless applied against those who were unfortunate enough to be known as **mamzerim**.

1   On the universalization of moral rules see R. M. Hare, **Moral Thinking**, (Oxford: 1981), ch. 6; M.G. Singer, **Generalization in Ethics**, (New York: Knopt, 1961); Brandt, **Ethical Theory**, pp. 28-35.

2   On situation ethics see B.A. Brody, **Moral Rules and Particular Circumstances**, (Englewood Cliffs, 1970); T.E. Davitt, **Ethics in the Situation**, (New York 1970); R.L. Cunningham (ed), **Situationism and the new Morality**, (New York, 1970); J. Fletcher, **Situation Ethics: The New Morality**, (Philadelphia, 1966); Schrey, **Einfuehrung**, p.116. On the concept of **epieikeia** see my **Dat haNetsach**, pp. 111-120.

3   BT Sanhedrin 32 b; cf. Federbush, p 154 ff.

4   M Bava Metsia 1:1.

5   M Bava Qama 5:1; Symmachos, BT Bava Qama 46 a.

6   **The Sages**, BT ibid.

7   JT Sanhedrin 1:1, 18 b: BT Sanhedrin 7 a ff.; Federbush, p.46 ff.; Urbach, **The Sages**, ch 16; and my **'Erkhey Mishpat**, p.70. See infra ch. 19 (c).

8   BT Bava Batra 35 a; Federbush, p.161.

9   Cf. my 'Erkhey Mishpat. p.90.

10   JT Ketubot 10:4, 33 d; BT Ketubot 85 b, 94 a; Qiddushin 74 a; see supra ch. 17 (a) on
     Situation Ethics.

11   BT Bava Batra 34 a; Federbush, p. 157; and my 'Erkhey Mishpat, p.68.

12   Mekhilta Neziqin 4, ad Ex. 21:14; M Bava Qama 4:3; Sanhedrin 9:2; JT Bava Qama 4:3, 4
     b; BT Bava Qama 38 a; 113 ab; on the rabbinic attitude towards Non-Jews see Michael
     Guttmann, **Das Judentum und seine Umwelt,** Berlin 1927; and Jacob Katz, **Exclusiveness
     and Tolerance: Studies in Jewish-Gentile Relations,** (Oxford: U.P. 1961).

13   Cf. Leon Roth, "Moralization and Demoralization", **Judaism** 11 (1962), pp. 291-302.

14   Sifra ad Lev. 19:18.

15   Cf. BT Sabbath 17 b.

16   M Chullin 2:7.

17   M 'Avodah Zarah 2:1.

18   BT Sukkah 30 a.

19   Mekhilta Bachodesh 5 ad Ex. 20:2; Sifre Deut. 343 ad Deut. 33:2; BT 'Avodah Zarah 2 a.

20   Luke 10:29-37.

21   BT Chullin 13 b; cf. Katz, **Exclusiveness,** ch. 3.

22   T Berakhot 5:21.

23   Mechilta deR. Ishmael, Neziqin 4, ad Ex. 21:14.

24   Cf. my 'Erkhey Mishpat, pp. 27-29.

25   CF. ET, s.v. **ben no'ach, ger, ger toshav, gerut** and **goy.**

26   BT Yevamot 47 b; cf. Tosafot Qiddushin 70 b, s.v. **qashin.**

27   After the lapse of ordination an argument was made that there was no longer a competent
     authority for accepting converts: Tosafot Qiddushin 62 b, s.v. **ger.**

28   The term was coined by W.G. Sumner, **Folkways,** (Boston: 1906); cf. Schrey, **Einfuehrung,**
     p.124.

29   On the status of women in Halakhah see R. Biale, **Women and Jewish Law,** (New York:
     Schocken, 1984); S. Heschel, "Feminism", in Cohen & Mendes-Flohr.

30   Sifre Num. 133, ad Num. 27: 1-5.

31   M Qiddushin 1:7; BT Qiddushin 35 a.

32   M Horayot 3:7; cf. Maimonides, **Commentary,** ad loc.

33   M Yevamot 6:6.

34   See my **Jewish Matrimonial Law in the MA,** (London: 1966); Tevi'at Gerushin mitsad
     ha'Ishah, (Jerusalem: 1973); **Law and Religion,** pp. 75-103; **Diney Nissu'in,** (Jerusalem:
     1983); and Si'ach Mesharim, 3, (1986).

35   Cf. L. Jacobs, **Tree of Life,** pp. 257-275; and supra ch. 14 (c).

36   Cf. M 'Eduyot 8:7; BT Pesachim 62 b; Qiddushin 69 b; Gen. Rabba 37:7, s.v. **ule'ever;**
     Ruth Rabba 8:1, s.v. **R. 'Abba.**

18. RABBINICAL VIRTUES

(a) Greek and Jewish Virtues

Aside from the discussion of the numerous norms of behaviour, rabbinical education included the discussion of a number of virtues and goals of life[1]. For instance, we find the "ways of peace" as a rubric of laws, viz. laws which have been promulgated to promote integration with others, and we also find the peaceful person as an educational ideal: "Hillel said, be among the disciples of Aaron, loving and pursuing peace, loving people and drawing them near to Torah"[2].

Such a virtue must, of course, be understood in a historical context, such as being a reaction to the militancy of the School of Shammai and of the zealots. It may also suggest an alternative to the martial virtues of Hellenism. Obviously, the ideal of peace could be cherished in the house of study, functioning outside the political arena and deploring the bloodshed during the anti-Roman revolts.

In general, the study of the highest virtue must have been discussed beside the study of the various norms of behaviour. Rabban Jochanan ben Zakkai was said to have asked his disciples which was the best path to follow, and the answers offered were as follows: R. Eliezer said, having a benevolent eye; R. Joshua, being a good fellow; R. Jose, being a good neighbour; R. Simon, foreseeing the future; and R. Elazar, having a good heart. Whereupon Rabban Jochanan ben Zakkai was said to have praised the latter view for being the most comprehensive[3].

Such a discussion of ethics probably did not spring up spontaneously during the study of Torah. It was similar in form to the traditions of the Greek philosophers, sought to define the concept of good and must have been formulated by an earlier model.

Perhaps the rabbis also discussed Greek virtues[4], and were thereby challenged to propose alternative formulations. There is a tradition describing Alexander the Great in discussion with Jewish spokesmen. He asked them who was wise, who was brave, who was rich and what was the behaviour promoting life[5]. One reply to these questions was ascribed to Simon Ben Zoma: Wise is he who learns from everybody, brave is he who overcomes his inclination, rich is he who is satisfied with his destiny, and honoured is he who pays respect to others[6].

The whole fifth chapter of the tractate 'Avot seems to be such a discussion of virtues, sometimes responding to Greek ethics[7]. The rabbinic term for virtues is **middot**, which literally means measures. A virtue is indeed a quantity of a characteristic which enables the person concerned to function, or a standard by which he is measured.

Take, for instance, the **middat chassidut** (measure of piety), describing the willingness to renounce one's right in favour of others[8], or **middat rachmanut** (measure of compassion), which has a similar meaning[9].

Although already mentioned in the Bible[10], the idea of the middle path is most probably a reflection of Greek ethics. According to a rabbinical formulation, "the Torah is like the path between a path of fire and another of snow. He who turns to the former will die of fire, and he who turns to the latter will die of snow. The answer is to take the middle path"[11]. In other words, in order to keep to the golden mean there was no need to abandon the Torah and turn to foreign models; it could be found within Jewish tradition itself.

A reaction to Greek and Roman ideals also appears in a saying of R. Simon bar Yochai: "Beauty, strength, riches, age and progeny are ornaments to the righteous and ornaments to the world"[12]. This means that these virtues are indeed of value, but primarily to the righteous, and only in a secondary sense to the world in general. This was a reply to the overwhelming impression of the Roman world, which certainly attracted many Jews.

A positive attitude concerning these virtues and the world is also reflected in the saying that at doomsday everyone will have to render account for any asceticism and withdrawal from the world[13]. The inference was that there was no need for assimilation to the Greco-Roman culture if one wanted to participate in this world. The Torah itself wants human beings to enjoy, only it should be done within limits and with the intention to serve God.

On the other hand, an ascetic ideal seems to have developed as a result of the destruction of the Temple and under the influence of pietists, sectarians and Christians. In this vein it was said that "those who bear insult without replying in kind, who hear their shame without answering, who act out of love and joyfully accept suffering, they are lovers of God, brave like the mighty sun"[14]. This virtue is also described as the willingness to restrain one's character traits by forgiving[15].

According to one tradition, "he who vows an optional fast deserves the title of holiness", while another view declared him to be a sinner[16]. Behind this controversy stood the idea of the middle-path.

Virtue was sometimes called the "path of life", and a specific type of ethical discourse dealt with this question: "When Rabbi Eliezer fell ill, his disciples asked him to teach them the paths of life, through which they would be worthy to enter into the life of the future world"[17]. Already the question seems to be a reaction to Greek ethics, dealing with virtues beneficial in this world. The disciples define paths of life as those leading to happiness in the future world. The corresponding question, however, who were "three whose life was not worth it" was meant in relation to life in this world[18]. This shows that the answers which are given in the spirit of practical ethics are based on the life experience of the respondents.

(b) The Tractate 'Avot

Having interpreted a number of sayings in this extraordinary part of the Mishnah, we would like to state that the entire tractate is a collection of ethical discourses offered by the rabbis as alternatives to their non-Jewish models. Certainly, the saying transmitted in the name of R. Elazar: "Know how to reject the arguments of Epicuros", is a reaction to the ethics of the said Philosopher[19].

By the same token, the saying of R. Judah the Prince can be interpreted: "Which is the straight way to be chosen? The one which gives glory to the person and through which he is glorified by others"[20]. Such a maxim could have evolved during a talk between the Rabbi and a learned Greek or Roman, and is therefore formulated in a universal way.

Likewise, the teaching of R. Matya ben Charash: "Be the tail of the lions, not the head of the foxes", was meant as an antithesis to the ambition of Julius Caesar and the philosophy derived from it[21]. The same was probably the background of the categories of characters which expressed universal insights rather than specific ideas of Judaism[22].

The polemical character of the tractate is perhaps reflected in its very name, 'Avot, referring to the tension between aristocratic and democratic viewpoints. The name has been interpreted as "parents" or general principles on the one hand, and as the sayings of the teachers, who could also be called parents, on the other. However, these interpretations do not fit the general custom of Jewish sources being named for a word at the beginning of the text. The question should therefore be raised as to where did the word 'Avot appear at the beginning of the tractate.

If we are not mistaken, the word can indeed be found in a parallel version of the tractate as transmitted in the School of Shammai. According to a saying which was put by the Shammaiites right at the beginning, one should admit into the academy only students of pedigree, of well-known ancestry, **Bnei 'Avot**[23]. The parallel version of the Hillelites quotes a saying of the Members of the Great Synagogue instead, namely that as many students as possible should be admitted[24]. The name of the tractate, however, as determined by the earlier Shammaiite version, remained even after the elimination of this saying, according to the Hillelite view.

(c) Hierarchies

An attempt of arranging ethical virtues into a progressive system has been ascribed to R. Pinehas ben Ya'ir, a pneumatic pietist living in the latter half of the second century C.E..[25] According to his system, once you developed certain virtues, other virtues would follow by necessity. This is an idea corresponding with that of the progression of meritorious or culpable acts[26]. Just as the consequence of any positive act is the performance of another act of the same category, certain virtues lead to the development of others, which are connected with the former.

Indeed, the concept of **imitatio dei** transfers the emphasis from the deontological concept of obedience, to the idea of adopting divine virtues[27]. A person who had been wronged, for instance, could refrain from reacting by remembering and imitating divine compassion, which is along the same line[28]. Instead of concentrating on the norm against taking revenge[29], which is limited in its application to kinsmen, he could set his mind towards the image of God as being compassionate towards every human being. Thus the system of virtues may be understood as being of a higher order than that of duties.

We have seen that a hierarchical order was needed between virtues promoting life in this world, and others promoting the spirit and the world to come. Ascetic attitudes and renunciation often compete with the idea of the golden mean, allowing for a certain degree of egoism.

A similar hierarchical order concerns altruism. Basically, Halakhah takes into account the personal needs of the individual, before caring for the needs of others. Since the individual is called upon to take care that he not become a burden to others, he may look after his own interests first, before those of others. However, the following remark changes this hierarchical order: "He who abides by this order, will eventually be in need of others"[30]. The ideas of lovingkindness put the interest of fellow-man over that of oneself, at least as far as possible without directly endangering one's own existence.

According to the classical order preserved by Rabbi Aqiva, a person in the desert should not offer his water to his fellow man, if he himself needs it to survive. He is supposed to see to it that his fellow could live along with him, but his own life is his first priority. A view reported in the name of an unknown sage, Ben Petora, on the other hand, called for self-sacrifice in favour of one's fellow man[31].

Likewise, the alternatives of adjudication and compromise show a different setting of the hierarchical order. According to some opinions, justice should always be administered, while others advised the judge to bring about a compromise[32]. Thus, in the latter view, the values of consensus and peace are greater than those of truth and justice.

1. On the ethics of virtue cf. Frankena, **Ethics**, pp. 63-69; and Hoffe, **Lexikon**, pp. 257-259.

2. M 'Avot 1:12.

3. M 'Avot 2:9. See my "'al Limmud haTorah shebe'al Peh", **Sinai** 86 (1980) pp. 167-173.

4. Cf. Plato's Dialogues, **Charmides, Laches** and **Protagoras**; and Aristotle's **Nicomachean Ethics**.

5. BT Tamid 32 a.

6. M 'Avot 4:1.

7. Especially 10-15.

8. M 'Avot 5:10; cf. Federbush, pp. 117-119.

9. JT Bava Qama 8:5, 6 c top; BT Ketubot 50 b; Federbush, p. 119 f.

10. Cf. supra ch. 2 (d).

11. JT Chagigah 2:1, 77 a. On the middle-way see Steven S. Schwarzschild, "Moral Radicalism and 'Middlingness' in the Ethics of Maimonides", in **Studies in Medieval Culture**, 11, (1977), pp. 65-94.

12. M 'Avot 6:8.

13. JT Qiddushin 4:12, 66 d; cf. BT Ta'anit 11 a quoted below.

14. BT Yoma 23 a, quoting Jud. 5:31.

15. BT Pesachim 113 b, Megillah 28 a, Qiddushin 71 a, Bava Metsia 30 a.

16. BT Ta'anit 11 a.

17. BT Berakhot 28 b.

18. BT Betsah 32 b.

19. M 'Avot 2:14; cf. my **Law and Religion**, p. 36.

20. M 'Avot 2:1.

21.   M 'Avot 4:15.

22.   M 'Avot 5:10-15.

23.   'Avot deR. Nathan, A 3; B 4.

24.   M 'Avot 1:1.

25.   BT 'Avodah Zarah 20 b; M Sotah 9 end.

26.   'Avot 4:2.

27.   Lev. 19:2; Deut. 13:5; 28:9; Sifre ad Deut. 11:22; Mekhilta ad Ex. 15:2; BT Sotah 14 a; Gen. Rabba 8:13; Lev. Rabba 24:4; Deut. Rabba 1:12.

28.   R. Joshua b. Levi, BT Berakhot 7 a; cf. Maimonides, **Mishneh Torah,** De'ot 1:6.

29.   Lev. 19:18.

30.   BT Bava Metsia 33 a; Spero, p. 359 n.63.

31.   Sifra ad Lev. 25:36; cf. Shelomoh Pines, **Beyn Machshevet Israel leMachshevet ha'Amim,** (Jerusalem: 1977), pp. 9-11; Achad Haam, **Haposechim 'al shney hase'ifim.** HaShiloach 23 (1910), and 'Al **Parashat Derakhim** 2, trans. L. Simon, (1946), p. 132; Rabbi A.I. Kook, **Mishpat Kohen,** 143; Spero, **Morality,** pp. 218-227; L. Jacobs, "Greater love hath No Man" and Chaim Z. Reines, "The Self and the Other", both in Kellner, pp. 175-183, 162-174; Jakob J. Petuchowski, "The Limits of Self-Sacrifice", in Fox, **Ethics,** pp. 103-118; see infra ch. 19.

32.   BT Sanhedrin 6 b.

19. CONFLICT OF HALAKHIC DUTIES

(a) Categories of Conflict

In this chapter we will discuss the phenomenon of ethical conflict in relation to Halakhah[1]. The most important category of conflict is the **machloqet** (controversy), between individuals or schools of thought. The rule of second order to solve this problem is **halakhah** in its primary meaning, i.e. the norm which should be followed[2].

Another category of conflict is the distinction, previously discussed, between the legal and moral norm, such as **din** and **lifnim mishurat hadin, bediney 'adam and bediney shamayim, or din and derekh tovim.** As already mentioned, the rule of the second order calls upon the conscientious person to prefer the norms of the second type. Sometimes these norms led to a change of the law, so that the norm of the second type actually became one of the first type[3].

We have also spoken of the distinction between the **Noachide Commandments** and the Halakhah leading to a number of conflicts[4]. While we would have liked to see the rule of the second order in favour of the former, the prevalent view in rabbinic literature is often in favour of the latter.

A similar category of conflict is that between **dina demalkhuta** (the law of the kingdom), and Halakhah, and here again, opinions differ as to the exact rule of the second order to solve the conflict[5]. Likewise, **minhag** (custom), causes conflict when people of different places meet, or when a person moves from the area of one minhag to that of another. The rules of the second order, in these cases, remind us of those of Private International Law[6].

Conflicts may likewise arise between Halakhah and individual needs or conscience as a result of the generality of the former and the variety of the latter. In such instances, the rule of second order will be chosen by the individual, either by intuition or according to some rational principle established by himself. The choice may often reflect a basic attitude adopted by the person as a result of genetic or environmental factors.

Finally, a conflict may arise in Halakhah, as in other legal or moral systems, between different values and goals of the system, or between different duties which cannot be observed simultaneously. A rule of the second order is therefore needed to determine which of the two should be preferred.

(b) Rules of the Second Order

The oldest rule of second order for the solution of conflicting views is mentioned in the Torah: "If a legal case is too difficult for you... of any dispute in your gates, you shall go up to the place chosen by God, to the levitical priests and to the judge in office at that time... you must abide by the decision they pronounce for you..."[7].

According to the rabbinical interpretation, not the litigants but the judges of the lower court refer their controversy to the supreme court. They were to report: "Thus was my interpretation of the law, and thus my colleague's..."[8]. In theory, therefore, every conflict had to be solved by an authoritative decision of the highest court, and the many controversies, such as of the Hillelites and Shammaiites, were thought to be deplorable[9].

On the other hand, a more pluralistic attitude towards the controversies could also be perceived. Both views were said to express the will of the Living God[10], who was obviously able to establish the unity beyond the diversity, to make **unum ex pluribus**.

Moreover, according to a later formulation, the very process of Halakhah was in need of controversy: "If the Torah had been given (clear-)cut, it would have missed a leg to stand on... Finally, the Halakhah is according to the opinion of the majority. (The existence of the controversies) is needed in order to allow the Torah be interpreted even in forty-nine conflicting ways"[11].

While this rule of the second order follows from the need to maintain the unity of the people and to free the agenda from the controversies of the past, other rules of the same category are needed to bridge the conflict between Halakhah and individual needs or conscience.

Thus, a person may feel that obedience to Halakhah, at a certain moment, would desecrate the Divine Name and constitute a far greater evil than the act of disobedience. In such a situation, he is to decide for himself which is the lesser evil or the ethical preference: "Better to commit an offence in secret, than to do so in public, lest the Divine Name be desecrated... If a person feels that his evil inclination overcomes him, let him go to a place where he is unknown, let him wear black clothes and do what his heart wishes, lest the Divine Name be desecrated"[12].

While the above-mentioned text probably refers to the predicament of sexual deviation, the following even includes idolatry as a viable option:

"King David, after the rebellion of Absalom, intended to commit an act of idolatry (and to perish), rather than to permit the desecration of the Divine Name (by God having permitted such an injustice)"[13].

Another text speaks of King David having extradited the sons of King Saul to the Gibeonites, and thereby having violated the rule that children should not be responsible for their parents' sins. The justification was that "it was better to extract a letter of the law than to desecrate the Divine Name"[14]. The idea, that the extradition was necessary to prevent a desecration of the Name, seems to refer to the fact that the Gibeonites were strangers and should not be discriminated against. David was said to have violated a rule of the law as the lesser evil.

In this context, the use of the term **letter of the law** needs to be explained. In order to stress the seriousness of the desecration, reference should have been made to a whole commandment, or a whole sentence which must give way, while the extraction of only a letter is not really the strongest alternative. Here, the speaker probably had in mind the Pauline argument against the rabbinic preference given to the letter, rather than to the spirit[15]. While in general, according to the Jewish attitude, every letter counted and should not be disregarded in favour of the spirit, where the desecration of the Divine Name was concerned, the letter had to give way.

An example for the possibility of disregarding a rule in order to prevent greater evil, is the decision to record the oral law in writing. Here, too, it was said that "better to extract the Torah, than to let the Torah be forgotten"[16]. We should note the former alternative vis-a-vis the one just mentioned. In this case, the idea was that you could violate even the Torah in general, not only a single rule, word or letter, to keep it in mind. This was similar to the preference given, at the time of Ezra, to the Assyrian-Babylonian version of the Torah, which was more readable than that of the tradition of the Holy Land, preserved by the Samaritans[17].

On a less ideological level, one expressed the idea that "the **chaver** (member of the brotherhood of the rabbis) should sometimes commit a minor transgression, to save the unlearned from committing a major one"[18]. This is a practical example of the conflict between the general norm and the needs or conscience of the individual, as solved by giving preference to the latter[19].

(c) Conflicting Values

Indeed, the Halakhah did not always insist on strict obedience. Sometimes the negative consequences were thought to justify a deviation from the law, even a **priori**. In the decision-making process of such cases, preference was given to teleological over conceptual thinking, and ethical considerations surmounted purely legal reasons.

Perhaps the best example of such an orientation is the problem of sharing food with sinners, which was also discussed in Christian teaching[20]. According to a rule of the pious, a member of their brotherhood had to refrain from eating at the table of an unlearned person, lest he eat any food before tithing[21]. Nevertheless, if such an unlearned person is so annoyed by the refusal that he vows never again to share a meal with the pietist[22], the latter should once accept the invitation of sharing the Sabbath meal, to show his good intention[23].

Likewise, the strict rules of the pietists did not permit them consumption of wine or oil of the unlearned, because of their disregard of the laws of purity[24]. Nevertheless, no objection was made against accepting donations of wine and oil for libations in the Temple without distinguishing between learned and unlearned donors[25]. This was done lest those whose donation were rejected build a sanctuary for themselves, including their own purification ceremonies[26]. Therefore, in Jerusalem, even the unlearned were considered trustworthy concerning the purity of earthen vessels and of heave-offering[27], and this was justified by the need to promote the sense of solidarity[28].

A similar attitude can be traced in the rule that the learned person should be restrained in criticizing the unlearned for disregarding rabbinical commandments. The reason is that the technique of admonition had been forgotten[29]. This was definitely so where the unlearned had mistakenly refrained from something which was actually permissible[30]. The reason given for this self-restraint of the rabbis was their apprehension, lest such permission lead to a general attitude of permissiveness on the part of the unlearned.

But even in cases where the practice of the unlearned violated rabbinical law, the learned were warned not to rush forward with criticism. The rule was established that the unlearned should rather break the law out of ignorance, than through the criticism come to transgress on purpose[31]. A similar formulation of the same approach is the saying that Jews should rather eat meat which was ritually slaughtered, though there be another ritual flaw in it, than to eat meat which was not even ritually slaughtered[32]. Both formulations are purpose-oriented, and illustrate the practical approach of the speakers.

Another conflict of values is that between truth and peace. While truth is seen as the Seal of God[33], a person should sometimes say an untruth, if that is what is necessary to promote peace[34]. This is not only an expression of the higher ranking of peace than of truth in the rabbinical hierarchy of values, but equally of the social orientation and the teleology of the speakers.

The same idea found expression in the preference given to compromise over adjudication[35]. This view was based on the assumption that a solution worked out by the parties themselves would serve peace better than a solution imposed from above. The opposite view, viz. that a judge should not be satisfied with arranging compromises, emphasized the violation of truth by any compromise, and the duty of the judge to discover the truth.

Likewise, many halakhic innovations were introduced for the sake of peace, although in each case this meant a deviation from law and tradition[36]. A discussion had probably preceded the decision as to whether these innovations were justified, and finally the value of peace was preferred to that of authenticity.

A similar conflict emerged between the values of obedience to the Torah and that of saving a life, which had to be solved by an ethical decision. Such a resolution was made during the Maccabean revolt, to give precedence to the needs of warfare over the Sabbath[37]. That decision became the basis for the general rule of the second order, that saving a life was preferable to the observance of the Sabbath[38]. There are a variety of reasons for this rule, one of them, that one should desecrate for the person in danger one Sabbath, in order to enable him to observe many Sabbath days, reflects the teleological discourse[39].

The rule must have been extended as situations demanded[40], until it was finally said that nothing should prevent the saving of a life except for idolatry, sexual offences and killing[41]. This decision was connected with the famous controversy of "two people being together in the desert, one having a bottle of water"[42].

Again, the same tension between the values of obedience to Torah, on the one hand, and utilitarian thought on the other, can be seen in a series of legal innovations, which were justified **mipeney tiqqun ha'olam** (in order to improve the world)[43]. Each of these rules was the result of a discussion between traditionalists and innovators, the latter prevailing by the said reason.

An existential and theological controversy likewise arose among the rabbis, as to whether love of God or awe of God should be chosen as educational goals of Jewish life[44]. Both values were emphasized by the Torah[45], but the choice between them depended, certainly, upon the character of each person, which in turn reflected genetic and environmental factors.

Even ordinary conflicts between two duties of Halakhah were probably solved by reference to their respective values. Thus, the rule that a person should prefer the mandatory over the prohibitive commandment when the two clashed with one another, was not just a matter of formality[46]. As shown by Nachmanides, the positive form of worship was better adapted to express the love of God, while injunctions usually raised feelings of awe or fear of God[47].

Likewise, wherever Halakhah gave precedence to one rule over another, there must have been an argument about the respective value of each of them. For instance, the rule that the offering or the prayer which occurs more often is to be given preference[48]. The ordinary person would pay greater attention to the unusual item, but the educational goal of the rabbis was to realize the great ideas in everyday life, rather than those being elevated on special occasions[49].

A series of rules of the second order in conflict of duties is listed in the Mishnah[50], where the moral evaluation can easily be detected in all three items[51].

1   On the problem of conflict see Schrey, **Einfuehrung,** 153-163; R. Dahrendorf, **Society and Democracy in Germany,** (New York: 1967), chs. 9-13; W. Vossenkuhl, "Konflikt", in Hoeffe, **Lexikon,** 132-133; D. Mieth, "Konflikt", in Stoeckle, **Woerterbuch,** 162-164.

2   Cf. **ET,** s.v. **halakhah.**

3   Cf. supra ch. 13 b.

4   Cf. supra ch. 13 c.

5   BT Gittin 10 b. Cf. **ET,** s.v. **dina demalkhuta dina;** S. Shilo, **Dina demalkhuta Dina,** (Jerusalem: 1975).

6   Cf. M Pesachim 4:1-5; and my **Introduction,** ch.1.

7   Deut. 17:8-10.

8   Sifre Deut. 152.

9   T Sanhedrin 7:1.

10 BT 'Eruvin 13 b.

11 JT Sanhedrin 4:2, 22 a.

12 BT Qiddushin 40 a.

13 BT Sanhedrin 107 a.

14 BT Yevamot 79 a.

15 2 Cor. 3:6; Rom. 2:29; 7:6.

16 BT Temurah 14 b.

17 T Sanhedrin 4:7; JT Megillah 1:11, 71 bc; BT Sanhedrin 21 b.

18 BT 'Eruvin 32 b.

19 In this context see the discussion of Maimonides' **'al derekh harov** (Guide 3:34) in my **Dat haNetsach**, 22 ff. and infra ch. 23 (d).

20 Mt. 9:10-11; Marc 2:15-16; Luke 5:30; 15:2.

21 M Demai 2:2.

22 See M Nedarim 9:1; Mt. 15:5; cf. my note in **HarvThR** 59 (1966) p. 309, and my "Binding and Loosing", **JJS** 25 (1974) p. 92 ff.

23 M Demai 4:2.

24 M Chagigah 2:7; cf. Luke 11:37 ff.

25 M Chagigah 3:4.

26 R. Jose, BT Chagigah 22 a.

27 M Chagigah 3:6.

28 BT Chagigah 26 a, quoting Jud. 20:11, saying that all the men of Israel gathered, united as one man.

29 BT 'Arakhin 16 b.

30 BT Pesachim 50 b - 51 a.

31 BT Sabbath 148 b.; Betsah 30 a (applying the rule even to biblical commandments).

32 BT Qiddushin 21 b.

33 BT Sabbath 55 a.

34 BT Yevamot 65 b; note the three traditions in the name of R. Elazar ben Simon, that one should not say something which will be rejected, that one could sometimes say a falsehood and that one should indeed do so. See also BT Ketubot 17 a.

35 BT Sanhedrin 6 b; cf. supra ch. 17 (a).

36 M Gittin 5:8-9; Shevi'it 4:3, 5:9; Sheqalim 1:3. cf. ET 7, pp. 712-724; Jacobs, **Tree**, p. 38 ff., and my "'al hashalom", in **Levav Shalem: Divrey Torah le'illuy nishmato shel Shlomoh Bacharach**, (Jerusalem: 1971), pp. 63-67.

37 Cf. my "Mimishnat Chassidim".

38 JT Yoma 8:5, 45 b top; BT Yoma 82 a, 85 b.

39 JT Yoma 8:5, 45 b.

40 Another formulation, Mekhilta deR. Ismael, Ki Tissa; BT Yoma 85 a.

41 BT Yoma 82 a.

42 BT Bava Metsia 62 a top; supra ch. 18 (c).

43 M Gittin 4:2-9, 5:3, 9:4; 'Eduyot 11:13.

44 BT Sotah 31 a; cf. infra the rule that the mandatory commandment takes precedence over the prohibitive one, and Nachmanides ad. Ex. 20:8.

45 Deut. 10:12.

46 BT Yevamot 3 b.

47   Nachmanides ad Ex. 20:8.

48   M Zevachim 10:1; CF. ET, Subject index, S.V. **tadir.**

49   Cf. the preference of the awe of the mother and the honour of the father, Sifra Lev.
     19:3.

50   M Zevachim 1:7.

51   The preference of substituting another animal for the firstborn donkey means a choice
     of making a sacrifice, rather than killing the donkey without apparent purpose. The
     preference of the outshoeing ceremony over the levirate marriage probaly reflects Greek
     and Roman rejection of the levirate marriage. The preference of the marriage of the
     female servant over her redemption is in accordance with the woman's expectations,
     while redemption would be treacherous behaviour.

20. CHOICE AND INTENTION IN RABBINICAL THOUGHT

(a) Omnipotence

The problem of free choice, as well as of will and intention, occupied an important place in rabbinical thought[1]. The main difficulty was the reconciliation of the idea of indeterminism with that of divine omniscience and omnipotence. According to the formulation ascribed to R. Aqiva, "everything is subject to omniscience, yet freedom is given"[2]. The intention of the author was probably to distinguish between ordinary prescience, which seems to be in conflict with human freedom, and the particular prescience ascribed to God. The latter could be a kind of knowledge totally different from our own, i.e. it could be a prescience without impairing the freedom of human will.

As a result of divine self-restraint, one could also understand that "everything is dependent upon the will of Heaven except for the fear of Heaven"[3]. While the disposition of every person is predetermined, his conscience and spiritual life are open-ended. Moreover, even the external situation of a person, though predetermined by divine omnipotence, nevertheless reflects the will of the person concerned. "Everyone is led on the path which he himself has chosen"[4]. God is perceived as exercizing self-restraint in order to respect the will of the person, and man is told not to rely on divine intervention, but to accept responsibility for his own life.

A determinist attitude expresses itself in various prayers asking for divine intervention. For instance, there is a prayer for being saved from temptation, and for the victory of the good over the evil inclination of the person[5]. There would be little sense in such prayers if we presumed complete freedom of will. Take, for instance, the saying of Simon ben Zoma that the virtue of bravity consisted of overcoming one's inclination[6]. The brave do not need divine intervention, and would therefore be precluded from developing this particular virtue.

Obviously, freedom of will is not identical with freedom of action. Even if we accept an indeterminist viewpoint, it applies only to good or evil intentions, not to their execution. The latter depends upon the situation, the resources of the person, lucky or unlucky circumstances, etc. The prayer may therefore refer to the act, rather than to the will itself. This is the meaning of the following formulation: "Master of the Worlds, You know that we would like to act according to Your will, and that the leaven in the dough and political oppression prevent it. May it be Your will to save us from both, so that we will return to the cordial observance of the laws of Your will"[7].

We could define the system of free will, against the background of omnipotence, as a kind of **soft determinism**, which imposes responsibility in spite of the genetic and environmental factors determining human behaviour. Although any act is seen as conditioned by these causes, it also reflects the will of the individual to transcend them, even if his will is often unsuccessful. The will to change, not the change itself, counts as fear of Heaven, for "the Compassionate One acquits the accused, if he has acted under constraint"[8]. Moreover, omnipotence is interpreted in a way respecting human will, therefore granting support to the aspiration of the individual, in spite of the limits imposed upon the act due to some degree of determinism.

(b) Presumptions of Behaviour

Like any legal system, Halakhic discourse developed a number of presumptions concerning human behaviour, and these presumptions derived from determinism. This is in line with the modern behavioral sciences, such as psychology, sociology, biology, anthropology and economics. We tend to explain human action by way of various concepts derived from psycho-analysis, such as aggression, neurosis, repression, complex and frustration. The behaviorist manipulation of human reaction in particular, as developed by B.F. Skinner, has had a great influence on our understanding of the causality of human behaviour.

While in principle Halakhah accepted human freedom of choice, it nevertheless took notice of these factors. This was primarily the result of observation of human behaviour and its regularity. If one declared, for instance, that the rebellious son was to be executed because otherwise he would end up as a murderer[9], for this purpose one disregarded the factor of free choice. The justification of this approach was the fact that the situation had to be taken care of by teleology, which demanded foresight rather than retrospection.

Likewise, the biblical rule justifying the killing of the thief while he was breaking in at night, is based on such a presumption, viz. that the owner would defend his property and that the thief would in turn kill him[10]. Such a presumption is expressed in the idea that certain forms of human behaviour can be expected, as fitting the concept of determinism. A similar rule of Halakhah is derived from the presumption that any person would protect his property[11].

Without a minimum of foreseeability regarding human behaviour, Halakhah, as well as other rational normative systems, could not function. Hence, the series of presumptions about what a person usually avoids[12], and what he or she usually does[13], is quite essential.

Rabbinical thought explained the observance of each commandment as the result of the prior observance of another commandment, and the violation of a commandment as the result of another violation on an earlier occasion[14]. This again means that human action is predetermined by factors beyond one's control at the time of the decision. Every single act is seen as part of a sequence. Responsibility for every act follows from the failure to make an effort to break out of such a chain of cause and effect. In spite of determinism, human will is credited with the ability to wish to do good. This wish, rather than its realization, is what is required from everyone.

In summation, while rabbinical thought started from an indeterminist position, it took notice of various causes to human action, and developed a system of prediction. It was as if the sages held freedom as a possibility, which did not, however, affect statistics. Most people use their freedom of choice in a predictable way, so that determinism can be applied in social planning.

At the same time, Halakhah appealed to the individual and to the group to transcend this regularity, by making use of the potential of free will. The above-mentioned rules were based on the principles of **rov**, i.e. that you rely on statistics and probability[15], and of **chazaqah**, i.e. the presumption based on experience[16]. But the acts of individuals and groups are not totally explained by these principles; they also reflect the free choice of the people concerned.

(c) Responsibility

Obviously, if an individual is deprived of his freedom of action by another human being, he can not be held responsible for his deeds. We have already mentioned the rule of Halakhah, that "God acquitted any person who had committed an offence under constraint"[17]. Therefore, responsibility for an offence demands not only freedom of will but also of action. Where there is freedom of action, freedom of will can be presumed.

The question must be raised, however, as to whether undue influence on the will of the actor should also be considered as a case of duress. If the accused argued, for instance, that his freedom of will had been negated because of some of the above mentioned factors, he should perhaps be considered as having formed his will under coercion.

This is the reason why some rabbis are willing to exempt a person who had been kidnapped and brought up by Gentiles from any responsibility for the violation of Torah. Their view developed because "he who thinks that a certain act is permitted, cannot be held guilty, because he made his decision under duress"[18]. In this respect, we may say that **ignorantia iuris neminem excusat** is not applied in moral discourse. In law, however, especially in the law of tort, the maxim is accepted in Halakhah, as we will describe below.

The same reason was given to refrain from application of the rules of non-fraternization with Gentiles. It was held that idolatry outside of the Land of Israel was not practised with a guilty mind, but only as a tradition passed on from the earlier generations[19]. Hence, the responsibility for idolatry, and perhaps for other offences committed by non-Jews, actually rested on their ascendants as well, and therefore less on our contemporaries.

An **error of law** is not accepted as an excuse for the commission of an unlawful act. In this respect the act, though committed in ignorance, is deemed to be willful[20]. This is the logical conclusion from the commandment of constantly studying the law[21], and from the need of atonement for sins committed in error[22]. According to another opinion, ignorance or error equals a voluntary act, but only where it has caused a desecration of the divine name[23], and we have found acceptance of ignorance as an excuse in moral judgment.

A similar concept is **mistake**, which is recognized as an excuse. Mistake is called "coercion of the heart", i.e. an involuntary act[24]. A minor is considered as incapable of making a free decision. Therefore, the seduction of a minor was seen as coercion[25]. Both concepts are based on the notion of free will as a prerequisite for legal responsibility.

An exception to this rule is the giving of effect to a divorce with only the fictitious consent of the husband. In such a case, the husband was pressured by the rabbinical court until he uttered the formula of consent, and this was considered to be sufficient[26]. Halakhic paternalism and care for the freedom of the woman justified this legal fiction. A conditional divorce was likewise considered to be voluntary and effective, even if the husband did not want to fulfill the condition.

Take, for instance, the case of the husband who had stipulated that the divorce would be effective if he did not return from his trip abroad within a year. If he was prevented from returning in time by an act of God, the divorce nevertheless came into effect, as if he had wanted it[27]. This rule was introduced in order to prevent uncertainty of status, but the claim of volition as a prerequisite of divorce was not waived.

The readiness to identify fictitious consent with true consent was even applied to the disposition of property. If the transferor of value had been coerced, he was nevertheless thought to be bound by his declaration of consent. Following the precedent of the enforced divorce, one of the rabbis held the enforced consent to the transfer of property to be equal to real consent[28]. The legal fiction, having emerged from equitable considerations, acquired a life of its own, and even invaded situations where it caused injustice. This is an example of the high price paid for the employment of legal fictions, viz. the corruption of legal thought and the substitution of legalism for justice.

Likewise, responsibility for damage caused during sleep is not diminished because of the absence of free will: "A human being is always forewarned to bear responsibility, whether he is acting inadvertently or with premeditation, whether he is acting while awake or while sleeping. Thus, if he deprived another person of his sight or if he destroyed his goods, he must pay the full damage"[29]. The assumption seems to be that before falling asleep the defendant could have taken precautions, so that the damage caused during sleep was the indirect outcome of the earlier negligence. Here, we have the equivalent to the above-mentioned idea, that the commission of an offence was the effect of another committed on an earlier occasion.

Ethics justifies the extension of responsibility in torts beyond the boundaries of volition. This rule is not justified from a utilitarian point of view only, in order to raise awareness of responsibility, but also from a deontological point of view. Even if an act did not result from the free will of a person, this person should assume ministerial responsibility. This is linked to the idea that "a meritorious act is brought about through the agency of a good person, and a bad act is brought about through that of a bad person"[30]. The fact, therefore, that damage was caused through the agency of a sleeping person or a person who acted inadvertently, is reason enough for this person to search for the reason as to why he had been chosen for this purpose. The proper reaction to this situation is making good the damage, and though without fault, assuming responsibility.

A drunk person is bound by his acts in contract, tort and crime[31]. However, according to a later view, acts committed in extreme drunkenness will not be considered as willful acts[32].

(d) Intention

The mental element plays a major role in the rule concerning creative work, which is prohibited on Sabbath. If work has been done without the proper intention, it cannot be defined as creative work. Digging a hole, for instance, can be such a creative act constituting violation of the Sabbath. However, this is so only if the person digging had the intention of making the hole; if he merely had in mind to use the excavated earth, this was neither creative work nor a violation of the Sabbath[33].

Even with regard to other prohibitions, intention is, according to certain opinions, of the essence. The commission of the act without intention, or with an intention unrelated to the act, does not constitute an offence[34].

Proper intention is needed in prayer and in the observance of other mandatory commandments[35]. Scripture must be copied by the scribe with such an intention, and the same is necessary when writing a letter of divorce[36]. In the latter case, there is also a utilitarian reason, viz. to impose a cooling-off period, by prohibiting the use of ready-made forms.

Although proper intention is desirable in the fullfilment of any commandment, the value of the good deed undertaken without the proper intention is also understood. Therefore, it was said that a person should study Torah and observe the commandments even out of ulterior motives, for as a result he would be doing so in the future with the proper motive[37].

By the same token, it is said that God accepts the good intention which could not be realized, as if it had been, but not vice versa[38]. The evil intention is not considered as an evil act, even if the realization of the intention had only been prevented by external factors.

However, **a priori**, an evil intention is harshly criticized as a choice of evil by the free will. In this sense, "evil thoughts are worse than evil deeds"[39], which is an emphasis of the mental element of sin over that of the physical element. The author of the latter statement was probably in favour of a morality of intention, though he may have exaggerated in order to stress the need for mental purity.

In terms of intentional morality there was a tradition saying that "it is the same whether you do much or little; all depends upon the direction of your heart to God"[40]. The morality of intention is described through a number of rabbinical anecdotes and lives[41]. An evil intention, even if taking the form of a permitted act, was considered to be a moral evil and in need of expiation.

The corollary of this idea is the statement that "the commission of an offence for the sake of some good is of greater moral value than the observance of a mandatory commandment without good intention"[42]. This notion, corresponding with the view that the end justifies the means, could, of course, lead to anarchy. If the good intention could make up for the illegal act, the whole system of Halakhah would be replaced by an individualist and anomian approach. The last time that Judaism in fact experienced such an approach, was the Sabbatean movement during the 17th century[43].

It should be noted that the intention was important, so as not to blur the distinction between the will of God and that of man[44]. By identifying too much with the contents of the commandments, a person was in danger of losing touch with the concept of submitting to the divine will. The observance of the rule would then become an ontological necessity of his character, and not an act of worship. The latter was possible only out of a tension between natural behaviour and the obedience to positive commandments[45].

1   On the freedom of will and on responsibility cf. Frankena, **Ethics**, pp. 71-78; Raphael, **Moral Philosophy**, pp. 85-104; O. Hoeffe, "Freiheit", and A. Schoepf, "Wille", in Hoeffe, **Lexikon**", pp. 62 f., and 280 f., respectively. On Jewish Thought cf. D. Winston, "Free Will", in Cohen & Mendes-Flohr, pp. 269-274; M. Halevi Spero, **Judaism and Psychology: Halakhic Perspectives**, (New York: Ktav, 1980), p.39 ff.

2   M 'Avot 3:15; cf. Urbach, **The Sages**, ch. 11; this and the following quotations are discussed in Spero, **Judaism and Pshychology**, pp.39-41.

3   BT Berakhot 33 b.

4   BT Makkot 10 b.

5   BT Berakhot 60 b; JT Berachot 4:2, 7 d; BT Qiddushin 81 b.

6   M' Avot 4:1.

7   BT Berakhot 17 a.

8   BT Nedarim 27 a.

9   M. Sanhedrin 8:5.

10 BT Sanhedrin 72 a.

11 BT Pesachim 11 a.

12 E.g. BT Ketubot 10 a; Bava Metsia 5 b; Bava Batra 5 b; and see ET, 1, s.v. 'eyn 'adam......

13 BT Yevamot 25 a; and see ET, vol. 13, s.v. **chazaqah**, (c), pp. 693-713, and vol. 1, s.v. **umdena**, pp. 295-302.

14 M 'Avot 4:2; BT Yoma 39 a, 86 b. See also BT Yoma 38 b at the end, where the human effort is shown to cause divine support.

15 Cf. M. Taharot 5:7; Makhshirin 2:11; Tvul Yom 2:3.

16 Cf. ET, s.v. **chazaqah.**

17 BT Bava Qama 28 b.

18 BT Sabbath 68 b.

19 BT Chullin 13 b.

20 M 'Avot 4:13; cf. Justinian, **Digesta** 22:6:9 pr.

21 Deut. 6:7; 11:19; Jos. 1:8.

22 Lev. 4:27-31.

23 M 'Avot 4:4.

24 BT Shevu'ot 26 a.

25 BT Yevamot 33 b.

26 M 'Arakhin 5:6.

27 BT Ketubot 2 b.

28 BT Bava Batra 47 b ff.

29 M Bava Qama 2:6; cf E.E. Urbach, **The Halakhah**, ch. 12.

30 T Kippurim 4 (5):12, and parallels quoted by Lieberman.

31 T Terumot 3:1.

32 BT 'Eruvin 65 a, cf. G. Leibson, "The Criminal Liability of the Drunkard", DI, 3 (1972) pp. 71-89.

33 BT Chagigah 10 b top.

34 ET 6, s.v. **davar she'eno mitkaven,** p. 637.

35 BT Berakhot 13 ab; 'Eruvin 95 b-96 a; Pesachim 114 b; Rosh Hashanah 28 a-29 a; cf. Bachya ibn Paquda, **Duties of the Heart**, trans. M. Hyamson, (New York: Bloch, 1945), Introduction; H.G. Enelow, "The Struggle for Inwardness in Judaism", in **Kaufmann, Kohler Festschrift**, (Berlin: 1913), pp. 82-88; I. Tishbi, **Mishnat Hazohar**, (Jerusalem 1961), vol. 2, p. 247 ff.; and Robert Goldenberg, "Commandment and Conscience in Talmudic Thought", HarvThR 68 (1975) pp. 261-271.

36 BT Gittin 23 a.

37 BT Pesachim 50 b.

38 T Pe'ah 1:4; BT Qidushin 40 a; cf. R. Sa'adyah ben Josef Ga'on, **Book of Doctrines and Beliefs**, 5:8; Urbach, op. cit.

39 BT Yoma 29 a; Nazir 23 a bottom.

40 BT Berakhot 5 b; M Menachot 13:11.

41 BT Qiddushin 81 b.

42 BT Nazir 23 b; cf. Urbach, **The Sages**, ch. 13 end.

43 See G. Scholem, **The Messianic Idea in Judaism**, New York 1971, 78-141.

44 Sifra Qedoshim 11:22, ad Lev. 20:26; cf. M 'Avot 2:4 cf. supra ch. 14 (a).

45 Cf. Maimonides, **Mishnah Commentary**, Introduction to 'Avot, ch. 6.

21. EMOTION AND CONSCIENCE IN HALAKHAH

(a) Moral Intuition

According to one school of thought, ethics is a matter of emotion and intuition, rather than reason and cognition[1]. The question should be raised as to whether such a theory could be reconciled with Halakhic thought, or must be seen as contradicting its basically authoritarian and rational tendencies[2].

Rabbinical language locates moral considerations in the heart and kidneys, which seems to indicate emotion as a source of moral insight. Every person was said to have two kidneys, one to advise him to do good, and the other to advise him to commit evil deeds[3]. This statement corresponds with the distinction between the good and the evil **yetser** (inclination), located in the heart, both describing emotion rather than intellect.

Abraham was said to have known the rules of Torah through his kidneys, which God had created for this purpose: "Neither did his father teach him, nor did he have a teacher to study Torah. Therefore, God prepared his two kidneys to act as teachers to pour forth wisdom"[4]. This is a clear reference to the intuitive character of moral insights, at least in the absence of other sources of information.

In a psalm, King David was described as saying: "My God, I always wanted to do your will, and Your Torah was in my bowels"[5]. Since his rules of behaviour were described as being **Torah**, viz. revealed by God, we may infer that there could be revelation through intuition. This is the same virtue as that of the righteous person "having the Torah of his God in his heart"[6], and that promised by the prophet as a part of the new covenant[7].

In this sense, even an unlearned person could have a share in the Torah by observing its commandments: "If a person regrets that he has acquired wisdom but not learned Torah, and if he fears what he would do there (probably in the future world), his consolation should be the oath delivered by God to Israel, that Wisdom and Torah would be seen as one. Whoever fears God and observes rules of Torah, Wisdom and Torah are said to be in his heart"[8].

This is probably a reaction to Christian claims, that Gentiles had the Torah inscribed in their heart, while Jews, who actually studied and followed the sources, were really estranged from Torah[9]. Whereas Christians claimed they had the intuition of Torah, the rabbis ascribed this intuition only to those Jews who observed the commandments, even if not learned in Scripture or Oral Law.

Intuition is also a guide for the proper treatment of a person's body. If, for instance, the patient himself feels that he cannot keep the fast on the Day of Atonement, even though the doctors tell him that he can, he should break the fast and rely on his intuition[10]. The same should probably be said regarding a person's soul and its problems, which could also best be understood by the individual[11].

On the other hand, the rabbis called for the control of emotion by the intellect. The evildoers, they assumed, were **hem bireshut libbam** (under the control of their hearts), while the righteous **libbam bireshutam** (they controlled their hearts)[12].

(b) Feeling or Obedience

We have mentioned the view of some rabbis interpreting the commandment of the bird's nest as a call for compassion, while others rejected such an emotional approach and asked for an unconditional obedience to the divine will. The former understood the rule as an appeal to emotion, by ascribing the reason of the commandment to divine compassion, and calling upon man to imitate this attribute of God. The other held this rule to be, first and foremost, an opportunity for human beings to submit to the commandment[13].

This need not be understood as a rejection of the emotive approach altogether, but could be taken as an expression of preference of one emotion (dependence), over another (compassion). The observance of the **gezerot** (rules), though, reflects a deontological approach to the commandment, while the practice of **rachamim** (compassion), means the cultivation of a virtue.

The element of obedience also appears in the previously mentioned question and answer ascribed to R. Elazar ben Azaryah, with regard to the motive of refraining from prohibitions[14]. Again, this should not be taken as a rejection of emotion as a motive of religious activity. It is rather a recognition of the common element in the fulfillment of the commandments: the wish to express love to the Father in Heaven.

Perhaps we could say that the text demanded a certain distance between one's inclination and the performance of the divine will. By total internalization of the rules, we might lose their didactic effect and actually forget their divine source.

According to another formulation, the distance between the wills of God and man was not to be overemphasized. One should rather aim at "making the will of God ones's own will", so that God "would make the will of man His own"[15]. Such a total identification with the will of God, could obviously be realized only through emotion.

The emotive approach to ethics can be found in the central role played by the commandment of loving one's neighbour as oneself[16]. According to a tradition related to Hillel, this was the most important commandment of the Torah[17], which means that emotion is more important than action. Hillel's negative formulation, however, viz. that you should not do unto others what you would not like to experience from them, referred to action rather than to emotion[18].

Another preference for the emotive element is the prohibition of desiring the wife or property of the other[19], but here again, some interpreters belived this commandment to refer to action and not to mere feelings[20]. Their reason must have been to justify the inclusion of this commandment among the cardinal offences, which would be difficult if it concerned mere feeling.

The rabbis expressed, however, a number of warnings against sinful thoughts[21]. They even said that sinful thoughts are worse than the sinful act[22], referring to sexual desires[23], which emphasizes the greater importance of the **mens rea** than that of the **actus reus**. But this should be seen as a moralizing exaggeration, to impress those who felt no need at all to sanctify their thoughts and feelings.

(c) Intuition in Lawfinding

The above-mentioned attitude of R. Tarfon is an example of the emotive approach in law and morals. According to his view, a judge should use his intuition to deliver a socially justified judgment. In a case of conflicting claims as to the ownership of certain property, the judge should award it to the party who most needed help, instead of awarding it to the party having the best legal title. The opposite view was held by R. Aqiva, namely that the judge should not use compassion in the legal process, but only rely on rational and legal thought[24].

In this controversy the tension between **rachamim** (compassion), and din (justice), comes out well. While R. Tarfon aimed at the integration of emotion and reason, R. Aqiva called for a clear separation of the two functions. The judge could only decide according to reason, leaving his emotion to other situations. Only in exceptional circumstances, where the facts could not be determined, were the judges referred to their intuition[25].

Emotion is often understood to be a reflection of divine inspiration. We have mentioned the story about the 'Akhnai Oven, where the legitimacy of prophetic and metaphysical arguments was discussed[26]. Even after the rationalization of the halakhic process, we still hear about rabbis "being told from Heaven" which decision to make. Thus, inspiration and emotion were still important factors in the history of rabbinical law[27].

In any event, a judge was supposed to refrain from making a decision if he felt that he was deceived by one of the parties, even though the evidence and the law would seem to be in his favour[28].

The idea of inspiration is one of the innovations of Chassidism vis-a-vis traditional halakhic scholarship. The rulings of the **rebbe** (leader of a chassidic sect), are accepted by his followers without question, as a kind of revelation through intuition.

At present, certain decisions by ultra-orthodox rabbinical authorities without scriptural or traditional roots are being justified by reference to **Da'at Torah** (knowledge of Torah). This is an almost mystical concept, referring to the inspiration of a rabbi who is both scholar and pious, and studies Torah as a way of worship.

(d) Conscience

A special form of emotion is conscience, which can be divided into two: reflection about the past, and about the future. The former is a feeling of guilt for an act or an omission, the latter a feeling for the need of future action or forbearance. According to Erikson, the conscience develops in reaction to the ideal concepts and the reality as presented to the child from outside. While originally the views of the authority are accepted in their totality, gradually the child develops his own feeling of reality and of ideals, and of what should be selected out of those authoritative statements. At this stage autonomy is developed in the moral decision-making process[29].

Although rabbinical thought did not develop a concept of conscience, it had a number of concepts with a similar meaning. In a homily referring to Num. 21:27, R. Jochanan spoke of those who "master their inclination, and who account for the loss incurred by observing a commandment vis-a-vis its reward, and for the benefit incurred by committing a sin vis-a-vis its punishment"[30]. This **accounting** is a kind of probing of one's past behaviour carried out by conscience.

Conscienciousness is also known as the attitude of being troubled in one's heart as to whether one has acted correctly, and the opposite of **qalut rosh** (being frivolous)[31]. This means showing constant care for one's deeds and a seriousness in one's approach to life. Before engaging in prayer, a person should meditate and attain **weightiness in his head**[32], which is again a function of his conscience.

Of a number of commandments it was said that they were "given to the heart", which means that they were justiciable only in **foro interno** or in conscience[33]. There could be no legal enforcement, so that a special reference to the fact that God knows what is in the heart became necessary[34].

1   C.L. Stevenson, **Ethics and Language**, (New Haven: 1944); Frankena, **Ethics**, pp. 102-107; Schrey, **Einfuehrung**, pp. 99-107; Ricken, **Allgemeine Ethik**, pp. 30-35; M. Forschner, "Gefuehl", in Hoeffe, **Lexikon**, p.71.

2   Cf. Spero, **Morality**, p. 68, in favour of intuitions in Halakhah.

3   BT Berakhot 61 a.

4   Gen. Rabba 61:1; cf. Urbach, **The Sages**, ch. 13:1.

5   Cf. Ps. 40:9; Tanchuma Re'eh 14; Tanchuma Buber, Re'eh 12.

6   Ps. 37:31.

7   Jer. 31:32.

8   Deut. Rabba 11:6, ad Deut. 33:1 (description of Moses' death).

9   Rom. 2:14-16. But see already Deut. 30:14.

10   BT Yoma 83 a, referring to Prov. 14:10.

11   This follows from Prov. 14:10, speaking of grief and joy, not of physical matters. Cf. my **Law and Religion**, p. 131, referring to Rozenzweig's attitude.

12   Gen. Rabba 34:10, ad Gen. 8:21.

13   M Berakhot 5:3; on the other hand cf. Lev. Rabba 27:11 ad Lev. 22:28; cf. Urbach, **The Sages**, ch. 13; cf. ch 14 (a) and 15 (a).

14   Sifra Qedoshim, end, ad Lev. 20:22. See supra ch. 14 (a).

15   M 'Avot 2:4.

16   Lev. 19:18; cf. my '**Erkhey Mishpat**, p. 22.

17   BT Sabbat 31 a; the tradition is ascribed to R. Aqiva, JT Nedarim 9:3, 41 c.

18   On the negative formulation cf. Federbush, **Hamusar**, p. 41 ff. The reason for this limitation seems to be the context, i.e. the prohibition of revenge.

19   Ex. 20:14; Deut. 5:18.

20   Mekhilta deR Ishmael, **Bachodesh** 8.

21   Cf. BT Berakhot 12 b; Bava Batra 164 b; 'Avodah Zarah 20 b.

22   BT Yoma 29 a.

23   Rashi, ad loc.

24   M. Ketubot 9:2.

25   See supra ch. 17 (a).

26   BT Bava Metsia 59 b.

27   On metaphysical proof in the halakhic process see BT Sanhedrin 11 a. Cf. also E.E. Urbach, "Matai paseqah haNevu'ah?", **Tarbits**, 17, a. (1945), pp. 1-11; A.J. Heschel, "'Al Ru'ach ha Qodesh biyemey haBenayim": **Alexander Marx Jubilee Volume**, (New York: 1950); G. Scholem, **Uspruenge und Anfaenge der Kabbalah**, (Berlin: deGruyter, 1962), p. 210 f., and p. 218; I.B. Marcus, **Piety and Society: The Jewish Pietists of Medieval Germany**, (Leiden: Brill, 1981), p. 70, 163 n. 59; L. Jacobs, **Hassidic Thought**, (New York: Behrman, 1976), pp. 210-213; I. Englard, "Mysticisme et droit; reflexion sur les Liqute Halakhot de l'ecole de R. Nahman de Bratslav". **Melanges Marcel-Henri Pre'vost**, (Paris: 1982), pp. 191-205; Y. Elman, "R. Zadok Hakohen of Lublin on Prophecy in the Halakhic Process", **JLA Studies** 1 (1985) pp. 1-16.

28   Cf. Josef Qaro, **Shulchan 'Arukh, Choshen Mishpat** 15:3.

29   E.H. Erikson, **Childhood and Society**, 2nd. ed, (New York): 1963).

30   BT Bava Batra 78 b.

31   BT Chagigah 13 a.

32   M Berakhot 5:1.

33   Sifra, Qedoshim, ad Lev. 19:14; BT Bava Metsia 58 b.

34   On conscience in Jewish thought see R. Artzt, "Imperative and Conscience in Jewish Law", in J.A. Sleeper & A.L. Mintz (eds.), **The New Jews,** (New York: Vintage, 1971), pp. 144-151; M. Greenberg, "Rabbinic Reflections on Defying Illegal Orders: Amasa, Abner, Joab", **Judaism** 19 (1970) pp. 30-37; M.R. Konvitz, "Individual Conscience and Group Consciousness", **Judaism** 20 (1971), pp. 153-166; M.R. Konvitz, **Judaism and the American Idea**, (New York: 1980), pp. 139-159; R. Goldenberg, "Commandment and Conscience in Talmudic Thought", **HarvThR** 68 (1975) pp. 261-271.

22. EVIL IN RABBINICAL THOUGHT

(a) Monism

The rabbinical concept of **ra'** (evil), describes first and foremost defectiveness. In this sense one speaks of a bad chattel, of a calamity or misfortune which happens to a person[1]. Evil is therefore something falling short of our expectation, and a failure in the expected function of a thing or a human being.

Acts of God are felt to be behind many such phenomena, and one should express one's submission to the divine will causing evil, just as credit should be given to God for anything positive[2]. When receiving bad news a person should say the blessing describing God as a truthful judge[3], which points to the divine source of evil and the human need for self-criticism and repentance.

The recital of the blessing does not, however, mean that evil is actually a means of finally causing good and therefore an expression of divine benevolence. The intention is rather to accept the evil as a just punishment, or as an otherwise legitimate act of God. In any case, the blessing ascribes the evil to the divine will, which is ultimately an expression of monism.

Indeed, rabbinical thought included mostly monist perceptions of evil. If one had to recite a blessing over bad news, it was on the assumption that God had acted as judge according to the stern measure. The term was **middat pur'anut** (measure of retribution), which is the antonym of **middah tovah** (measure of benevolence), and probably a synonym of **middah ra'ah** (measure of evil)[4]. Hence, good and evil form part of one system of divine justice, and are not two conflicting powers. Both, however, are often described as personal entities in dispute with each other.

An extremely monist attitude is reflected in a statement denying the existence of evil altogether, and claiming that whatever God does is for our benefit. Thus it was said that "whatever God does is for the good"[5], and that even death and suffering are included in the attribute of creation being very good[6]. The **middat yissurin** (measure of inflicting suffering), was beneficial for "bringing human beings into the future life". In this sense, not only the angel of death, but even hell was given the predicate very good[7]. The perception of evil was sometimes understood as an illusion, only due to human lack of understanding[8].

(b) Dualism

Sometimes, however, the source of harm is found in human action or intention. An evil eye and evil inclination are charged with the calamity befalling other persons[9], and the evil tongue is blamed for much harm[10]. Thus, evil as a source of suffering can be ascribed both to metaphysical and to human factors.

Sometimes God was even said not to have used His name in conjunction with darkness and evil. Thus, just as God had declared light to be good after it had become an independent entity, darkness, another creation and independent entity, functioned as a synonym of evil[11].

This was probably meant to ascribe evil to divine creation at the beginning of the world, and henceforth as an independent entity, like light and darkness. While having originated once in the divine will, evil is now an independent force, whether a cosmic or human entity.

Likewise, God was said to be the source of **middot tovot** (measures of good, benevolence) but not of **middah ra'ah** (measure of evil). The latter does not originate from God, for "all His ways are **'emet** (in this context, a synonym of **chesed,** i.e. consistency). "Through the evil deeds of people, the measure of evil goes out against them"[12].

With regard to falsehood in particular, the entire responsibility was put upon the human party. "God is the Creator of everything, except for **middat sheqer** or **middat shaw** (measure of falsehood), which is the invention of mankind"[13].

Hence, evil was perceived by the rabbis in a dualist as well as monist way, though the concepts of monotheism and omnipotence pointed in the former direction, and the latter must have been the result of the tendency of concretization and personification.

(c) Theodicy

The belief in the omnipotence, omniscience and benevolence of God sometimes made it difficult for rabbinical thought to grasp the concept of evil[14]. It can be seen as a punishment for individual or national sin, as a divine test of his saint, or as another execution of the will of God which may be beyond human understanding. The Book of Job developed the idea of the last alternative. In the present day, the problem has taken on a special urgency through the **sho'ah,** which destroyed a third of Jewry during World War II.

The first thing in traditional thought to be reexamined is the monistic approach, namely that evil is actually part of the comprehensive harmony of the world. The opposite is the dualistic approach, that evil is always in conflict with, and sometimes triumphing over the good.

As a result of the experience of the **sho'ah**, perhaps a third interpretation of the doctrine of divine attributes is preferable. According to the psalmist, "God judges the righteous and God is angry every day"[15], so that any evil wish or evil idea as expressed and carried out at the time of anger, may indeed be realized with divine acquiescence[16].

On the basis of this teaching, the Holocaust could be seen as an example of divine ire, which exists beside divine benevolence. Indeed, this same ire is said to have led God to want to destroy Israel on several occasions[17], and only the prayers of Moses prevailed upon Him to change His mind. The Holocaust could therefore be perceived as an analogous event, only without the corresponding intercession.

When we say that God is good[18] and benevolent, we use an anthropomorphism, which does not do justice to the freedom of God. God is what He chooses to be[19], and cannot be pressed into any concept or doctrine. He is given the attributes of stern judgment as well as compassion, which means that we do not really know how to offer a consistent definition of His ways. According to one formulation, He would like us "to pray that His compassion might overcome His stern judgment"[20], which means that His attitude is actually open-ended.

This is the meaning of the statement: "I am God, and there is none else. I form the light, and create darkness; I make the whole and create evil. I am God who does all these things"[21]. Therefore Job asks: "What, shall we receive good at the hand of God, and shall we not receive evil?"[22].

One of the possible ways to relate to the **sho'ah** is by putting the blame on God, as well as on ourselves, and hoping for a **tiqqun** (reparation), to make up for the evil of the past through additional good in the future. In a daring statement of Resh Laqish, God Himself is said to be in need of atonement for having committed an injustice during creation[23]. In the same vein, God may be said to be in need of atonement for the evil of the Holocaust, and we are the ones to help Him atone.

A similar expression, putting the blame for human cruelty upon God for not having intervened, is quoted in the name of R. Simon bar Yochai. The verse describing the complaint of Abel's blood is taken as an accusation of God together with that of **Cain**: "Though it is difficult to say so and to give such an interpretation, this was like the case of the two athletes fighting with each other in the presence of the king. If the king had wanted to do so, he could have stopped the fight, but he decided not to interfere, so that one of them prevailed and killed the other. The dying athlete had kept crying, why had'nt the king listened to his voice"[24].

By no means should the guilt-sharing on the part of God lead to the evasion of human responsibility. While the Creator may have a right to destroy His creation, no such right has ever been granted to a human being. We could even imagine the possibility of acquitting God for human crime by the insight that the grant of free will to man was a kind of abdication by God as direct administrator of the world. It was like a declaration of non-interference by God, and called for the human assumption of responsibility for evil.

According to one formulation, the prophetic warning "not to trust the neighbour"[25], referred to one's own evil inclination, which must be suspect. The source of evil advice is in ourselves[26], and evil is not metaphysical, but moral. But every person also has good inclinations, and is able to opt against evil. Indeed, there can be no good without the freedom to choose evil, so that even the evil inclination can be seen as good[27].

The concept of evil is needed for the reeducation of mankind in order to prevent another Holocaust. The emphasis put upon the behavioural sciences in contempory society, especially psycho-analysis, has spread the value-free approach in other spheres of life as well. Similarly, the prevalent ideologies of individualism, relativism and pluralism have all undermined the ideas of absolutes, duties, responsibility and guiltfeeling, so that little is being said against evil, and the talk about it is quite unpopular.

The concepts of duty, virtue, sin and evil have been misused by religious, political and family authorities for too long, and the attitude of the present generation is the reaction to such misuse. However, even if they have been misinterpreted and misused, they still remain the foundations of human society and of human rights. Without a clear condemnation of evil, the concept of duty and the feeling of guilt, there is little hope for a moral future of mankind. All this depends upon our faith in God and our feeling of responsibility, so that theodicy can become a model for our own conscienciousness.

1   E. g. Gen. 41:3-4, 19-21; Lev. 27:33; Jer. 24:2; M Me'ilah 6:4; BT Bekhorot 14 b.

2   M Berakhot 9:5.

3   BT Pesachim 50 a.

4   BT Berakhot 48 b; Yoma 76 a.

5   BT Berakhot 60 b, cf. Ta'anit 21 a; Gen. Rabba 3:6; Midrash Ps. 5:7 (edition of S.
    Buber, 54).

6   Gen. Rabba 9:8-9.

7   Gen. Rabba 9:8-9.

8   BT Sotah 35 a, referring to the positive intention in the death of the people of
    Canaan: Num. 13:32.

9   M 'Avot 2:9,11.

10 BT 'Arakhin 15 a.

11 Gen. Rabba 3:6. This saying and those quoted hereafter may represent Parsee influnces,
    perceiving the constant struggle between the forces of good and evil.

12 Seder Elijah Rabba 7(8), referring to the plagues of Egypt.

13 Pesiqta Rabbati 24, end, referring to the two descriptions of false testimony in the
    Decalogue. According to medieval Jewish philosophy (e.g. Gersonides, **Milchamot Hashem,**
    Bk. 4, trans. J.D. Bleich, **Providence in the Philosophy of Gersonides,** (New York:
    1973), pp. 59-61; quoted by C. Sirat, **History of Jewish Philosophy in the M.A.,**
    (Cambridge: U.P., 1985), p. 297), evil is the deprivation of good. According to Jewish
    Mysticism, as shown by G. Scholem, evil has an existence of itself; cf. Sirat, p. 249.
    Abraham ibn Ezra and Abraham ibn Daud declared evil and defect to be independent
    from God and not to be caused by Him; cf. I. Husik, **A History of Medieval Jewish
    Philosophy,** (New York: 1930), pp. 195, and 228-231. See also Harry Blumberg, "Theories
    of Evil in Medieval Jewish Philosophy", HUCA 43 (1972) pp. 149-168.

14 Cf. Richard L. Rubenstein, **The Cunning of History,** (New York: 1978); Rubenstein,
    "Evil", in Cohen & Mendes-Flohr, pp. 203-210; B.L. Sherwin, "Theodicy", in op. cit.,
    pp. 959-970; Eliezer Berkovits, **Faith after the Holocaust,** (New York: Ktav, 1973);
    Harold S. Kushner, **When bad things happen to good people,** (New York: 1981).

15 Ps. 7:11.

16 BT Berakhot 7 a.

17 E.g. Ex. 32:10; Num. 14:12; 16:21; 17:10.

18 Cf. L. Jacobs, **A Jewish Theology,** (New York: 1973), pp. 125-135.

19 Ex. 3:14.

20 BT Berakhot 7 a.

21 Is. 45:6-7.

22 Job 2:10.

23 BT Chullin 60 b, refering to the offering of atonement on the day of Newmoon: Num.
    28:15.

24 Gen. Rabba 22:9.

25 Mic. 7:5.

26 BT Chagigah 16 a.

27 Gen Rabba 9:7.

D. POSTTALMUDIC ETHICS

23. MEDIEVAL PHILOSOPHY AND ETHICS

(a) Rational Criticism

Medieval Jewish philosophy is the result of the encounter between Jewish and Greek thought. This encounter had already taken place in antiquity, and its most important creative outcome had been the oeuvre of Philo of Alexandria[1]. A similar encounter took place during the 10th century through the spreading of Greek writings in Arabic translations and the study of Muslim philosophers. The result of the latter was R. Sa'adyah Ga'on's **Book of Doctrines and Beliefs**. A similar willingness to encounter general philosophy and use it for a new interpretation of Jewish sources persisted among Spanish Jewry.

Reason as a source of information and as a legal authority played an important role in the **Qara'ite** argument against Halakhah. Take, for example, the epistle of Sahl ben Matsliach (910-990 C.E.), and its call against the reliance on tradition instead of personal examination of each problem[2]. The author emphasized the personal responsibility of every individual towards God. Everyone must follow Scripture and reason, he claimed, rather than rely upon the authority of parents and teachers. According to his view, custom was not a source of law, but required investigation, whereas no such investigation was necessary for Torah[3].

This was obviously the reaction of the sectarians against what they considered to be the prejudice of the rabbinic leadership regarding the interpretation of Torah. Talmudic tradition, as handled by the **Ge'onim**, had spread many unproven opinions, against which Qara'ites offered rational criticism.

(b) Sa'adyah Ga'on

Sa'adyah Ga'on (882-942 C.E.), accepted the challenge of the Qara'ites by adopting rational methods of exegesis and philosophical discourse in matters of faith. He was even ready to reinterpret the Mishnah and to differ from the interpretation of the Talmud[4]. Similarly, some of his decisions in

Halakhah were truly innovative, and met with the criticism of his colleagues[5].

Nevertheless, the legitimacy of his rationalist endeavour was undeniable, owing to the great recognition accorded to his knowledge of Jewish law. Sa'adyah was both the leading scholar and teacher of Halakhah, and at the same time a spokesman of Judaism. It was through this combination that he became the founder of medieval Jewish theology.

Sa'adyah indeed recognized the authority of reason, and thereby came to develop his synthesis of Halakhah and philosophy. In terms of what we have been studying, first in the Bible and then in Talmud and Midrash, this was also a synthesis between theonomy and autonomy. The Bible, i.e. theonomy, is said to have assented to human thought, as based on **yedi'at hanir'eh** (sensation), **madda' hasekhel** (nous, intuitions), and **yedi'at ma shehahekhre'ach mevi' 'elaw** (necessary inference)[6].

As a result of this referral, any anthropomorphic or deterministic passages of the Bible should be reinterpreted in order to harmonize them with reason. However, this referral does not justify the abolition of commandments, the doctrine of creation or the denial of miracles and resurrection[7]. We could say that the use of reason for the latter purposes was **ultra vires** the basic norm, that being theonomy. Autonomy is granted only for the better implementation of theonomy, not in order to replace it.

As already mentioned, most Halakhists did not follow Sa'adyah's lead, but preferred to dispute the value of reason. In order to defend Jewish legal tradition they rejected the right of rational criticism altogether, and thereby not only occupied an inferior position vis-a-vis their adversaries, but even constituted a regression as opposed to their rabbinic predecessors. This irrational position, the loss of creativity and the reluctance to rely on reason, as developed among those rabbinical authors, was due to the hardening of the front against the Qara'ites, and later against Christian and Muslim attackers.

However, the impeccable halakhic credentials of R. Sa'adyah allowed him to create a rationalist school within the tradition of Halakhah. He thereby established a certain independence from authority and tradition. A synthesis was subsequently made possible between faith and reason, and the groundwork was laid for a Jewish ethics.

Alas, this independence of thought did not last very long. As of the 13th century, moral discourse merged in the exegesis of tradition and sources. For Nachmanides and R. Jonah Gerondi, for example, there was no longer room for an independent ethics.

Nachmanides, in his Torah Commentary, still explained that the Great Flood had been imposed, even though mankind had not broken any positive law. Their sin had been having broken rules of reason, which had preceded Torah and prophetic authority[8]. On the other hand, his interpretation of the Law of Holiness[9] offered a prooftext for the moral duty of being holy, and his interpretation of the phrase calling for straight and good behaviour[10] derived the moral duty of acting beyond the letter of the law from the law itself.

Hence, according to Nachmanides, at the time of the flood morals had still enjoyed an independent authority, but after the giving of the Torah, all moral concepts could and should be traced in the source itself. This actually meant the extension of Torah (not necessarily Halakhah), over all moral questions, and the transformation of ethics into hermeneutics.

But even so, the development of a Jewish ethics between the 10th and 13th centuries had enriched halakhic Judaism and universalized its vision. In the following, we will trace some of the insights and items of self-understanding resulting from this phase of the history of Judaism.

The third chapter of Sa'adyah's **Book of Doctrines and Beliefs** presents his conception of Jewish legal philosophy, which is a combination of utilitarian and deontological thought. According to his view, the goal of creation was to benefit creatures by leading them towards complete happiness and perfect bliss in the future world. The observance of the commandments gave man the satisfaction of having laboured and having been justly rewarded, while divine blessing without any human effort would have led to less happiness and bliss[11].

His is therefore a teleological, even egoistical, interpretation of the Halakhah, unlike the deontological approach demonstrated by Leibowitz in our time. But actually, both describe the same phenomenon from different angles: Sa'adyah refers to the theological, Leibowitz to the psychological meaning of the mitswot. In other words, Sa'adyah describes the divine, while Leibowitz speaks of the human intention.

Sa'adyah's conception was the result of his wish to follow both the biblical system of reward and punishment, and the Aristotelian teaching about the central function of happiness in ethics. However, he could also have given a deontological legitimation of Halakhah, as follows from the rabbinical demand of serving God without expecting any reward[12]. Indeed, Sa'adyah interpreted the commandments not only as a means of achieving happiness, but likewise as a demand of reason, viz. as a form of gratitude to the Creator[13]. The latter argument goes beyond teleological thought and comes closer to the deontological approach.

The moral and rational value of the rational commandments, and even of those **mitswot shim'iyot**, explained by reason, remained independent of, and unaffected by, their religious formulation. An atheist could therefore have found and observed a great part of the Torah. Sa'adyah really developed an ethical system, which could also be considered as part of religion[14].

His distinction between **mitswot shim'iyot** (commandments of obedience or revelational commandments), and **mitswot sikhliyot** (rational commandments), obviously followed from his philosophical approach. On the other hand, Halakhah itself had already differentiated between legal, religious and moral rules, as well as between commandments which should have been written in any case, and commandments which are questioned by the Gentiles or by the Jew's evil inclination.

On the basis of the referral from theonomy to autonomy, Sa'adyah Ga'on developed an independent ethics in the tenth chapter of his book. This was really done outside the system of Jewish tradition and Halakhah as a reflection on Greek philosophy. He found his legitimation on the grounds of the Halakhic differentiation itself, and in following the examples of the talmudic sages. But it was an extraordinary phenomenon that a halakhist, like Sa'adyah, was able to transcend Halakhah and determine good and proper behaviour according to the thinking of Plato and Aristotle about harmony, reason, teleology and individualism.

The human-centered or autonomous character of Sa'adyah's system appeared in the last chapter, which is actually **devarim bifrishut min ha'olam** (a discourse on asceticism), **or sefer perishut shalem** (a full treatise on asceticism)[15], almost a separate work. The idea that one should make full use of all human faculties, following from the composite disposition of any creature, was derived from the idea of the Aristotelian **middle path**[16].

God Himself, being Creator and Legislator, was said to have commanded the use of the golden mean. Just as a house must be built of diverse materials, he argued, human beings must create an equilibrium between their conflicting virtues and tendencies. Sa'adyah listed thirteen goals which determine human life, begining with asceticism and various passions, and showed the extent given to each of them by reason[17].

As already mentioned, the choice of the middle path was most probably a reflection of Greek ethics, though similar ideas had prevailed among the rabbis of the Talmud. According to a rabbinical formulation, "the Torah was like a (middle-) path leading us between a path of fire and another of snow. He who turned to the former would, therefore, die of fire, and he who turned to the latter, would die of snow. The answer was, of course, to take the middle path"[18].   In other words, in order to declare the value of the golden mean, Saʿadyah could have relied on a Jewish tradition, which served in itself as a model for a Jewish ethics. However, his teaching about the balance of the different faculties was certainly influenced by the Platonic idea of **harmony** between wisdom, courage, moderation and justice, as well as by the Aristotelian concept of the **middle path**.

As a result of the idea of the equilibrium, Saʿadyah developed his concept of **secularity** as a necessary corollary of Torah and Halakhah. He rejected the exclusive devotion to the study and practice of Jewish law, because in his opinion the other aspects of life were necessary to provide the material basis for the worship of God. A balanced way of life was a prerequisite to the observance of the commandments. A person devoting his life to Torah, he said, might argue that he did not have to practice what was necessary for the observance of certain commandments; instead, he could teach others how to serve God through these rules.

The author replied that God would then be worshipped by the others, rather than by the person totally engaged in Torah. The service to God should not consist only of spiritual, but also of material acts. A person should care for the preservation of his body, ensure that he had the necessary material goods, build a family and engage in other worldly activities. While it is true that God could, by way of a miracle, preserve a person's body without the individual making an effort of his own, this would not change the rule of nature.

Thus, the ethics of the middle path was reconciled with the otherwise totalitarian system of Halakhah[19], and this was due to the existence of free space in the Halakhah itself. Moreover, the reconciliation of Halakhah and the idea of temperance also represented the possibility of combining theonomy with human autonomy.

One of the ideas of Saʿadyah Ga'on was the classification of Jews according to their attitudes toward the commandments, thereby creating a series of types or virtues. One of these types is the servant, another the perfect. The opposite types are the obstinate, the sinner, etc.[20]. Universalist ethics led Saʿadyah to reject the concept of Israel's chosenness and special relationship to God. These ideas in his view, were used to praise Israel or the righteous people, but should not be taken at face value[21].

In contrast to Saʿadyah's rejection of asceticism, was his quite pessimistic attitude towards this world, which he saw mainly as an antechamber for the world to come. Here, Saʿadyah felt that philosophy was still in need of religious faith and hope.

Sa'adyah's rejection of asceticism was adopted and continued by Maimonides, who even included it in his code[22]. On the other hand, a Jewish philosopher could not free himself from the idea of total devotion to God, from the maximal aspiration of certain virtues and from the concept of endless progress and moral ascent. The totality of the idea of acting for the sake of Heaven and of the commandment of loving God, as developed by Maimonides[23] and ibn Paqudah[24], more or less meant asceticism, though it is in conflict with the idea of the golden mean.

The question could of course be raised as to why have a system of revealed law at all if God wanted man to develop an ethics and assume responsibility; and why does the Torah include rational laws, which could have been discovered by human effort without any need for revelation. Sa'adyah Ga'on replied that norms of reason were too general and needed to be specified by revelation. Revealed law was also a unifying force, while the discussion concerning reason very often led to conflict. The creation of a rational code would have taken some time, and would not have been understood by everyone. Moreover, by transforming rational laws into divine commandments, the value of obedience to God was added and the reward was enhanced[25].

Hence, revelation was necessary, even with regard to the rational commandments, or we might say that autonomy referred us to theonomy.

(c) Internalization and Universalization

Another result of criticism against rabbinical legalism was the emphasis upon intention and motive in religious life. While tradition had formalized, quantified and objectivized the observance of the commandments, little had been said about the spirit and inner life of the Jew. Meanwhile the spiritual religiosity of Muslim **Sufis** had influenced some of the most sensitive rabbis and led them to new insights.

The outstanding among them, R. Bachyah ibn Pequdah (c. 1050-c. 1156), devoted a whole book to this topic[26]. The quantity was less important, in his view, than the quality of the act[27]. The emphasis upon the spiritual dimension led the author to inward abstention, or asceticism, and to the interpretation of various prohibitions as steps in this direction[28]. This was in line with an ethics based on virtues rather than on deontology.

Bachyah maintained the rationalism of Sa'adyah with one significant innovation: in order to know the divine Torah and law, God had referred us "to the sane and sound mind, to the written Torah delivered to Moses, and to the traditions which our ancestors received from the prophets"[29].

Here, the human mind, i.e. reason, is mentioned even before the Written and Oral Torah as a source of information. Similarly, the author counts the arguments for the discourse about the unity of God in the same order: haSekhel, haKatuv, haQabbalah (reason, scripture, tradition)[30].

Thus, Bachyah's system emphasized the human and subjective aspects of religious life and philosophy. Instead of simply submitting to theonomy, we are expected to take an active part in doing God's will. This leaves a certain area free, to be filled by the reason and will of the individual, i.e. autonomy, to a certain degree.

The emphasis upon virtues also appears in Joseph ibn Tsaddik's (d. 1145) Microcosm[31]. Again, human beings are advised to meditate upon themselves, rather than only to engage in the study of Bible and Tradition. By considering oneself, the microcosm, one can better understand the macrocosm, and God. Everyman's soul represents the spiritual world and could reflect upon it. Instead of the four Platonic virtues of wisdom, courage, temperance and justice, the author counted four biblical virtues: knowledge of God, righteousness, hope and humility.

During the 12th century, Jewish thought tended towards universalism and recognition of moral values outside the rabbinic tradition. In Yemen, Nethanel ben al-Fayyumi (d. 1165) declared that God had many messengers, according to the special needs of the various nations. Muhammad had been sent by God to teach Islam to the pagan world, just as Moses and the Prophets had given the Torah to Israel. Revelation, therefore, had to differ from people to people because of the particular character of each of them[32].

His Spanish contemporary, Abraham bar Chiyya, wrote at the beginning of the 12th century about the superiority of Israel, adding however the following caveat: "I do not say that such superiority is not available for the rest of mankind, for that would be wrong; we must believe that the gates of repentance are open for all who seek it; as it says 'Let him return unto the Lord and He will have mercy on him and to our God for He will abundantly pardon'(Is. 55:7). He has mercy on all who repent"[33].

This attitude follows from the principle of universalism, which is a major test of ethical thinking. It is by no means self-evident, taking into consideration Muslim pressure towards converting the Jews and the consciousness of the Jewish minority. Judah Halevi's insistence upon the superiority of Israel is much more in line with the existential needs of his contemporaries, but less creative in ethical thought[34].

(d) Maimonides

Moses ben Maimon (1135-1204 C.E.) adopted a similar attitude to explain the providential role of Jesus and Muhammad[35]. The divine scheme of human salvation was therefore larger than that of Torah, and called for a universalist interpretation of the Jewish tradition.

Maimonides, accordingly, offered a rationalist interpretation of Torah and commandments, which was based on his universalist approach. The goal of the commandments, according to him, was to promote the spiritual perfection of human beings, which was again an expression of ethics[36].

Hence Maimonides also understood the need for living inside the line of the law, as a moral value beyond that of obedience to Torah. The pious were not satisfied with keeping to the middle path, but leant a bit towards that extreme which was opposite their inclination. Instead of observing the law, they tended toward asceticism; instead of being courageous, they tended to take some risk; instead of being benevolent, they tended to be more than benevolent; and instead of being humble, they tended to demean themselves a bit[37].

An application of ethical thought to Torah was the adoption of the golden mean[38]. However, unlike the Greek middle path, which is a value by itself, the Maimonidean golden mean was the result of a temporary reaction to a negative extreme, by turning towards the opposite one. Hence, it was a kind of medicine, to be prescribed according to the spiritual needs of the individual, while the same middle path followed in the wrong case by someone else could harm the person concerned.

Likewise, Maimonides chose a special way to develop a synthesis between the philosophical approach to virtues and the rabbinical teaching on repentance. The problem was which of the two types is of greater value, the one who in his piety feels no desire to sin, or the one who overcomes his inclination to sin. While the philosophers chose the first, the rabbis came out in favour of the second. According to Maimonides, with regard to moral laws it is preferable not to feel attraction to sin, whereas with regard to positive religious norms, the person overcoming his attraction to sin is of higher quality[39].

The meaning of the commandments, religious as well as moral, is teleological, said Maimonides. Even those laws which seem to be justified only by the lawgiver, i.e. by deontological considerations, do have a utilitarian meaning, which could, however, be beyond our perception[40]. The goal of moral laws is spiritual not social. The final perfection of the person observing the law is neither behavioural, nor does it concern his virtues, but refers to the perception of the divine[41]. This transcendental end of the Torah at the same time represented a synthesis of theology and ethics.

According to Maimonides, obedience of the Noachide Commandments as a result of ethical discourse is insufficient. It is lacking in piety and recognition for the function of Torah, even for the Non-Jewish world. This would mean that human perfection depended on direct contact with God, not on ethical and rational thought alone, that it demanded recognition of the Sinai Covenant, and that theonomy was higher up in the hierarchy of human perfection than autonomy[42].

An interesting idea of Maimonides is his recognition of the general concept of **derekh 'erets** (way of people, trade, morals), as a prescriptive statement for the control of behaviour; not only as a guidance **praeter legem**, but even **contra legem**. The concept was used as a kind of equitable norm to correct an unsatisfactory legal rule. He advised the readers of his code not to always make use of the halakhic law. They should not divorce a sick wife in order to save further medical expenses, as strict Halakhah allowed them to do, because of the call for **derekh 'erets**[43].

Maimonides thus felt that sometimes there was need for a balance to Halakhah, and we would call this balance a moral norm above and beyond the law described in the Code. This is a further example of theonomy, here represented by the Code, referring to autonomy, or ethics, as represented by **derekh 'erets**. By the way, this special meaning of **derekh 'erets**, viz. morals, has not yet been listed in the dictionaries[44].

(e) Further Ideas

We have mentioned the moral concepts of Nachmanides and R. Jonah Gerondi, both returning from ethics and autonomy to the authority of theonomy. In the same century, R. Moses of Coucy explained the moral character of Jewish existence in the world: "The Holy One, Blessed be He, sows Israel in the various lands, so that proselytes shall be gathered unto them; but so long as they behave deceitfully towards their neighbours, who will cleave unto them?"[45]. This was an attack against the double morality which was often practiced by Jews towards their Gentile neighbours. The speaker relied upon his ethical insight to assess the halakhic standard of behaviour.

The adoption of moral philosophy as a criterion for the understanding of Jewish tradition led Chasdai Crescas (d. 1412), in his book[46] of 1410-14, to put love above knowledge as the highest principle of religion. This was an ethical insight vis-a-vis the intellectual and rational tradition of Jewish philosophers. Learning from the teaching of the renegade, Abner of Burgos (1270-1340), who justified his conversion to Christianity by the doctrine of predestination[47], Crescas examined the necessity of free choice as a central tenet of Judaism. Crescas could have adopted determinism by following the method of Maimonides and Averroes, viz. that some philosophical truths should be kept hidden from ordinary people. Determinism would be understood by most listeners as an invitation to licentiousness, but nevertheless, it had to be taken into consideration as a possible interpretation of human behaviour.

Joseph Albo (1380-1444) classified the Torah as a divine law vis-a-vis natural and conventional laws[48]. Hence Jewish religious tradition was explained in universal terms of law and ethics, instead of maintaining its unique character and being **sui generis.** This was the obvious result of Albo's experience at the disputation, but it also reflected the tendency of universalization.

After the great break caused by the experience of the **Marannos** and their contact with Christian thought, Barukh Spinoza (1632-1677) introduced human ethics as an alternative to the traditional concept of divine law, and thereby came to deny metaphysics per se. Declaring the love of God as the only legitimate goal of Philosophy, Spinoza perhaps made use of the idea of Crescas, and was probably following Maimonides when he rejected the prevalent motivation of reward and punishment. Moreover, he declared divine law as being universal, i.e. common to all men. Accordingly, it could also not depend upon revelation or any other historical narrative, neither could it include the performance of acts which from the ethical point of view were indifferent[49].

In other words, Spinoza developed the universal elements of Jewish tradition to their Christian extreme, meaning the rejection of the Jewish doctrine of election and revelation. As a logical result of the idea that divine law must be perfect, and as part of his ethics, he developed a concept of divine human rights based on the supremacy of human reason. Theonomy was thereby merged in the autonomy of reason.

---

1   See supra ch. 14.

2   "Tokhachah Megullah", in S. Pinsker, **Liqutey Qadmoniyot: Zur Geschichte des Karaismus und der karaeischen Literatur,** (Wien: 1860), App. 3, p. 33; L. Nemoy, **Karaite Anthology: Excerpts from Early Literature,** (Yale UP, 1952), pp. 111-122, and p. 118.

3   "Tokhachah Megullah", pp. 33-34; cf. my **Introduction,** p. 17.

4   B.M. Levin, **Otsar haGeonim,** Ketubbot, p. 310.

5   Cf. M. Zucker (ed.), **Hasagot R. Mevasser ben Nissai**, (New York: 1945).

6   'Emunot weDe'ot, trans. by S. Rosenblatt; **Saadia Gaon: The Book of Beliefs and Opinions**, (Yale UP, 1948), Introduction 5-6, Rosenblatt, pp. 16-33; cf. I. Efros, **Saadia's Theory of Knowledge**, in JOR Saadia Studies, (Philadelphia: 1943), pp. 25-62, 162-163.

7   'Emunot weDe'ot, chs. 2,5,7,9; Efros, ibid.

8   Commentary and Gen. 6:2; 10:13.

9   Lev. 19:2.

10   Deut. 16:18.

11   'Emunot weDe'ot, Introduction and ch. 3, Introduction (A Altman, in **Three Jewish Philosophers**, New York: Harper Torchbooks, 1965, p. 94).

12   M 'Avot 1:3.

13   'Emunot weDe'ot, 3:1; Rosenblatt, p. 138.

14   See also H. Ben-Shammai, "Chaluqat haMitswot uMusag haChokhmah beMishnat Rasag", **Tarbiz** 41 (1972) pp. 170-182.

15   'Emunot weDe'ot 5:10, quoted in J. Guttmann, **Die Religionsphilosophie des Saadia**, (Goettingen: 1882), pp. 258-259.

16   Ch. 10 s. 1; ch. 10, s. 8:19. Cf. Aristotle, **Nicomachean Ethics**, 2:6-9; cf. Agus, **The Vision**, p. 169 ff.; Lenn E. Goodman, "Saadyah's Ethical Pluralism", **Journal of the American Oriental Society** 100 (1980) pp. 407-419.

17   Cf. Sirat, **History**, pp. 31-33.

18   JT Chagigah 2:1, 77 a. On the middle-way see Steven S. Schwarzschild, "Moral Radicalism and 'Middlingness" in the Ethics of Maimonides", in **Studies in Medieval Culture**, 11, (1977), pp. 65-94.

19   'Emunot weDe'ot 10:15.

20   'Emunot weDe'ot 5:4.

21   'Emunot weDe'ot 2:11.

22   **Mishneh Torah**, De'ot 1:4.

23   Commentary to 'Avot, ch. 5; cf. L. Jacobs, **A Jewish Theology**, ch. 11.

24   Bachyah ben Joseph ibn Paquda, **Chovot haLevavot**, trans. M. Mansoor, **The Book of Direction to the Duties of the Heart**, (London: Routledge & Kegan Paul, 1973) 8:25; 9:7; 10:7.

25   'Emunot weDe'ot, Ch. 3, Intro pp. 1-3; A. Altmann "Saadya Gaon", in **Three Jewish Philosophers**, pp. 93-108; A. Altman, "Saadya's Conception of the Law", **Bulletin of John Rylands Library** 28 (1944) pp. 1-24; cf. Fox, **Ethics**, pp. 174-187; Greenberg, **The Ethical**, pp. 43-48.

26   Bachyah ibn Paquda, **Chovot haLevavot**.

27   Cf. H.G. Enelow, "Kawwana: The Struggle for Inwardness in Judaism", in **Kaufman Kohler Jubilee Vol,**. (Berlin, 1913).

28   Cf. Sirat, **History**, pp. 81-82.

29   **Chovot haLevavot**, Introduction.

30   **Chovot haLevavot**, 1:3.

31   **Ha'Olam haQatan**, A. Jellinek (ed.), (Leipzig: 1854); S. Horovitz, **Der Mikrokosmos des Josef Saddik**, (Breslau: 1903). The concept had already been mentioned by Solomon ibn Gabirol (11th century) in his **Tiqqun haMiddot**, trans. N. Braun, (Tel Aviv: 1951).

32   **Gan haSekhalim**, trans. Joseph Kafich, (1954); English trans. D. Levine, **The Garden of Wisdom**, (New York: 1908); cf. Sirat, History, p. 92.

33   **Hegyon ha-Nefesh ha'atsuvah**, G. Wigoder (ed.), (Jerusalem: 1971); trans. G. Wigoder, **The Meditation of the Sad Soul**, (London: Routledge & Kegan Paul, 1969); quoted by Sirat, History, p, 101.

34   **Kuzari: The Book of Refutation and Proof in Defence of the Despised Faith**; I. Heinemann, in **Three Jewish Philosophers**, (New York: 1969); 1:11-12; 2:10-14; Sirat, History, p. 117 and 124.

35   **Mishneh Torah**, Hilkhot Melakhim 11:4, (according to the uncensored text).

36   **Guide of the Perplexed**, trans. S. Pines, (Chicago: UP, 1963), 3:26,27,54. This idea was developed by Chasdai Crescas (cf. Sirat, **History**, p. 368).

37   **The Eight Chapters of Maimonides on Ethics**, trans. J.I. Gorfinkle, (New York: 1966), ch.4.

38   **The Eight Chapters**, ch. 4, beginning; **Mishneh Torah**, Hilkhot De'ot 1:4; 2:2.

39   The Eight Chapters, ch. 6. England "The Interaction of Morality and Jewish Law", JLA 7 (1988) p.121, sees this statement as an affirmation of law vis-a-vis morals, but it is only with regard to cultic commandments that Maimonides makes his rating, whereas with regard to moral commandments he thinks higher of the person acting out of his natural inclination. England's interpretation fits R. Jacob Emden's criticism levelled against the distinction of Maimonides, not Maimonides' statement.

40   **Guide**, 3:26. Cf. against this the deontological view of Y. Leibowitz, **Yahadut**, 13-36, and his "Commandments", in Cohen & Mendes Flohr, p. 70; cf. Isadore Twersky, **Studies in Jewish Law and Philosophy**, (New York: 1982), pp. 52-75; Miriam Galston, "The Purpose of the Law according to Maimonides", JQR **69** (1978) pp. 27-51.

41   **Guide**, 3:27,54 Cf. **Milot haHigayon**, trans. I. Efros, **Proc. American Academy of Jewish Research** (1938), ch. 9.

42   See Spinoza, **The Theological-Political Tractate**, ch.5; A. Lichtenstein, **The Seven Laws of Noah**, (New York: 1981); S. Schwarzschild, "Do Noachides have to believe in Revelation?" JQR 52-3 (1962) pp. 297-308, and 30-65; D. Hartman, **Maimonides: Torah and Philosophic Quest**, Philadelphia: JPS, 1976, p. 222, n. 62; I. Twersky, **Introduction to the Code of Maimonides**, Yale, 1980, p. 455; M. Fox, "Maimonides and Aquinas on Natural Law", DI 3 (1972) pp. 5-36; M. Levine, "The Role of Reason in the Ethics of Maimonides", JRE 14 (1986) pp. 279-295; J.D. Bleich, "Judaism and Natural Law", JLA 7 (1985) pp. 5-42.

43   Maimonides, **Mishneh Torah,** Hilkhot 'Ishut 14:17.

44   Cf. E. Ben Iehuda, **Millon Halashon Ha'ivrit;** A. 'EvenShoshan **HaMillon Hachadash.**

45   **Sefer Mitswot Gadol,** quoted in Agus, **The Vision,** p. 18.

46   **'Or Hashem,** Bk.2; Sirat, **History,** p. 367.

47   Cf. Sirat, p. 308, and 312.

48   **Sefer ha'Iqqarim,** trans. I. Husik, (Philadelphia: 1929); cf. Sirat, p. 376.

49   **The Theologico-Political Tractate,** ch. 4, quoted in Agus, **The Vision,** p. 230.

24. PIETISM AND MYSTICISM

(a) Chassidey Ashkenaz

Just as Maimonides had declared certain moral principles to be graded above the Halakhic norms, the pietists of Germany and France, during the 12th and 13th centuries, followed the **din shamayim** (heavenly law), or **retson habore'** (the will of the Creator), where strict Halakhah contradicted their conscience[1]. The strict rule of the Torah was sufficient for ordinary people, but the pious were supposed to abide by a higher norm ascribed to "heaven", which was a synonym of "God".

The pietists believed that there was a Torah for the masses, another for the scholars, and a third for them. The latter was encoded into Scripture by **remazim** (ciphers), to be discovered by the initiates[2].

According to the law of Torah of the second category, for example, fact-finding in court depended on the rules of evidence. Once these rules had been satisfied, there was no room for further reasoning[3]. Nevertheless, the pietists recited a story about a case where the defendant had been allowed to keep a certain property for lack of competent witnesses to support the plaintiff's claim. Their comment was, that later on the defendant had lost all his property, "for there are matters beyond the jurisdiction of the human court, which are taken care of by the celestial court. Likewise, there are matters ·which are legal but nevertheless punishable (in the celestial court), viz. the commission of an act which one would not like to experience from another person"[4].

By telling such a story, the pietists criticized the formalism of the Halakhah and expressed their hope for divine intervention in favour of the wronged party. They were making use of a talmudic statement referring to the celestial court all those criminal cases which could not be adjudicated by a rabbinical court[5].

The second statement is even more far-reaching than the first. The defendant may have been justified by legal standards, but he had violated the moral rule of loving his fellow, as formulated by Hillel[6]. This is not only to say that the decision according to the Halakhah might be morally wrong, but that it violated the central rule of the Torah, viz. the commandment to love one's fellow like oneself. The rules of evidence should give way to the golden rule, in order to refrain from injustice.

Halakhic penal law provided for equal punishment, whether a thief had acted in order to enrich himself or to break his fast. The rule of Heaven, on the other hand, demanded individual modes of punishment according to the motive of the person on trial. The Torah of Moses spoke to the ordinary court, but the pietist wished to understand the higher rules of divine justice. This was discussed with reference to extra-marital sex, in particular with the argument that the offender had acted under an irresistible impulse[7].

Likewise, the reward for the observance of the commandment, said the pietists, **lefi yetser levavo**, would depend on the intention and effort of the person, not on the criteria mentioned in the law[8]. The least significant act might therefore be of the highest quality, while the fulfillment of an important act without intention and effort could be meaningless.

However, the pious circle did not create a law and court for themselves, rather the heavenly law would be applied in the ordinary court in cases where the parties belonged to the pietist circle: "If two litigants come before the sage, he should decide according to the law of the Torah, even though according to the celestial law the decision would be in the opposite direction. However, if the litigants are good and God-fearing people who listen to his advice, he should decide according to the celestial law, although the law of the Torah is the opposite. For example, if a man died in a village in the presence of women only and made his will in their presence (without male witnesses), or a will was made before two male witnesses and one of them died. If the sage knows that the women or the single man spoke the truth, he should rather decide according to the celestial law"[9]. The listeners to these moralizing stories, and the readers of the **Book of the Pious**, were ordinary people who tried to implement in their own lives all or some of the aspirations of the pietistic teaching.

According to the norm of the pious, the poor should be exempt from communal taxation, whereas Halakhah had not provided for this exemption. "The Torah corresponded with the popular view, therefore it imposed upon rich and poor to give the tithes... But if the Israelite is poor and the Priest rich, how is it possible to impose upon the poor to support the rich?... the text made no distinction. Likewise, if the community imposes a duty, even the poor... must pay from each pound a given percentage, for their exemption would set an example to others to refuse payment, and destroy all public business. Therefore, the poor should rather participate in the levy. However, if the evildoers would listen to the good people, they would refrain from pressuring the poor. The good people should pay the poor, secretely, what they had to pay, lest the evildoers know about it..."[10]. Here we have a moral criticism of the common usage, as based on Halakhah.

A pious litigant was supposed to pay, even if his obligation was doubtful, and he should always agree to compromise. "Suppose a person owed another person an amount of money, and does not remember whether he paid the debt, and the other also does not know and does not summon him to court. The first should free himself from the celestial debt and pay the other. If the other is also a good person, he should not accept the money... They should release each other and split the amount"[11]. Again, this pietist advice is based on moral concepts and on conscience, which are of greater authority than the law of Torah.

The strict Halakhah prohibited cohabitation of a **kohen** (priest), with his wife, if she had been held captive by Gentiles[12]. However, in the middle of the 15th century, during the Austrian persecution of Jews, rabbinical authorities permitted the resumption of marital relations even to priests. This was done **contra legem** because of the historical circumstance and out of concern for the poor woman. The decision was made with regard to the future of captive women and to their need for protection by their husbands. The restrictive attitude of Halakhah would have caused the corruption of these women, and the innovation was probably introduced on humanitarian grounds[13].

The duty of reciting the daily prayer was made subject to the right intention. Everyone was to judge for himself whether he could pray with the necessary feeling. If he lacked the proper disposition of the mind, he should rather refrain from praying, than recite the words without meaning. Moreover, if one felt a dislike of prayer, one should reduce the prayers to twice weekly or once daily. Likewise, a person feeling a dislike of Torah should learn only a bit every week[14].

(b) Spanish Kabbalah

In Spain, Nachmanides (1194-1270) criticized the legalism and positivism of some people. He declared that one could be fully observant of the rules of Torah, and nevertheless be disgraceful. For instance, the Torah had provided for the observance of the impediments and the dietary rules, but it had not restricted sexual relations between husband and wife or the consumption of meat and wine. A glutton could therefore justify excessive sex with his wife or wives, and be "among the winebibbers and gluttenous eaters of meat"[15]. He could use filthy language, which was not expressly prohibited in the Torah, and "be a disgrace within the optional region of the Torah". Therefore, following the detailed prohibitions of Torah, a general rule was laid down requiring one to sanctify oneself beyond these prohibitions[16].

Joseph ben Abraham Gikatilla (1248-c.1325), one of the founders of Spanish Jewish mysticism, described the letters of the Torah as its body and God Himself as its soul. A presumption was thereby made that one should relate to God in a more spritual way, than by mere observance of the practical commandments.

In a similar manner, the **Zohar** distinguished between the "open" and the "hidden" Torah, the latter to be studied and applied by the mystics. This referred to the tension between the legalistic interpretation of the law and that based on conscience. Mysticism not only claimed that there was an additional meaning to the commandments, but that it occupied a higher rank in the hierarchy of meanings[17].

The disciples of the Kabbalah criticized the rabbis and judges for lacking in their private and social morals: "Woe to those eating the straw, the spices of Torah, those donkeys of Torah posing as super-wise, without grasping the secrets of Torah, who only know the lighter and harsher prohibitions of Torah"[18]. Likewise, a distinction was made between the masters of the bodily parts of the Mishnah, and those masters of its intellect, referring to the deeper understanding of the traditions.

The study of Torah, according to the mystics, should help in the redemption of the divine presence from its exile, otherwise the effort was in vain. Some of the teachers "shouted day and night questions regarding the Oral Law, they barked like dogs and like hell for riches in the present and in the future world. Nobody studied Torah to elevate the divine from its exile and restore the unity, because their eyes were blind and their hearts blocked"[19].

According to an alternative formulation, a distinction should be made between the **Torah of Creation**, i.e. the Torah including the norms of behaviour, and the Torah of the **atsilut**, i.e. the **Torah of Inspiration** or the Meta-Torah. The latter does not exist in the present world and does not refer to practice[20].

All these statements express moral criticism against the intellectual leadership of Spanish Judaism and the legalism of Halakhah. The mystic did not accept the positivism of the halakhists, and demanded a say in the interpretation of the commandments as well as of the Torah[21].

As in the 13th century, Kabbalists likewise distinguished between our Torah and that before the sin, or that of the Messiah. Even every **shemittah** (seven thousand years), according to this system, had a Torah of its own, which is a way of justifying change in the law. Some of the things missing in our Torah would appear in the Torah of the next seven thousand years. For instance, in our Torah, we do not have a letter shin with four vertical strokes, such as is impressed upon the phylacteries, but this letter will appear in the Torah of another **shemittah**[22].

An implied criticism of Halakhic legalism can be noticed in the different accent set by Kabbalists upon some institutions, and the metaphysical meaning given to them. The strict observance of the middle days of Passover and the Feast of Tabernacles, even without observing the duty of donning phylacteries, the assistance of the Levites at the washing before the priestly blessing, and the repetition of the last words of the **shema'** are examples of this spiritualisation and internalization[23].

In all of these instances, Kabbalah adopted a kind of supreme good, using it for the derivation of new norms and criticism of the old ones. If, for example, **devequt** (holding on to God), was the supreme good, Halakhah has to give way if it presented an obstacle. While Halakhah mainly appealed to the community, Kabbalah tended to attract the individual. It also stressed the intention rather than the act itself, which was the main concern of the rules of Halakhah. In these points Jewish mysticism follows the attitude of ethics, vis-a-vis the legalist attitude of Halakhists.

(c) Chassidism

The relationship between law and morals plays a central role in the identity of Chassidism, both as a matter of principle and as a practical guide in particular situations. While rabbinic Judaism in the 18th century primarily emphasized the act of the commandment, rather than the intention[24], Chassidism stressed the intention of the person fulfilling the commandment, sometimes even at the expense of the act itself. Moreover, normal rabbinic Judaism had adopted a deontological attitude towards the commandments. Chassidism, however, took a teleological view, considering the commandments to be the means to achieve certain virtues, such as **devequt** (attachment to God).

A tradition of R. Israel Ba'al Shem Tov (1700-1760) ran as follows: "Even if a person studies diligently, prays and castigates himself, it is all in vain if he has no **devequt** (attachment to the Creator...)"[25]. "One should always keep in mind that everything is permeated by the Creator, done by His wish and under His control. Therefore, if something should happen against the person's will, he should realize that it is from God and for his benefit... Whatever a person is doing, he should have in mind to satisfy and worship God, and to attach his thought to the Upper World of God"[26].

According to R. Menachem Mendel of Vitebsk (1730-1788), "attachment to God can occur only after everything that separates has been removed. But as long as anything else is held on to, there can be no real attachment. Man's pleasure in having material or other things is so strong, that it permits no distraction of the mind from them, and therefore prevents him from cleaving to God". The Ba'al Shem Tov gave this illustration: "When two pieces of silver are to be soldered together, they must be scraped clean at the place where they are to be joined. If there is tarnish or any other dividing matter on the silver, the join is bound to be ineffective. Hence the verse says: 'If you seek her as silver...' (Prov. 2:4). For attachment to God, man must first scrape away something of his self, only then can **devequt** be achieved"[27].

R. Nachman of Kosov (before 1750), called for always keeping God before oneself[28], not only during prayer and while fulfilling commandments, but also during work and trade. When asked how this was possible, he replied with a little irony: "While being at prayer at the synagogue, are you not able to think about your business, why should you not be able to think at your business about God?"[29].

This is the idea that one can worship God by performing acts which are indifferent from the point of view of Torah. If such an act is performed with the intention of serving God, it thereby becomes a meritorious act. This idea had already been ascribed to Hillel, for whom having a bath was a **mitswah**.[30] Especially in the mystical tradition, the possibility was given to concentrate on the intention even in otherwise neutral acts. The first Chassidim used to quote the mystic R. Isaac of Acre, who spoke of a shoemaker meditating during his work, and thereby worshipping during his worldly activity[31].

Likewise, in particular circumstances, a person could be seen as worshipping God **contra legem**, or of having to have to violate the law in order to follow some moral concept. "God wants to be worshipped in all forms. Sometimes a person must interrupt the study of the Torah to speak to others, or to go to some place where he cannot pray and learn as usual. Let him not be sad, for God wants him to worship in various forms, and to remain attached to Him even while talking and walking"[32].

Chassidism inherited from the **Kabbalah** the mystical concepts of divine immanence, the doctrine of **tsimtsum** (contraction), and of **nitsotsot** (sparks of holiness). God could therefore be found everywhere, even in the material and so-called secular sphere. Every phenomenon is a challenge, to be redeemed and brought back to its divine source. While Lurianic mysticism considered the nitsotsot to be the result of a cosmic catastrophe, i.e. **shevirat hakelim** (breaking of the vessels), for Chassidism it became a beneficial event. It provided man with the opportunity to mend the world and become a partner to the Creator.

"Whatever exists in this world includes sparks of holiness resulting from the breaking of the vessels, even wood and stone. The same applies to any human act, even a sinful one, its sparks being repentance. By repentance for a sin, the sparks included in this sin are elevated to the Upper World"[33].

Hence, sin or evil was no longer perceived as an element independent of God's benevolence, but as benevolence covered by **kelipot** (husks, shells), really being good. "Evil is good of a lower rank. By doing good, evil turns into good, but by acting badly, it turns into real evil. This is like a broom for cleaning the house, which is a good of the lower rank, and which becomes really bad if it is used to punish a child"[34].

Just as the world is seen as a carriage serving God, evil could be seen as a carriage serving the good. In other words, there is no essential evil, and one can serve God through one's evil inclination; by putting aside the shell and redeeming the sparks of holiness residing even in evil.

This idea too, already had talmudic roots[35], but was drawn to the extreme by Chassidic thought. Since a saying, quoted in the Talmud, declared the Torah to be an antidote to the evil inclination[36], R. Dov Baer, the Maggid, declared the evil inclination to be the main entity, and more important than Torah itself. The real worship was to take place in the transformation of the evil inclination, rather than in fulfilling the Torah: "It was said that God created the evil inclination, and made the Torah its seasoning (BT Qiddushin 30 b.), why is not the Torah likened to the main dish? The answer lies in the necessity of the evil inclination for the maintenance of the world, for without the evil inclination, there would be no procreation"[37].

Thus, God was said to have created the evil inclination of man as his major challenge, and as a requisite for His service. Sin was not only a possibility, but almost a necessity, because through sin there arose the possibility of repentance.

The saying probably demonstrated that Chassidism had preserved certain antinomian tendencies, similar to those of Sabbatai Tzvi's teaching. These included, firstly, the teaching about the special Torah of each **shemittah**, taken from the **Sefer haTemunah** of the 13th century, and developed by the followers of the reputed Messiah[38]. Secondly, the idea of the evil inclination, or of sin, as a necessary requisite for the attachment to God, was in line with Sabbatean teachings concerning **mitswah haba'ah be'averah** (commission of a meritorious act by sin), or the lapse of Torah in the time of the Messiah[39].

This possibility means priority of moral over legal principles, and autonomy rather than heteronomy. Since the decisive element of worship is the intention, individual moral concepts and individual conscience could earn religious legitimation for being directed toward God.

The idea of serving God through the overcoming of one's evil inclination also meant an individualization of worship, instead of the standardization perscribed by **Halakhah**. According to R. Mordekhai Josef Leiner of Izbice (d. 1854), "man must engage in reflection and increase his understanding while he is still a young man, before his evil inclination has gained too much of a hold on him. At this time of life he should learn how to discern between that for which he has a powerful desire, and that from which his heart is remote. From it he will come to appreciate exactly what it is that God has prepared as a test for him, so that he can thereby refine his character. It is with regard to this particular thing that he is called upon to gain self-control and exercize vigilance. For God has given each man some special means of refining his character, and each man is obliged to make himself aware of his own special task"[40].

This referred every individual to his own moral intuition. Every Jew has the root of his soul in the souls of the Patriarchs, who offered their lives to God. He might, therefore, rely on his intuition by surrendering to God and expecting divine enlightenment[41].

Just as overcomming the evil inclination and responding to one's own special challenge was seen to be superior to the standard of Torah, the institutions and commandments of Torah were considered to be below the individual attachment to God. Already in the Talmud, Halakhah had been given a lower rank than the relationship to God: "Do not fear the Sabbath, but He who warned you to keep the Sabbath; do not fear the Sanctuary, but He who warned you to build a sanctuary"[42].

In the same vein, R. Judah Loew of Prague (c.1525-1609) spoke of the "attachment of the learned to Torah, which is liked by its students, so that their love of Torah prevents them from the love of God... because one cannot love two at once. For love means total attachment to the beloved, and if you are attached to one, you cannot be attached to another"[43].

The Chassidim quoted the Ba'al Shem Tov as criticizing a certain rabbi for being so engaged in the study of Torah, that he forgot that there was God in the world. Likewise, R. Mordekhai Josef Leiner warned his listeners

lest they make idols out of the Sabbath, the Sanctuary, or in fact any rule
of Halakhah[44].

As a result of the doctrine of **devequt**, Chassidic teachers called for
freedom from legal restrictions regarding prayer, and even encouraged their
followers to disregard certain rules, in order to emphasize the greater
importance of the intention. This was not a completely new idea, but was
popularized by Chassidism.

In talmudic times, there had already been a controversy between the
rabbis as to whether prayer should be regulated or spontaneous[45]. It was
said that "every person should evaluate by himself whether he could have
the proper intention during prayer, only if the answer was positive should
he pray, otherwise he should refrain from praying"[46]. This meant that a
person returning from a voyage should wait three days to calm down, and
then start prayers again. Moreover, French teachers of the 12th century
advised their audience that rather than feeling aversion to prayer, they
should only pray some days in the week, or once daily[47].

Accordingly, the Ba'al Shem Tov was quoted as saying that one cannot
prescribe to a child when it might come to his father, but that he may
come whenever he likes. R. Israel of Ruzhyn (1797-1850), used the
following metaphor: "There was once a great and benevolent ruler who
permitted everybody to visit him. Thereupon his ministers decided that this
was below his dignity and provided for fixed hours. Once a beggar came
and asked for admission outside of these hours. When he was refused, he
told the gatekeeper that the hours did not apply in his case because he
came on a matter of state security, so that they had to bring him
immediately before the ruler. This convinced them so that they let him
in"[48].

This was not only a critique of the strict rule providing for the times of
prayer, but also of the contents of prayer. One should pray not for one's
own wellbeing, but for the general welfare, and in this case the prayer
should be independent of a particular time. Likewise, the Chassidic view
was that "if one cannot pray together with the congregation, because for
them prayer is a matter of routine, one should pray with a private group of
ten or by oneself"[49].

Another result of Chassidic ethical thought was the rejection of sadness
and asceticism, and the promotion of serenity and joy: "Sometimes the evil
inclination says to you, you have committed a great sin, although you have
only violated the strict norm... The intention of the evil inclination is to
make you sad... You must understand this deception, and tell the evil
inclination that you do not wish to follow the strict rule... Even if this is a

bit of a sin, you should say that God did not want you to keep this strict norm"[50].

According to another formulation: "Do not engage in trivialities, for this is the advice of the evil inclination... Even if you have sinned, do not be too sad... There is sometimes a meritorious act linked with some sin. In such a case, do not listen to the evil inclination keeping you from this act, but tell the evil inclination that you do not intend to annoy God by the act, on the contrary: you want to please God by the act... In any case, you must use your reason as to whether to do the act or not"[51].

The latter referral to the rational judgement of the individual is a clear indication of ethics within a theocentric belief system. The value of pleasing God takes precedence over the rules of law, and the normative inference from this value is within the autonomy of the individual[52].

The need for a joyful mood, though much more complicated, was especially stressed by R. Nachman of Bratslav (1772-1811): "One should try with all one's might always to be joyful, for by nature man is drawn towards melancholia, because of sad events and suffering... True, it is also good for man to have a broken heart, yet this should only happen in certain hours. He should set aside an hour each day to break his heart and pour out his speech to God... But for the rest of the day he should only be in a state of joy"[53].

Hence, Chasidism presented an example of an ethics of virtue within the system of Halakhah, and of autonomy within theonomy[54].

1   The pietists were the descendants of R. Kalonymus of Lucca headed by R. Judah ben Samuel of Regensburg (1150-1217). See J. Dan, **Sifrut haMusar vehaDrush**, Jerusalem, 1975, p. 143; and see s.v. "Hasidei Ashkenaz" in **Encyclopaedia Judaica**; Agus, **The Vision**, pp.128-166; I.G. Marcus, **Piety and Society: The Jewish Pietists of Medieval Germany**, (Leiden: 1981); Chaggai Ben–Artsi, "Perishut beSefer Chasidim", **Da'at** 10 (1983) pp.39-46.

2   Marcus, **Piety and Society**, p. 25 f., and 67.

3   Cf. Maimonides, **Mishneh Torah**, Hilkhot Sanhedrin 24:1.

4   **Sefer Chasidim** (Das Buch der Frommen), herausg, J. Wistinetzki, (Frankfurt M., 1924), 1005.

5   BT Sanhedrin 37 b.

6   BT Sabbat 31 a.

7   Op. cit. 1989.

8   Op. cit. 43.

9   Op. cit. 1381.

10 Op. cit. 914.

11 Op. cit. 1214.

12 BT Ketubot 14 b; Maimonides, **Mishneh Torah**, Isurey Bi'ah 18:6; ET, s.v. **zonah.**

13 R. Moses Isserlis, **Darkhey Mosheh**, Tur 'Even ha'Ezer 7:13. The decision was probably made by R. Israel Isserlein.

14 R. Jacob Tam, **Sefer haYashar**, (Jerusalem: 1967), p. 77, pp. 62-63, and 116; cf. BT Berakhot 30 b.

15 Prov. 23:20.

16 Nachmanides, Commentary ad Lev. 19:2.

17 Cf. I. Tishby, **Netivey Emunah uMinut**, (Ramat Gan: 1964), p. 18.

18 I. Baer, "Hareqa' hahistori shel haRa'ya Mehemna", **Zion** 5 (1940) pp. 6-10, 14-16, and 36-39; I. Tishbi, **Mishnat haZohar**, (Jerusalem: 1961), vol. 2, p. 363 ff., 385, and 429 ff.

19 **Zohar Chadash, Tiqqunim,** quoted by Tishbi, **Mishnat haZohar**, vol. 2, p. 386.

20 Tishbi, **Mishnat haZohar**, vol. 2 pp. 388-394.

21 Cf. also the reputed text from **Sefer haQanah**, p. 22 b-23 a, (see also op. cit. p. 71, and **Sefer haPeliah**, p. 74) quoted by H. Graetz, **Geschichte der Juden**, vol. 8, p. 463: "God had been asked why he had created poor woman, who did not receive reward and punishment. For woman was exempt from those commandments linked to a special time, and did neither receive reward for observing the commandments nor punishment for disregarding them, because she was exempt from them. God had indeed imposed the duty of study of Torah, which was the most important of the commandments, on woman, but our sages exempted her... and gave her the status of servants". I have not found the text in our edition, and according to the opinion of S. Eidelberg in an oral communication, it may be apocryphal. See however I. Zinberg, **Toledot Sifrut Israel**, vol. 2, p. 209, and 371; (English trans. B. Martin, A History of Jewish Literature, vol. 3, (Cleveland: W Reserve U, 1973), p. 266; and on the book in general A. Markus, **Der Chassidismus**, 3rd ed. Harburg 1927; and G. Scholem, **Major Trends in Jewish Mysticism**, (New York: Schocken, 1961), p. 211, and 400 n.20.

22 **Sefer HaTemunah** (c. 1250); see G. Scholem, **On the Kabbalah and its Symbolism**, (New York: Schocken, 1965), pp. 77-86; id., **Urspruenge und Anfaenge der Kabbala**, (Berlin: W. de Gruyter, 1962), pp. 417-419.

23 J. Katz, **Halakhah veKabbalah**, (Jerusalem, 1984).

24 R. Chayim of Voloshin, **Nefesh Hachayim**, (Jerusalem: 1973), p. 89.

25 **Tsawa'at haRivash**, Jerusalem, 1948, 74.

26 **Tsawa'at haRivash**, 84.

27 **Pri ha'Arets**, Ki Tisa, p. 34; L. Jacobs, **Hasidic Thought**, New York: Behrman, 1976, p. 95.

28   Ps. 16:8.

29   R. Jacob Josef of Pulnoye, **Toledot Jacob Josef,** Warsaw 1881, Wayera, p. 20 a; **Ben Porat Josef,** Koretz 1781. Gedalyah Nigal, **Torot Ba'al Hatoledot,** (Jerusalem: 1974), pp. 19-25; Samuel H. Dresner, **The Zaddik,** New York: Schocken, 1974.

30   'Avot deR. Nathan B 30; Lev. Rabba 34:3.

31   R. Jacob Josef of Pulnoye, **Tsofnat Pa'ne'ach,** Koretz 1782, p. 118 c.

32   **Tsawa'at haRivash,** 3.

33   **Tsawa'at haRivash,** 141.

34   **Tsawa'at haRivash,** 130.

35   BT Berakhot 54 a.

36   BT Qiddushin 30 b.

37   **Maggid Devarav le-Ya'akov of the Maggid Dov Baer of Mezhirech,** R. Schatz-Uffenheimer (ed.), (Jerusalem: Magnes, 1976), 51, p. 72.

38   Cf. I. Tishby, **Netivey Emunah uMinut,** pp. 204-226, especially pp. 215-217 and 226.

39   G. Scholem, **Mechqarim uMeqorot leToledot haShabtaut veGilguleha,** (Jerusalem: Bialik, 1982), pp. 9-67.

40   R. Mordekhai Josef Leiner (d. 1854), **Mey haShiloach,** Liqqutim, p. 139; Jacobs, **Hasidic Thought,** p.202.

41   A.J. Heschel, **A Passion for Truth,** (New York: Farrar, Straus & Giroux, 1973), p. 60.

42   BT Yevamot 6 b, top.

43   **Tif'eret Israel,** (Bnei Brak: 1980), Introduction, p. 3.

44   **Beth Jacob,** vol. 2, Yitro, 113; Jacobs, **Hasidic Thought,** p. 205.

45   M. Berakhot 4:3-4; BT Berakhot 29 b.

46   BT Berakhot 30 b.

47   R. Jacob Tam: **Sefer Hayashar,** p. 77, cf. pp. 62-63 and p. 116.

48   **Knesset Israel,** p. 19; cf. Jacobs, **Hasidic Thought,** p. 193.

49   R. Jacob Josef of Pulnoye, **Toledot Jacob Josef,** Nasso, p. 133 a.

50   **Tsawa'at haRivash,** 44.

51   **Tsawa'at haRivash,** 46.

52   The view of the **mitnaggedim** is formuled in R. Chayim of Volozyn, **Nefesh Hachayim,** passim. See in particular between Gate 3 and 4 in chapters 6-7.

53   **Liqutey Moharan,** Bney Braq 1965, Tinyana, 24; Jacobs, **Hasidic Thought,** p.62.

54   See also I. Englard, "Mysticism et Mort: reflections sur les pisque Halakhot de l'ecole de rabbi Nahman de Bratslav", in **Melanges Prevost,** (1982), pp. 191-205; Y. Elman, "R. Zadok Hakohen of Lublin on Prophecy in the Halakhic Process", in **JLA Studies** 1 (1985) pp. 1-16.

25. ENLIGHTENMENT AND ETHICS

(a) Universalists

During the French Enlightenment period, stress was laid upon the distinction between religion and morality. Pierre Bayle (1647-1706), spoke of the crimes committed in the name of God and of the hatred promoted by religion against the believers in other faiths. The followers of the Enlightenment aimed at the formulation of a humanist morality based on reason and the idea of humanity.[1] German Enlightenment, on the other hand, mainly desired to create an interconfessional community consisting of Protestants and Catholics. Some of its speakers, e.g. G.E. Lessing (1729-1781), also invited enlightened Jews to take part, and their spokesman became Moses Mendelssohn (1729-1786).

Mendelssohn's main innovation vis-a-vis the rabbinical tradition was the idea that there was an ethics beside Torah, that reason should be relied on beside revelation, and that Jews could participate in humanism beside theonomy. He felt himself to be a human being and a member of the cultural elite of Europe, not only a Jew[2].

His way of life was based on the assumption that the rules of separation between Jews and Gentiles, such as the dietary laws and the rejection of inter-religious marriage, though still in force, were to be practised in an unoffensive way. Though divided from the non-Jewish world by these rules, the Jews should feel united with them by their common ground: ethics, reason and humanism.

Mendelssohn's ideas about ethics were first expressed in his prize winning essay on the form of evidence in metaphysics, submitted in 1764 to the royal academy: "Whether metaphysical truths in general, and the first principles of natural theology and morality in particular, are susceptible of the same evidence as mathematical truths, and in case they are not, what is the nature of their certitude; which degree can it attain; and whether this degree is sufficient to impart conviction?".

He, inter alia, used a theological argument to show that moral principles could be demonstrated. From the concept of God's benevolence followed His intention that His creatures would aim at perfection. When human beings make themselves more perfect, they agree with the design of God and are imitators of Him[3].

Aside from the arguments derived from reason, reference was made to the **purpose** of divine creation, which was stated as being the perfection of all creatures and **imitatio dei**. Being the property of the Creator, man has an obligation to follow the divine law, to be virtuous and perfect[4].

For Mendelssohn, Christians living according to the law of nature were true **Noachides**, and of the same rank as pious Jews[5]. He probably belived natural law to be identical with the **Noachide Laws** of the rabbinical tradition. Revelation was necessary for the law of Judaism, but not for the universal norms of Noachides.

Although Mendelssohn believed in the superiority of Judaism, he rejected any form of missionary activity and religious pressure. Religious tolerance, even pluralism, could be justified according to his opinion, by the sources of Jewish law, and should be implemented by the Jewish community as well as by the civil authority[6].

According to Mendelssohn, Judaism was mainly a system of behaviour, consisting of law and morality, while the eternal truths and metaphysics were in the realm of reason, common to all mankind, and not particular to the revelation to Israel. Ethical principles were to be demonstrated by reason and to be universal, so "that Judaism was one of the many ways to reach the goal of human striving... one of the ways of establishing the ethical principle..."[7].

Samuel David Luzzatto (1800-1865), "relegated religion unreservedly to the sphere of ethics, and at the same time stressed the ethical content of the commandments over their ceremonial and legalistic character... the Jew is judged not by his acceptance or rejection of metaphysical tenets or theological dogmas, but by his moral activity... Religion is dear to God... not because of its truths, but because of its usefulness for morality"[8].

Luzzatto based Jewish morality on the emotion of pity and the belief in reward and punishment, as well as on the election of Israel. He distinguished between Jewish morality, based on revelation and the belief in God on the one hand, and Greek or Western morality, based on rationalism, human autonomy and the worship of art and beauty, on the other[9].

The universalist interpretation of Judaism was stressed by the Italian rabbi Elijah Benamozegh (1823-1900). According to his opinion, both particularist and universalist tendencies can be found in all parts of the Bible. This is due to the double function of Israel, as a people by itself and as an educator of mankind in general[10]. Besides the particular message to the Jewish people, the Torah includes a message to mankind at large, the concept of **Noachism**, which is the expression of biblical and rabbinic universalism and egalitarianism[11].

Therefore, the moral norms of the Torah, the Prophets and Wisdom literature apply to all of mankind. "The moral norm demands of Israel to practise justice and grace regarding pagans and religious enemies, though they are in most cases also political enemies of Israel. Perhaps, it is the unity and universality of the moral norm, which was the cause for the emphasis on the ethnic element in the Torah of Moses. The moral norm is presumably known to all, owing to the natural inclination of mankind and the common traditions of all nations..."[12].

Even within the framework of Torah itself, Benamozegh stressed the human element, which could be understood as a justification of ethics as a part of the theonomic system. According to his conception, man was called upon to become a partner with God, even in the realm of Torah.

"Divine law and human law are both one system, for collaboration is possible only if both have the same thought and move in the same circle... There is no need to mention again the idea of **imitatio dei**, imposed upon man as a duty. We should mention, however, the other side of this truth, as grasped by our sages, viz. that God Himself observes the commandments, and that He used the Torah as a plan of creation..."[13].

Before being given to man, the commandments belonged to God and were called His laws. Once they were given to man, they became his (man's) laws... The sages described the human soul, perhaps the whole human being, as a "scroll of Torah" and declared that the law did not apply where human life was in danger. This means, that there exists something which is more important than the text of the law"[14].

(b) Lazarus and Cohen

The idea of ethics within the context of Jewish theonomy was developed for the first time by Moritz Lazarus (1824-1903). Accepting the Kantian notion of ethical autonomy, he resolved the tension between theonomy and autonomy by declaring God Himself to be bound by ethics. God was said to have given the commandments, because they were in accordance with ethics, not because of His arbitrary will. The duty of being holy was justified by the fact that God Himself was holy, in other words, by the ethical value of holiness, not by ethical voluntarism. While it is true that the ethics of Judaism followed from theonomy, theonomy applied to man and not to morals. The former was under the rule of God, hence perhaps heteronomous, but the moral norm was derived from the human spirit, and was therefore autonomous[15].

Although ethical holiness was seen by the author as autonomous, he gave a voluntarist meaning to ritual holiness. Theonomy, therefore, besides applying to human beings, was also the characteristic of the a-moral elements of the Torah. In the terms of the rabbis, these would be the rules which were criticized by the evil inclination and by the nations. However, just as Sa'adyah had given reason to mitswot shim'iyot, Lazarus gave an ethical meaning to a-moral commandments: they were symbols of ethical ideas[16].

Instead of developing his system from medieval Jewish philosophies, such as that of Maimonides, Lazarus discussed biblical and mainly talmudical sources from the point of view of western ethical theory. Metaphysical concepts, which had been the concern of the philosophers of Judaism, had prevented them, according to his view, from a systematic study of the ethics of Judaism. While the science of Judaism had addressed historical and literary problems[17] he felt that the ethical meaning of the sources needed explication. His own attitude was determined by his specialization, national psychology.

Lazarus tried to express the "general spirit" of the sources of Judaism and the concepts of their "national soul". He therefore used a method of selectivity, rather than accounting for all viewpoints[18]. His object was the presentation of Jewish thought on duties and virtues, the teaching of how to be good rather than which goods should be aspired to.

Hermann Cohen (1842-1918) wrote a devastating critique of Lazarus' Ethik[19], which cannot be explained by his scholarly insights alone. At that phase of his life, Cohen perceived God only as an idea giving support to morals. According to his view, Christian ethics was possible, being derived from dogma and trying to harmonize it with reason. No such discipline could be developed for Judaism, however, since there was no dogma.

Instead of the dogmatic-systematic treatment of Lazarus, thought Cohen, there was first of all a need for a differentiation of the historical sources of Judaism. The central place should be occupied by the medieval philosophers of Judaism, whose concepts of Jewish religion should serve as the point of departure for the discourse on Jewish ethics. Hence, it would appear that each of these philosophers had been influenced from outside, and no "general spirit" of Judaism could be established in the totality of rabbinical literature. While Lazarus had tried to develop his system of Jewish ethics mainly from rabbinical quotations, Cohen would have liked to see one

Jewish ethics develop from the philosophy of Maimonides, and another from that of Philo or Sa'adyah for instance.

For Cohen, there could be no ethics without Kantian autonomy, which Lazarus had wrongly claimed as a basis of his system. To him, autonomy emancipated the ethical scholar from historical prejudice or anthropological discoveries. He was to rely only upon epistemological principles and thereby to allow ethics to be a scholarly undertaking, to develop the concept of human being and of humanity. Scholarly ethics, according to Cohen, could not use God as a principle of morals, but must develop its rules from the concepts of man and mankind.

In this review, Cohen considered religion as a means towards ethics. Later on, however, he came to differentiate between the two, and to realize the intrinsic value of religion. It created the idea of the personal God, and thereby gave the individual a status independent from mankind. "The God of ethics is the God of humanity and not of the individual"[20]. The prophets of Israel were shown to have developed the concept of man, which became the basis of modern ethics. Likewise, the possibility of love from man to God and vice versa, as well as of atonement, are the creation of the religion of Israel beyond the insights of universal ethics[21].

(c) Rosenzweig and Breuer

The problem of ethics and Jewish law was fundamental in the system of Franz Rosenzweig (1886-1929), though a different terminology was employed. In his epistle on the law, **The Builders**, responding to Martin Buber's Jewish **spiritualism**, he had the following to say: "The circle of the things which can be done is much much larger than the circle of the duties of (Jewish) orthodoxy... In the space outside the border established by orthodoxy enters the **minhag** (custom), and the **ta'am** (sense), which means something positive, instead of the negative sphere of **hetter** (permissible). Where there was a living Judaism, this was always so; but whereas in the past, officially, one was critical and mildly ironic vis-a-vis **minhag**, in the future it will be met by the seriousness of a principle... Even the inner border of this limitation will have to change and no longer be a mere borderline vis-a-vis the permissible... After custom will have adopted the dignity of the law, the law will receive some of the positive qualities of custom. The character of the law will no longer be determined by the prohibitions, but by the mandatory commandments. Even the prohibition will become positive. Work on the Sabbath will be omitted, because of the positive commandment of rest; refraining from prohibited food will be linked with the joy of being Jewish in the daily and human sphere of material life. Hence, the omission becomes an act... The area of what can be done (both in what is permissible and what is prohibited) will become one... The law must become again a commandment, which is fulfilled at the moment of hearing it... After all, this does not depend upon our will, but here too upon our ability. Here too the decisive thing is the selection, according to ability, among all those things which could be done. This choice can only be individual, for it applies to the ability, not to the will. A general law could demand from the will, but the ability has its own law. It concerns my, your and his ability, which is the basis of our ability, but not the ability of all..."[22].

By this demand of freedom, both regarding the spirit of the law and the factual aspects of what can be done, Rosenzweig uses ethical principles within the application of divine law. While custom may be understood as a recognized source of the law, the reference to the sense of the law is part of ethical considerations. As previously mentioned, the use of **ta'ama diqra** had been part of R. Simon bar Yochai's method, which had been rejected by his colleagues. This was, therefore, a selective statement of Rosenzweig, following from his ethical conviction.

Likewise, the emphasis upon the positive rather than the negative rules of Jewish law had been raised by Nachmanides, to explain the preference for the former in cases of conflict. The use of this idea, again, is part of the ethical freedom of human reason vis-a-vis divine law.

Rosenzweig, therefore, may be said to have qualified theonomy by a certain measure of autonomy, and thereby provided a viable option for modern Jews wishing to observe part of traditional rules. His assumption was that divine law indeed applied in its totality, but that it included certain referrals to individual autonomy.

In a sense, Rosenzweig presented the **teshuvah** (turning back), from enlightenment to Jewish learning and commandments. However, his concept demanded making use of whatever insight had been gained by ethics and general culture for a new and better understanding and observing of Torah.

A radical turning back from enlightenment to Jewish tradition was presented by Isaac Breuer (1883-1946), in an early paper on **the philosophical foundations of Jewish and modern law**[23]. The occasion was a court decision in a divorce case between Jews, declaring Jewish law to be inapplicable for violating the moral concepts of monogamy and equality. Breuer, at that time a young intern in the German legal service, undertook to explain the attitude of Jewish law, without violating his belief in its superiority over modern law.

He first put the problem of Jewish polygyny within the context of the corresponding attitude of Judaism to slavery and to Gentiles. The idea of equality of human beings in modern law, he went on to explain, followed from the ethical concept of humanity, and ethical concepts took human beings to be the measure of human action. Equality was "the triumph of ethics in law", therefore, "the idea of humanity was a formal principle of law as well as of ethics"[24]. Jewish distinctive treatment of husband and wife regarding extra-marital sex, just as Jewish toleration of slavery, was necessarily in contradiction with the morals of the modern judge.

Breuer first declared the idea of humanity to have been taken from Jewish tradition, and deplored the fact that this very idea was now used to criticize Judaism. In Judaism, the idea of humanity was one among other ideas, it was a presupposition and a prerequisite for the concept of human beings being servants to God. The idea functioned to implement divine service, which was its goal. The end was God, not man, and human dignity consisted in the function of carrying out divine goals on earth.

Modern autonomous ethics, on the other hand, based on the same idea of humanity, was to serve for the limitation of human power, and the definition of individual rights towards each other. For ethics the idea of humanity was fundamental and absolute, and human beings as such were its highest and absolute goal.

While ethics dealt with the actor, law regulated the action, so that both were separate. Hence, law had become profane, and had been left with utilitarianism as the sole criterion of action. Ethics applied to law only in marginal situations, such as the recognition of foreign law.

Jewish law, according to Breuer, was never separated from ethics, and Jewish ethics never became autonomous and merely a formal principle. It was so totally ruled by ethics, that it had no concept of powers, but only of duties. Human dignity was not dependent on the extent of the duties of the person, but on the extent of their fulfillment. Jewish ethics, says Breuer, was the theoretical teaching about being children and servants of God, while Jewish law was the applied teaching of the duties resulting thereof. Both were the creations of God.

Breuer admits that this system of Jewish law and ethics could be misused, to extend the power of the one at the expense of the other. Quoting a moral appeal to the master to treat the slave in a brotherly way, and to the slave to behave as befits a slave[25], he declared brotherhood to be a principle regulating legal relations between those unequal in their frame of duties.

In Jewish law, goes his argument, the prevention of misuse was not the object of law and enforcement, but of the free and moral decision of the person in power. In one of his paradoxes, Breuer described this situation as Jewish law actually being autonomous and Jewish ethics heteronomous, while modern law was heteronomous and modern ethics autonomous.

In conclusion, Breuer admits that the Jewish people did not meet these high expectations, and declares that this was the reason for the warning of the prophets and the loss of Jewish independence. He adds that rabbinical legislation, therefore, had to limit this autonomy through the use of legal sanction. In other words, we may call his paper a utopean construct, which left those in need of care and protection at the mercy of their adversaries. While defending an ideal system, Breuer did not answer the challenge of the court, that present-day Jewish law violated ethical principles. The correct response would have been a call for rabbinical legislation to prevent further desecration of The Name.

1   Schrey, **Einfuehrung**, p.32.

2   See Mendelssohn's letters to Herder and Lavater, and his introduction to Menasse ben Israel, **Rettung der Juden**, Berlin, 1782; and J. Katz, **Exclusiveness and Tolerance**, (New York: Schocken 1962), p. 170, and 179.

3   A. Altmann, **Moses Mendelssohn: A Biographical Study**, (Philadelphia: JPS, 1973), p. 127.

4   M. Fox, "Law and Ethics in Modern Jewish Philosophy: The Case of Moses Mendelssohn" in **Proceedings of the American Academy for Jewish Research** 43 (1976) pp. 1-13.

5   Maimonides, **Mishneh Torah**, Hilkhot Melakhim 8:11, had declared the observance of the Noachide laws to also demand their acceptance as part of the revelation of Sinai. The observance of the Noachide rules out of ethical considerations was an act of wisdom, but not of piety. Mendelsshn, therefore, consulted R. Jacob Emden as to the Talmudic authority of this statement of Maimonides, and upon his negative reply, rejected Maimonides' view: J. Katz, **Exclusiveness,** pp. 175-177; cf. J.I. Dienstag, "Natural Law in Maimonidean Thought and Scholarship", JLA 6 (1987) 64-77.

6   Mendelssohn, **Jerusalem**; cf. J. Katz, **Exclusiveness**, p. 169; Tsemah Tsamriyon, **Mosheh Mendelssohn wehaIdeologiyah shel haHaskalah**, (Israel: 1984), p. 55.

7   Mendelssohn, **Jerusalem**, ch. 2; N. Rotenstreich, **Jewish Philosophy in Modern Times: From Mendelssohn to Rosenzweig**, (New York: 1968), p. 27 f.

8   Rotenstreich, p. 30; Agus, **The Vision**, pp. 4, and 271 ff. Cf. S.D. Luzzatto, **Ketavim**, edited and trans. by M. E. Artom, (Jerusalem: Bialik, 1976).

9   "Derekh 'Erets et Atticismos", in **Ketavim**, vol. 2.

10 Elijah Benamozegh, **Israel veha'Enoshut**, trans S. Marcus, (Jerusalem: Harav Kook, 1967), pp. 76-90, and 105-112.

11 Benamozegh, p. 196 ff.

12 Benamozegh, p. 238.

13 Benamozegh, pp. 160.

14 Benamozegh, pp. 180 f.

15 Lazarus, **Ethik**, 1, ch. 2, p. 83 ff., 98 ff.; J. Guttmann, **Philosophies of Judaism**, (New York: Schocken, 1973), p. 398 (who did not mention this distinction and therefore criticized Lazarus' claim of following Kant); Rotenstreich, p. 46 ff.

16 Lazarus, **Ethik**, p. 179 ff.

17 See my "Juedisches Lernen und die Wissenschaft des Judentums", in K. E. Groezinger (ed.), **Judentum im deutschen Sprachraum**, Suhrkamp, 1991, 347-356.

18 Lazarus, **Ethik**, vol. 1, p. 60; vol. 2, Introduction.

19 H. Cohen, "Das Problem der juedischen Sittenlehre: Eine Kritik von Lazarus' Ethik des Judentums", **Monatsschrift fuer die Geschichte und Wissenschaft des Judentums** 43 (1899) pp. 385-400, and 433-449.

20 Guttmann, p. 409.

21 Rosenzweig, "Das soziale Ideal bei Plato und den Propheten", in **Juedische Schriften**, vol. 1, (Berlin: 1924), p. 306 ff.

22 "Die Bauleute: Ueber das Gestz", **Der Jude** 8 (1924); also in **Zweistromland**, (Dordrecht: Nijhoff, 1984), pp. 699-712.

23 "Die rechtsphilosophischen Grundlagen des juedischen und des modernen Rechts", in **Jahrbuch der juedisch-literarischen Gesellschaft** 8 (1910) pp. 35-64; cf. A. L. Mittleman, **Between Kant and Kabbalah: An Introduction to Isaac Breuer's Philosophy of Judaism**, (Albany: SUNY, 1990), pp. 142-149, and 182-183; and my **Dat haNetsach**, p. 58.

24 Breuer, loc. cit.

25 Sifra ad Lev. 25:39.

BIBLIOGRAPHY

Agus, Jacob B. **The Vision and the Way: An Interpretation of Jewish Ethics.** New York: 1966.

Baeck, Leo. **The Essence of Judaism,** transl. V. Grubenwieser. New York: Schocken 1948.

Barton John. "Understanding Old Testament Ethics." **Journal for the Study of the Old Testament,** 9, (1978), 44-64.

Barton, John. "Natural Law and Poetic Justice in the Old Testament." **Journal of Theological Studies,** 30.1, (1979), 1-14.

Barton, John. "Approaches to Ethics in the Old Testament." Rogerson, J. **Beginning Old Testament Study,** (1983), 113-130.

Berkovits, Eliezer. **Not in Heaven: The Nature and Function of Halakhah.** New York: 1983.

Bloch, Abraham P. **A Book of Jewish Ethical Concepts: Biblical and Postbiblical.** New York: Ktav, 1984.

Brandt, Richard B. **Ethical Theory.** Englewood Cliffs, NJ: Prentice Hall, 1959.

Burkhardt, Helmut (Ed.) **Begruendung ethischer Normen.** Wuppertal: Brockhaus, 1988.

BZAW = Beihefte der ZAW

Chadwick, Henry. "Gewissen". **Reallexikon fuer Antike und Christentum,** 10, 1025-1107.

Chamberlayne, John H. **Man in Society. The OT Doctrine.** London: 1966.

Cohen, Arthur A. & Mendes-Flohr, Paul. **Contemporary Jewish Religious Thought.** New York: Scribner, 1987.

Cohen, Boaz. **Law and Ethics in the Light of the Jewish Tradition.** New York: JTS, 1957.

Cohen, Hermann. **Die Religion der Vernunft nach den Quellen des Judentums.** 2nd ed., Frankfurt M., Kaufmann 1929.

DI = Diney Israel.

Drewermann, Eugen. **Strukturen des Boesen. Die j-histische Urgeschichte in exegetischer, psychoanalytischer und philosophischer Sicht.** Muenchen: 1977-1980.

Duvshani, Menashe. "'iqarey hamusar bamiqra." **Bet Miqra,** 89-90, (1982), 267-273.

Eckardt, A. Roy. **For Righteous Sake.** Contemporary Moral Philosophies. Indiana: U.P., 1987.

Eichrodt, W. **Theologie des Alten Testaments.** Stuttgart 1964.

ET = Encyclopaedia Talmudit

Falk, Z.W. **Introduction to Jewish Law of the Second Commonwealth.** Leiden:Brill, 1972-1978.

Falk, Z.W. "MiMishnat Chassidim", in: **B. deVries Memorial Vol.** Jerusalem 1968, 62-69.

Falk, Z.W. **'Erkhey Mishpat weYahadut.** Jerusalem: Mesharim, 1980.

Falk, Z.W. **Law and Religion: The Jewish Experience.** Jerusalem: Mesharim, 1981.

Falk, Z.W. **Dat haNetsach weTsorkhey Sha'ah.** Jerusalem: Mesharim, 1986.

Federbush, S. **Hamussar wehamishpat beIsrael.** Jerusalem: 1947.

Fischer, James E. "Ethics and Wisdom." **Catholic Biblical Quarterly,** 40/3, (1978), 293-310.

Fox, Marvin. **Modern Jewish Ethics.** Ohio: State U.P., 1975.

Fox, M. **The Philosophical Foundations of Jewish Ethics: Some Initial Reflections.** Cincinnati: 1979.

Frankena, William K. **Ethics.** Englewood Cliffs, NJ: Prentice Hall, 2nd ed. 1973.

Gilbert, Maurice, et al. **Morale et l'ancien testament.** Lv.-laNeuve, 1976.

Green, Ronald M. **Religion and Moral Reason: A new method for comparative study.** Oxford: U.P., 1988.

Greenberg, Simon. **The Ethical in the Jewish and American Heritage.** New York: JTS, 1977.

Gordis, Robert. "A dynamic Halakhah." **Judaism,** 28, (1979), 263-282.

Gordis, Robert, et al. "Jewish Law: 18 Perspectives." **Judaism,** 29, (1980), 1-109.

Gordis, Robert. **Judaic Ethics for a Lawless World.** New York: JTS, 1986.

Gustafson, James M. **Theology and Ethics.** Oxford: Blackwell, 1981.

Heinemann, Yitschaq. **Ta'amey haMitswot beSifrut Israel.** Jerusalem 1942.

Hempel, Johannes. **Das Ethos des Alten Testaments.** BZAW 67, 2nd ed. 1964.

Herzog, I. **The Main Institutions of Jewish Law.** London: Soncino, vol. 1, 379-386.

Hoeffe, Otfried (ed.). **Lexikon der Ethik.** Muenchen: Beck, 3rd ed., 1986.

ILR = Israel Law Review

Jacobs, Louis. **A Tree of Life.** Oxford: 1984.

JJS = Journal of Jewish Studies

JLA = Jewish Law Annual

JQR = Jewish Quarterly Review

JRE = Journal of Religious Ethics

Kaiser, Walter C. **Toward Old Testament Ethics.** Grand Rapids: 1983.

Kaufman, Yechezqel. **Toledot haEmunah haIsraelit.** Tel Aviv 1956.

Kellner, M. **Contemporary Jewish Ethics.** New York: Sanhedrin, 1978.

Knight, Douglas A. "Old Testament Ethics." **The Christian Century,** 99/2, (1982), 55-59.

Konwitz, M.R. "Law and Morals in the Hebrew Scriptures, Plato and Aristotle." Ed. L. Finkelstein **Social Responsibility in an Age of Revolution.** New York: 1971, 1-37.

Korn, Eugene B. "Ethics and Jewish Law", **Judaism,** 24, (1975), 206-209.

Lazarus, Moritz. **Die Ethik des Judentums.** Frankfurt M. 1898-1911.

Lauterbach, Jacob Z. **The Ethics of Halakhah.** Cincinnati: HUC, 1951.

Leibowitz, Y. **Yahadut, Am Yehudi uMedinat Israel,** Jerusalem 1976.

Levenson, John D. "The Theologies of Commandment in Biblical Times." **Harvard Theological Review,** 73/1-2, (1980), 17-33.

Lightstone, Jack N. "Problems and New Perspectives in the Study of Early Rabbinic Ethics." **Journal of Religious Ethics,** 9, (1981), 199-209.

Maier, G. **Mensch und freier Wille.** Tuebingen: 1971.

Mattuck, I. **Jewish Ethics.** London: 1953.

McKenzie, John L. "The Ethics of the Old Testament." Burns, P. & Cumming, J. **The Bible Now.** 1981, 86-97.

Mendenhall, G.E. "The Conflict between Value Systems and Social Control". Baltimore: **John Hopkins NE Studies,** 7, (1975), 169-180.

Murphy, Roland. "Die Bildung des sittlichen Gewissens nach dem Alten Testament." **Concilium,** 13/12, (1977), 634-638.

Murray, John. **Principles of Conduct: Aspects of Biblical Ethics.** London: 1957.

Nissen, A. **Gott und der Naechste im antiken Judentum.** WUNT 15. Tuebingen: 1974.

Oyen, Hendrik van. **Ethik des Alten Testaments.** Guetersloh: 1967.

Pieper, Annemarie. **Ethik und Moral.** Muenchen: Beck, 1985.

Priest, James E. **Governmental and Judicial Ethics in the Bible and Rabbinical Literature.** New York: Ktav, 1980.

Rakover, Nahum. **The Multi-Language Bibliography of Jewish Law.** Jerusalem 1990, s.v. Ethics and Halakhah, pp. 79-85.

Raphael, D.D. **Moral Philosophy.** Oxford UP, 1981.

Reeder, John P. Source, Sanction and Salvation; **Religion and Morality in Judaic and Christian Traditions.** Englewood Cliffs, NJ: Prentice Hall, 1988.

Reeder, John P. & Outka, Gene, eds. **Religion and Morality.** New York: Doubleday, 1973.

Ricken, Friedo. **Allgemeine Ethik.** Stuttgart: Kohlhammer, 1983.

RIDA = Revue internationale des droits del'antiquite

Ryrie, Charles C. "Perspectives on Social Ethics." **Bibliotheca Sacra.** 134/534, (1977), 114-122.

Schmidt, Werner H. "Aspekte alttestamentlicher Ethik." Moltmann, J. **Nachfolge und Bergpredigt.** Kaiser Traktate, 65, (1981), 12-36.

Schrey, Heinz Horst. **Einfuehrung in die Ethik.** Darmstadt: Wissenschaftliche Buchgesellschaft, 2nd ed., 1977.

Schwartz, Werner. **Analytische Ethik und christliche Theologie.** Goettingen: Vandenhoeck & Ruprecht

Shepherd, John J. "Man's Morals and Israel's Religion." **Expository Times.** 92, (1980), 171-74.

Sigal, Philipp. **New Dimensions in Judaism.** New York: 1972.

Silberg, M. **Talmudic Law and the Modern State.** New York: 1973, 93-130.

Silver, D.J. **Judaism and Ethics.** New York: 1970.

Sirat, Colette. **A History of Jewish Philosophy in the Middle Ages.** Cambridge UP 1985.

Smend, Rudolf. "Ethik. AT." TRE, 10.

Spero, Schubert. **Morality, Halakhah and the Jewish Tradition.** New York: 1982.

Stendebach, Franz J. **Der Mensch... wie ihn Israel... sah.** Stuttgart: 1972.

Stendebach, F.J. "Ueberlegungen zum Ethos des Alten Testaments." **Kairos,** 18.4, (1976), 273-281.

Stoeckle, Bernhard ed. **Woerterbuch christlicher Ethik.** Freiburg: Herder, 2nd ed., 1980.

TRE = Theologische Realenzyklopaedie

Twiss, Sumner B.& Little, David. **Comparative Religious Ethics.** San Francisco: Harper & Row, 1978.

Urbach, E.E.. **The Sages.** transl. I. Abrahams. Jerusalem: Magnes

Vasserot-Merle, P. "La Bible et la decision morale." **Lumiere et Vie.** Lyon, 27, 136, (1978), 79-99.

VT = Vetus Testamentum

Wallis, G. "Erwaegungen zur Ethik des Alten Testaments." Rogge, J. & Schille, G. **Theologische Versuche.** 7, (1976), Er.-V., 41-60.

Waxman, M. **Judaism, Religion and Ethics.** New York: 1953.

White, R.E.V. **Biblical Ethics.** Exeter: Paternoster, 1979.

Wolff, Hans Walter. **Anthropologie des Alten Testaments.** Muenchen: Kaiser, 1973.

Wright, J.H. **Living as the People of God.** The Relevance of O.T. Ethics. Leicester: 1983.

ZAW = Zeitschrift fuer die alttestamentliche Wissenschaft